PRACTICAL AUTO & TRUCK RESTORATION

How to Plan and Organize Your Project to Save Time and Money

John Gunnell

HPBOOKS

HPBooks

Published by the Penguin Group
Penguin Group (USA) Inc.
375 Hudson Street, New York, New York 10014, USA
Penguin Group (Canada), 90 Eglinton Avenue East, Suite 700, Toronto, Ontario M4P 2Y3, Canada
(a division of Pearson Penguin Canada Inc.)
Penguin Books Ltd., 80 Strand, London WC2R 0RL, England
Penguin Group Ireland, 25 St. Stephen's Green, Dublin 2, Ireland (a division of Penguin Books Ltd.)
Penguin Group (Australia), 250 Camberwell Road, Camberwell, Victoria 3124, Australia
(a division of Pearson Australia Group Pty. Ltd.)
Penguin Books India Pvt. Ltd., 11 Community Centre, Panchsheel Park, New Delhi—110 017, India
Penguin Group (NZ), 67 Apollo Drive, Rosedale, North Shore 0632, New Zealand
(a division of Pearson New Zealand Ltd.)
Penguin Books (South Africa) (Pty.) Ltd., 24 Sturdee Avenue, Rosebank, Johannesburg 2196, South Africa

Penguin Books Ltd., Registered Offices: 80 Strand, London WC2R 0RL, England

While the author has made every effort to provide accurate telephone numbers and Internet addresses at the time of publication, neither the publisher nor the author assumes any responsibility for errors, or for changes that occur after publication. Further, the publisher does not have any control over and does not assume any responsibility for author or third-party websites or their content.

PRACTICAL AUTO & TRUCK RESTORATION

First edition: March 2010

ISBN: 978-1-55788-547-0

PRINTED IN THE UNITED STATES OF AMERICA

10 9 8 7 6 5 4 3 2 1

CONTENTS

ACKNOWLEDGMENTS

I would like to recognize the help of the following people in making this book a reality:

Accurate Alignment, Don Barlup, Bob Bennett, Lee Bestul, Dennis and Kathy Bickford, Stefano Bimbi, Bolt Locker, Jim Carlson, Circus World Museum, Colin Comer, Joe Curto, Tom Dietz, The Eastwood Company, Eclectic Motorworks, Rex Evchuk, Fondy Auto Electric, Mike Granlund, Dave Glass, Glassworks-The Hardtop Shop, Steve Hamilton, Jesse Gunnell, Fred Kanter, Paul Katzke, Al Knoch, Jerry Kopecky, Wayne Lensing, Michael Lutfy, Bob Marx, The Masterpiece of Style & Speed, McCloskey Auto Trim, Jewel Meetz, Terry Meetz, Mid America Motorworks, Mitler Bros., Jim Mokwa, Lou Natenschon, Nisongers, "Cowboy Bob" Norris, Dave Pugh, Ragtops & Roadsters, Rare Parts, Marv Richer, Vince Sauberlich, SEMA, John Sloane, Jim Summers, and John Twist.

INTRODUCTION

Today, more and more people who collect cars do not have the time or skills to perform an entire ground-up automotive restoration themselves. At the same time, they do not have the money needed to "hire out" all the work involved. This book represents a guide on what work they can job out and what work they can do themselves.

In a real-life example, I rebuilt a set of British S.V. carburetors for an MG. Working with a mechanic friend, we did the job in my home shop. Between the cost of my time and his time, the cost of an S.V. carburetor kit, cleaning and buffing time and machine shop costs, this job ran several hundred dollars.

When all is said and done, I could have sent the carburetors to commercial rebuilders in Milwaukee or New York and had them professionally rebuilt by an expert. The job would have been completed much faster and at just slightly higher cost. In addition, their work would have been guaranteed, should anything go wrong.

The purpose of this book is to expand on this concept. It looks at the restoration of a vintage car, truck or motorcycle in a new light. Which parts of the project does it pay to job out? Which parts of the project does it pay to do yourself?

In this book, I discuss how you can play the role of "general contractor" in planning and organizing your restoration. I have listed many reliable places that various parts can be sent for individual unit restoration work. In the Sources section at the end, you will find listings of people and shops that specialize in unit repair services.

—John Gunnell

To all of the talented "shade-tree" mechanics in the old-car hobby, who turn rusty relics into regal roadsters. And to Jerry Kopecky, and Dennis and Kathy Bickford: three expert restorers who help me learn the magic they do.

Chapter 1

Approaches to Classic Vehicle Restoration

During this every-nut-and-bolt restoration of a 1961 Chrysler 300 F convertible at Kopecky's Klassics, in Iola, Wisconsin, the car was completely disassembled and every single part from the car was replaced or restored.

Like everything else in life, the practical way to restore a car or truck has to have a direction—or an approach—to it. If you do what's called an every-nut-and-bolt restoration it is going to cost more, but virtually every piece on the car will be restored. That means you shouldn't have to worry about breaking down on your way to a show. On the other hand, you may have so much invested in the job, you won't want to drive the car.

In contrast to that, you can do a partial restoration in which you fix only the parts that seem to need fixing. This approach can give you a pretty nice car at a lower investment, but a part you didn't bother restoring might break the first time you use the restored car.

There are also other directions to go in with restoration work. You may favor strict originality over drivability enhancements or you may give more weight to using lead body filler, rather than plastic putty. There are no wrong or right choices, as long as you're doing quality work, but there are choices. Determining what approach you want to take is the first step in formulating a practical plan to restoring a classic car, truck or motorcycle.

This 1936 Pontiac six-cylinder engine has had a good amateur restoration, but the red-painted Indian embossment and chrome acorn nuts are non-authentic touches. The paint is thin and not up to professional standards.

Amateur, Professional and Hybrid

When it comes to restoring a vehicle, the only good amateur is a dead amateur. That's a play on words of course, but the message is clear. After you restore a car, you're going to drive it on the highway, so it should go without catching on fire, it should run without blowing up and it should stop when you need to stop it. You can call yourself an amateur if you're not getting paid for the work you do, but don't think

you can safely get by with amateur-quality work.

If you have never restored a car yourself and don't have the slightest idea how to start, you probably think of yourself as an amateur. However, if you are going to fix a car that drives on the road, you will have to learn both basic mechanical skills and specialized restoration techniques. Having a strong will to fix a car is just not going to make things happen. You can't wish it done, no matter how hard you squint your eyes

A large array of high-quality tools, such as shown here, is an important factor in getting a vintage vehicle restored. Neatness and organization contribute to a successful restoration as well.

and stamp your feet. In contrast, having the will to learn and following through on it will make the restoration hobby an enlightening one.

The biggest problem the amateur (or novice, which is a better term) restorer faces is a shortage of confidence. For years, I spent more time reading about repairs than doing them. I gathered so much reference material, I could write complete articles about a repair without ever doing the job. That helped me as an author, but my cars never got fixed. I could diagnose problems with my car or a neighbor's truck and 95 percent of the time I was right, but I didn't have the nerve to actually turn the wrenches for fear of screwing up.

This changed when I made friends with a veteran mechanic who worked on my cars once a week. In cases where I would just examine an assembly for weeks, read the shop manual, contact people on the Internet and check with a half dozen other friends, he would simply take the assembly apart. He rarely referred to a shop manual (unless he was doing something brand new to him) and he made any job seem like a simple matter of taking things apart, replacing the broken part and putting everything back together again.

One of the mechanic's other strengths was that nothing scared him. When a job was a bit challenging, it became an obsession with him to conquer whatever the problem was. If we needed a longer puller to yank a brake drum off, he undid the bolts in three different-sized pullers, mated them together like one long puller and made the resulting creation work. On the other hand, he could sense when a job had no practical solution and he was willing to walk away to think about it or to find another tool.

Tools—When it comes to auto restoration, the biggest difference between the novice and the professional is really the investment in tools. We've all heard the expression that the man with the most toys wins and I guess it's the same for the man with the most tools. However, in the real world, it's not only the number of tools that separates the beginner from the pro; it's also the quality of the tools. It is possible to go broke trying to equip your home shop with every trick tool to handle every job. For most of us, this wouldn't be practical and, luckily, it's not necessary either.

Many tools in my shop come from Harbor Freight or Northern Tool or swap meet vendors who sell foreign-made tools. To be honest, I've had some breakage problems with the latter category, but my purchases from Harbor Freight and Northern Tool have all been satisfactory. That doesn't mean perfect, but when I did have problems, the customer service people took care of it. I also have a number of problem-free Eastwood specialty tools that are designed for hobby-shop use and do what some big machines do for a whole lot less.

As my mechanic friend says, if I had to use these tools over and over again, every day, for weeks on end, I might consider upgrading them to commercial strength. But for the jobs I do in my shop—even some mighty big jobs—these tools are very practical and work fine. And making decisions like that is part of our practical approach to restoration.

We'll talk about tools and equipment in more detail later; the important thing here is to nail down the importance of having a practical approach to restoration work. As we've seen, you can consider yourself an amateur, but you still have to turn out professional-quality work, at least to the point of building a safe vehicle. If your paint is a little sloppy, you may not win a trophy, but you can take a night school class or pick up a good book and learn to paint better. That's practical. However, if your brakes fail, you're in a heap of trouble because you took an impractical approach (fixing a safety device you weren't up to speed on).

The Hybrid Approach—Most home restorers will actually find that a hybrid approach to restoration is most practical. This is a system in which you as the novice deals with the minor aspects of the restoration while farming out the tricky or more complex projects to someone who specializes in the restoration of that particular system. On the surface, this may sound like a costlier approach, but I don't think it is. Here's an example.

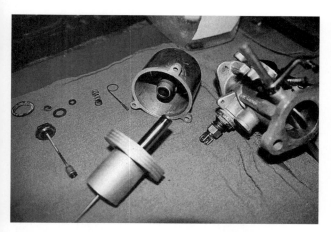

The inner workings of the British SU carburetor are a mystery to many sports car enthusiasts at first. However, there are many books, videos, CDs and seminars to teach you how to rebuild and tune SU carburetors.

Kopecky's Klassics, of Iola, Wisconsin, does high-dollar total restorations. With Chrysler Unibody construction, they can rebuild the chassis and engine unit—like this one for a '61 300 F—apart from the body of the car.

When I got my first MG, I knew absolutely nothing about SU carburetors and I sent them to Joe Curto, in New York City, to be rebuilt. This cost me about $375 at that time and that included some custom welding of one of the carb levers that was broke. The carburetors were mailed back in a few weeks and looked beautiful. They worked great, too. A year later, I bought a second MG and had its carburetors rebuilt by a man in a club I belonged to. This ran about $350 with shipping. They also looked and worked very nice.

A few years later, I bought a third MG and decided to do the carburetors at home with my mechanic friend. We had to buy a carb kit by mail order from Joe Curto. It was around $75. Later, we found we needed other pieces. Each time we ordered a few more parts, we paid more shipping. We had to buy white rogue to buff the aluminum carbs with my Eastwood buffer. It took us over 12 hours to rebuild the carbs. (I could have spent that time writing approximately two articles for $150 each.) When we finally put the carbs together, following the instructions in the parts kit, we had no idea if they'd work. Luckily, they did. All in all, counting the time we used, I think the carbs we rebuilt cost me around $400.

If I had taken the hybrid approach and worried only about the nuts-and-bolts removal of the carbs, before sending them out to either outside restorer, I would have saved money. And I could have spent 12 hours making money writing instead of trying to fix something I never fixed before. I'll admit that the math works more in favor of doing the job yourself, if you have 12 hours to spend. But that's rarely the case around my house.

The Total Restoration Approach

People who collect cars will tell you that they did a total restoration on a vehicle. However, you may later see another car of the same year, make and model advertised as totally restored and notice that doesn't look quite as nice as the first car. That can make you wonder exactly what the term total means. For a perspective on this, I visited Jerry Kopecky at his shop—Kopecky's Klassics—in Iola, Wisconsin.

Jerry Kopecky is a young man who restores old cars made before he was born. He learned his craft as a kid, working with his dad Dave, a former restorer, during the '80s. In January 2007, Kopecky gained local cult status and national notoriety when a '57 De Soto convertible that he spent a year restoring sold for $285,000 at the Barrett-Jackson auction. Based on that experience, Jerry decided to focus on complete nut-and-bolt restorations.

A total restoration starts with an analysis of the vehicle being worked on. Kopecky brings the car into the shop and assesses its strengths and weaknesses. Is the car worth restoring? Was the original factory build quality lacking in any way? How much has the car deteriorated over the years? Has the car been abused? Has it been damaged? Have modifications been made?

Kopecky says that the 1950s and 1960s cars he specializes in were notorious for poor-fitting body panels. He and his staff completely strip the car's old interior, take off the front and rear bumpers and begin to panel-fit the car. This is a process in which they take the doors, hood, trunk, fenders and other body panels off in order to rework the metal so that all of the panels have nice even panel gaps and super-straight seams.

The car's body will be taken apart and put back together at least four to six times. Parts like the doors will be reworked to fit the body. An inch and a half of metal may be added to the upper rear

Before the bodywork stage, deal with the engine, transmission, suspension and mechanical parts. Here we see once-pitted suspension pieces that were stripped to bare metal, epoxy coated, primed and painted.

Bolts, nuts and washers can be sandblasted, replated and used in a restoration. In some cases, when a car is being restored to strict judging standards, the nice-looking cad-plated hardware has to be painted black.

corner of a door skin so that the door-break opening will be perfectly straight and vertical from top to bottom. When the car is done, the straight seams enhance its beauty.

To aid in fitting panels, black edges—called margins—are used. When everything fits the way it should, the car will be taken apart one more time so that each body panel can be separately repaired or replaced. Then, each panel is individually refinished with new paint. This is called one-on-one work. It takes a lot of hours and a lot of pain to finish just one piece.

Before getting to the bodywork stage, Kopecky recommends dealing first with the engine, transmission, suspension and other mechanical parts. This is because the powerplant has to be sent out to a machine shop, the transmission rebuild gets jobbed out to another specialist and new suspension bushings have to be ordered. By dealing with repairs and parts orders first, you can be focusing on the body and paintwork while your contractors do the other jobs and while the parts orders are being filled.

Bodywork—other than parts replacements—involves stripping each and every original piece of the car to bare metal using sandblasting, coating them with epoxy primer, hand-sanding the primer as smooth as possible, adding high-build primer to make the pieces even smoother and—after many hours of doing this over and over again—wet-sanding the pieces with 400-grit sandpaper. The primer is applied with a gun in a large, professional-quality paint booth and the primed panels are hung throughout the shop for lengthy drying times.

Driveline and chassis parts are usually rust-pitted to one degree or another, so restoring them begins with sandblasting the part to bare metal to remove all rust. An epoxy primer is then applied over the raw metal. The epoxy primer is hand-sanded and then the first coat of filler primer is applied. This hand-sand-then-filler-prime process is done over

and over and over until there are no imperfections that the eye can see. For deep pitting, a body glaze may be applied. Of course, some parts require metal patches to be welded in before they can be refinished.

Jobs like welding in patches, fitting panels together with straight seams and building such things as replacement rocker panels require a good deal of metal fabrication. Usually, new rocker panels are installed on both sides of the car. Often, these are not available in the aftermarket and have to be made up. While '50s cars typically came with one-piece rockers, often two-piece replacements must be made in order to roll and shape exact copies of the originals. A stitch-welding technique is used to join the pieces together. This prevents the heat of the welder from warping the panels. A series of wide-spaced stitches is made. When things cool off, more stitches are added to the in-between spaces. This creates a nice, tight weld without getting the sheet metal too hot.

After the welding is done, the area is filed down, smoothed, rust-proofed, epoxy-primed, sanded, filled and glazed over and over and, finally, wet sanded. Of course, when the entire car is painted, the rocker panels will be refinished, too. Many cars have previously-repaired rocker panels, but Kopecky feels they all have to be redone to maintain his high quality of work.

Every original bolt, nut and washer that comes off the car in good shape is sandblasted, replated and used in the restoration. In some cases, when a car is being restored to strict judging standards, the nice-looking cad-plated hardware has to be painted black. "We can take a car to whatever level of authenticity the owner wants," says Jerry Kopecky.

A high level of eyeball appeal is delivered whether

To make the dashboard restoration work easy, Kopecky's Klassics designed this dashboard rotisserie. The shop workers can mount the entire assembly in it and flip the dash over to work at different angles.

A roomy shop is a must. Some restorers say it takes three car spaces to do one car properly. Shelves and cabinets help to clear up floor space and give a shop a nice look.

the car is done for authenticity judging by purists or strictly for show. Looking at the finish that Kopecky achieves on an A-arm or frame rail is like looking in a black mirror. Every rubber bushing, washer, nut and bolt looks like you just bought it at the hardware store. All lines are redone and all hoses are replaced and replacements use the latest rubbers that won't be affected by today's gas blends.

A total restoration also involves sourcing materials from outside suppliers and having carburetors, transmissions, electrical components and interior parts rebuilt by specialists. Kopecky can get interior kits for most of the Mopars he does. Bulk soft trim materials and padded dashboards are also available.

Kopecky has carburetors, engines and transmissions rebuilt by outside specialists. To make the dashboard restoration work easy, Kopecky designed his own dashboard rotisserie. He can mount the entire assembly in it and flip the dashboard over to work at different angles. As the dashboard is disassembled, every piece is sandblasted and refinished. The old brittle, faded and spliced wiring is replaced with a new harness. All chrome trim parts are replated and all gauges are rebuilt. When finished, he has a new dashboard.

Reassembly starts by attaching the totally restored subframe to the body. The frame rails bolt to the cowl and bolt up under a horizontal rib near the front of the floor pan. The A arms, torsion bars, steering components, etc., all bolt to the sub frame. The rebuilt and refinished engine and transmission are installed. The brake and wheel parts are added and tires and hubcaps are mounted. On a full-frame car, the body drops on the chassis and the power train is installed.

Restoring a car this way is expensive. Kopecky is

up-front with his clients. "I do not want to restore your car unless you want it done totally, and totally the right way," he tells them.

Jerry's shop has room. Experts say you need at least a three-car space to restore a vehicle, one for the parts you take off, one for the car and one for the restored parts you're putting back on. Kopecky's shop could probably hold 20 cars, but there is never more than one vehicle being restored at a time.

The shop is kept spotless. Wall shelves are provided for small parts storage. There are two separate rooms. One is used for small parts and chassis assembly. The other is where the body sits on the rotisserie. There's a paint booth at one end. Over the booth is a loft—accessible by stairs (which is nice)—for parts storage. There is plenty of open room to hang large body panels (like fenders and doors) from the rafters, after they are primed or painted. Bumpers, grilles, convertible top frames, etc., are mounted on hooks on the walls.

Kopecky keeps a visual record of all work done with digital photos and videos. He says that taking lots of pictures is a good way to keep track of your total restoration project. I agree and recommend it. I also back the idea of using a digital camera. I resisted getting one for years, but I now have two of them.

Digital cameras are perfect for keeping a visual record of restoration work. You can take hundreds of photos, store them on a memory card (about $25) until the job is done and you do not have to worry about spending hundreds of dollars to make prints.

The Rolling Restoration Approach

A rolling restoration doesn't mean that you're working on a body shell that you can roll around

John Sloane's white MG Midget is a real rolling restoration. Sloane was a Product Specialist for The Eastwood Company, which sells restoration tools and supplies. The little sports car was his product test bed.

One disadvantage to a rolling restoration is not doing everything all at once. After taking my '36 Pontiac's front end off to rebuild the engine, I had to disassemble much of it once again to fix this DuBonnet front suspension unit.

your shop on skates. Such devices—like Backyard Buddy's Easy Access fixtures (essentially a pair of jack stands on wheels)—are a great help with a total restoration, but a rolling restoration is a fully planned project during which you keep the car you're restoring on the road.

One advantage of a rolling restoration is that it is generally cheaper to do than a total restoration, because you will not be taking apart every nut and bolt on the vehicle. Instead, you'll be doing systematic unit repairs until every major unit on the car, truck or motorcycle is repaired. The big advantage is that you can continue to have fun with the car even while it is being restored. There may be some down time when you yank the engine and send it to a machine shop or restitch an interior, but if you plan a rolling restoration properly, the car won't be laid up for years and become more of a pain than a gain.

High Fun Factor—By keeping the car on the road, you'll also have the advantage of keeping your enthusiasm high. The importance of the enthusiasm factor shouldn't be overrated. Just check the classified ads that Gullwing Motors regularly places in publications like *Old Cars Weekly* and AutoTrader's *Classic Cars & Parts*. They often offer sports cars that someone started restoring years ago and gave up on.

Professional restoration shops keep total restoration projects going because they're a source of income to them. Amateurs have the opposite problem. After they rip a car apart, it tends to become a money pit and if they can't keep up with the expenses, they wind up letting the car sit for years. I'm going to get back to that someday, is the

typical response neighbors receive when they ask about the Dodge in the garage.

MG restoration expert Malcolm Green addresses this situation in his excellent book *MG T Series Restoration Guide*. "Most restorations take at least four times as long and cost three times as much as your original estimate," Green wrote. Many of the basket cases started off as perfectly sound cars before being pulled apart by people with more enthusiasm than sense.

Disadvantages—Being able to use the car while it's being restored has a practical aspect to it, but there are a few downsides to the rolling restoration concept. The car that gets totally taken apart, restored piece by piece and totally reassembled is probably going to impress concours judges more than a car that's been fixed up piece by piece. The latter car is probably going to show a little more dirt and wear and tear than the total resto. Also, since the motor may have been done in 2006 and the transmission in 2007, the roller can lack the same uniform level of restoration that the total restoration has. If the goal of your restoration is to win trophies, you should probably plan on doing a total restoration.

A frustration with the rolling restoration approach can be the part that breaks after the car is restored. Since most rollers involve some degree of selective restoration, it's possible for the restorer to skip something it turns out he shouldn't have. For instance, the water pump looked good, so it wasn't rebuilt and, a week after the engine is put back in, the water pump goes out.

This can be partly combated by proper planning. Consider that each part on your car, unless it's

If you're starting with a basket case like this '36 Nash, a rolling restoration is not going to work. You want to start with a fairly decent, operable car and do your restoration work from time to time, as your budget allows.

A rolling restoration works well in combination with the general contractor approach. That's when you remove a part like this Oldsmobile engine, send it out to a specialist to be rebuilt and then reinstall it, as is being done here.

defective, has an expected service life. A water pump is only going to last so long a time before its seals dry out and a starter is going to give you only so many starts before it needs to be rebuilt. When you reassemble your roller, consider the service life of the part rather than how good it looks or how well it seemed to work the last time the car was driven. If you think that water pump has been sitting a long time, the seals are probably weak and it's a beast to rebuild it before you put the engine back in the car.

Skimping on how many old parts you rebuild before reassembly is false economy. First of all, it is

going to be harder and cost you more to bolt a part to an engine once the engine is reinstalled. Secondly, if you get the replacements parts by mail order, it will cost less to ship them all at once than to buy one part now and one later and ship them separately. Don't fix something that doesn't need fixing, but don't try to skimp if your good judgment says it's getting to be time to replace a certain part.

The rolling restoration approach doesn't work very well if the car you're restoring is a basket case to start with. The term basket case means that it was taken apart and you're buying the pieces to put back together. In this case, you definitely can't keep the car going as you restore it. However, once you pass a certain point and it is suitable for street use, you can convert to a rolling restoration at that stage of the project.

In order to do a good rolling restoration, you must have a plan. "If you buy a complete car in working order you could, perhaps, consider doing a running rebuild (same as a rolling restoration) on just one section at a time," says Malcolm Green in his MG restoration book. For example, one year rebuild the engine and then have some fun with the car before starting, say, on the bodywork the next year.

In planning your rolling restoration, keep in mind that the goal is to disassemble the vehicle only to the point of taking off a part or group of parts, then to rebuild the sub-assembly you took off and finally to reinstall the rebuilt sub-assembly in the vehicle. Your overall goal is to rebuild all sub-assemblies on the vehicle. If you reach that point in a relatively reasonable time span, the restoration will be complete. (If it takes too long, the first sub-assemblies you did may have so much wear and tear that they'll need to be redone.)

It would be a good idea to start by mapping out the entire project in a notebook or a dedicated computer file. List each sub-assembly on the car, estimate the time it will take to do it and the likely cost of needed parts and services. This way, you'll know the order you're going to proceed in and you'll have a good idea of the budget you'll need.

Putting the plan on paper will also help you logic out the most practical order in which to deal with each section of the car. For example, it would be silly to finish the body and paintwork, and then deal with taking out and reinstalling the drivetrain. If you did the body first, your new paint might get scratched when the engine is lowered into the chassis and jiggled into proper position. By the same token, you don't want to paint the body tub after you've mounted new tires. If you did, the paint overspray may get on the new rubber.

After restoring four GTOs, Jim Mokwa built this '69 GTO Judge convertible as a mild resto-mod. The car has the overall look of a restored muscle car, but its engineering has been modernized. Thus, the term resto-mod.

A rolling restoration works well with the concept of the restorer functioning as a general contractor, which is the primary focus of this book. As each unit of the car is removed, it can be disassembled and the individual parts can be sent to the vendors who specialize in restoring particular units. The vendors will fix and refinish the part and send it back to the car owner to be reinstalled. Working this way is somewhat like building a model car kit. For many of us, it is the most practical way to match an automobile restoration to our skill level and still enjoy doing the jobs we can do. It can also make a quality restoration more affordable and easy to budget.

Resto-Mod Approach

In the early days of the collector car hobby, cars were put together or assembled. I remember that when I was about twelve years old, one of my favorite books was *How to Fix Up Old Cars* by LeRoi Tex Smith. I checked that book out of the library many times (and you can imagine how honored I was when Tex, by then my boss at *Old Cars Weekly*, asked me to supply a cover photo for an updated version of the book done in 1980). In *How to Fix Up Old Cars*, Tex talked of fixing and rebuilding cars, but he never once talked about building them. In contrast, nowadays, all you hear enthusiasts talk about is car builders.

To some degree, these changes in vocabulary are justified, especially when the car in question is a resto-mod. Craig Jackson of the Barrett-Jackson Auction Co. takes credit for coining this phrase to identify old cars that are modernized as they are being rebuilt. Although the "resto" part of the name comes from restoration, most of these cars do not represent a real restoration, which would imply that they are being put back to the way they originally left the factory. That simply isn't the case, since the finished cars are far from stock.

Resto-mods are created to mate vintage car designs with reliable modern engineering, powerful high-tech engines, up-to-date creature comforts and the latest convenience features. There are resto-mod cars and trucks and even resto-mod motorcycles. For instance, a California company called Kiwi Indian (www.kiwiindian.com) takes original Indian Chief motorcycles with their hard-to-handle tank shifters and suicide clutches and converts them to modern-type machines that baby boomers can ride safely. Owner Mike Tomas, a New Zealand native, has achieved great success with his Kiwi Indians. The idea of modernizing vehicles is really nothing new. Customizers did it years ago. However, the resto-mod type of vehicle is a very sophisticated custom car.

As authors Bill Holder and Phil Kunz pointed out in their book *Resto-Mod Muscle Cars*, The name of this class of modified cars is confusing to say the least. According to Holder and Kunz, other terms that have been applied to them include Pro-Touring Car, Retro-Mod, Resto-Rod, Retro-Rod, Continuation, Clone, Replica, Replicar, Recreation and Hybrid. Holder and Kunz listed six rules that generally apply to resto-mods:

1) Older close-to-stock body
2) No chopping, channeling or tubbing
3) Totally modern built-up engine
4) Custom modernized interior
5) Usually larger wheels
6) Upgraded chassis and suspension components, especially brakes.

In nine out of ten cases, the "resto" means only that the car looks a little bit stock. Usually, the bodywork is restored to one degree or another, while the chassis, tires and wheels, drivetrain and interior are modified to a much higher extent. Often, the amount of bright metal trim is reduced and the bodylines are smoothed out a bit. The OEM headlights and taillights are frequently exchanged for sleeker-looking units. Chopping the windshield and/or roof is common. Rarely does the new paint look anything like the finish that the factory sprayed on. The latest and greatest in high-style wheels and tires is a must. However, the body will still be more restored-to-original than the rest of the car is.

Some people say the "mod" part of the term means modified, but for me it stands for modernized. I'll discuss this more below, but there's no doubt that resto-mod builders pour it on when

Most resto-mods have crate engines like this 427 anniversary edition big-block V-8 that General Motors Restoration Parts division displayed at the 2008 Green Bay, Wisconsin, World of Wheels show.

Powder-coated finishes, as seen on this custom motorcycle engine, are popular for use on drivetrain parts. One reason for this is that they resist gas and oil spills. The parts will stay looking good after the car is driven.

Some resto-mod builders favor the two-tone look with a graphic flavor to the arrangement of colors that emphasizes the original body lines. This Mercury convertible's unique maroon and silver turquoise paint is eye-catching.

it comes to radical changes under the skin. This is where the art of car building really kicks in. These vehicles are not simply made-up of freshly rebuilt parts like a restored car—instead they are totally reengineered machines. They are built up piece by piece like a new car, but with some styling motifs from earlier eras reflected in the finished product.

Most resto-mods are fitted with brand-new, warranty-protected crate engines. The motors are linked to high-tech automatic transmissions ordered from the Internet or from catalogs. Some cars have brand-new frames that builders source from mail-order merchants. Others have modified original frames with coil-over rear suspensions, MacPherson-strut front suspensions and upgraded steering gears. Molded seats are commonly seen and the interiors are no longer reupholstered or trimmed. Instead, they are either custom-built or a kit with modern materials is installed. The cockpits are always fitted with the latest in audio technology, satellite navigation systems and usually a computer. Satellite TV and radio are a must.

Finishes applied to resto-mods generally fall into three basic categories. There is the stealth look with everything painted a dark monochromatic color and no bright metal trim to speak of. The bulk of the trim is either body color or matte black. A new process known as water transfer printing can even add a finish that looks just like carbon fiber, even though it has no real texture to it. Often, exotic paints are used to get special effects such as chameleon colors, ultra-shiny finishes and fadeaway

toning. Powder coating drivetrain and chassis parts is very popular. In many cases, the sheet metal in the engine bay and the engine block itself will be powder coated, with other parts chrome-plated.

Other resto-mods favor the two-tone look with a graphic flavor to the arrangement of colors that emphasizes the original bodylines. For instance, the fender and body sides may be in one color with the upper fender surfaces, hood, trunk, rear panel and roof done in another color. Usually, one of the colors selected is bright, like yellow, orange or red, and the other is a muted hue like gray, tan or white. Lightning bolt graphics are often used to separate the colors.

The third popular style is a wild finish with bright colors and graphic treatments like flames, scallops or stylized versions of popular OEM graphics from the muscle car era like Mopar hockey stick decals of bumblebee stripes, Camaro butterknife decals and Ford and Cobra racing stripes. Builders of resto-mods based on full-size '60s cars sometimes opt for candy apple colors or heavy metallic finishes. The solid-color metal flake

This Rat Rod pickup truck, built by Jim Summers of Michigan, looks like a real barn find in need of restoration. However, it was actually built to look that way and underneath it is solid and reliable as a shiny restored vehicle.

jobs seem to be the top choice for resto-mods based on earlier model cars dating back to the late-'40s.

This brings up the difference between resto-mods and resto-rods. Although there isn't uniform agreement on this opinion, I consider most cars with pre-World War II styling (even those built in 1946–1948) to be resto-rods, rather than resto-mods. But model years don't always tell the story, either. I have seen a 1946–1948-style Buick, several 1949–1951 Shoebox Fords and a few 1949–1951 James Dean Mercs that were definitely more resto-mod than resto-rod.

The cars I'm talking about in this case were radically altered to be low-slung and modern in appearance. Their builders totally abandoned any pretense of paying homage to a prewar look. In essence, they turned a car from one era into a car of a more modern era. To me, the "mod" part of resto-mod means modernized and if the vehicle has the toy-car-come-to-life flavor of a Viper or a New Beetle, to me it's a resto-mod and not a resto-rod. In fact, I would go as far as putting the Plymouth Prowler into this category. The Prowler never looked like a true prewar car—it looked like a modern interpretation of a prewar car.

Some people in the collector car hobby call the job of building a resto-mod a restification. This is another amalgamation of familiar terms, with the "resti" part meaning restoration and the balance of the term designed to indicate that a lot of modifications are being done.

While the term restification may sound a little bit awkward, it does get a point across. Resto-mods aren't restored, because that term means to be put

back to original. However, they do get some of the same attention that a restorer gives a car that's put back to original condition. At the same time, they undergo lots of modifications, too. So, restification works well to describe the process too.

What's important to the purpose of this book is the vision of building a car that evolved out of the resto-mod segment of the hobby. While restification is a legitimate approach to fixing up an old car to make it useful again, it is not what I'm focusing on in these pages. This book is about true restoration. However, the idea of using the same building block approach when doing a restoration is critical to planning a practical modern restoration.

What I am going to try to do in this book, as we go on, is to show how the home restorer can take a car apart, have many units restored by outside specialists and then build the car to like-new condition using the outside-restored units. This is very similar to building a resto-mod, except you'll be working with stock parts instead of updated ones. I believe that this type of restoration—which I call the general contractor approach—can be done at reasonable cost.

The Rat Rod Approach

Originally, a Rat Rod was a type of hot rod that had an unrestored look to it. When this branch of the hobby began, the idea was to build old-school hot rods that resembled the bitsa cars that enthusiasts built right before and after World War II. They were made of bitsa this and bitsa that and somehow they actually ran. In fact, some were pretty fast on the drag strip. These cars were often painted with flat black primer and used Indian blankets for upholstery.

About a decade or so ago, it came to be considered campy to make replicas of such early hot rods. Thus, the Rat Rod movement was born. Before long, cars were actually being restored with special paints that made them look rusty and with their trim powder-coated in black instead of plated with chrome.

Those that participated in the Rat Rod movement created their own culture around the cars. They dressed in old 1950s clothing, slicked back their hair with pomade and organized old-school shows and events that reflected their stylized interest in a bygone era. A whole slew of new magazines evolved and widened the interest in the movement. Publications with names like *Ol' Skool Rodz*, *Car Kulture DeLuxe* and *The Horse* gave the Rat Rodders much exposure.

From seeing such machines at shows, the term

Cowboy Bob Norris builds Ol' Skool flathead-powered Model T track roadsters at his Grade-A-Welding in Fond du Lac, Wisconsin. He has put together six such cars for friends and started a drag racing class for them.

This Old Skool rod started out as a Model A coupe. Cowboy Bob Norris gave it the look of hot rods he built as a teen-ager. A bungee cord holds the passenger door shut, but the '40 Ford dash took great skill to install.

Rat Rod is familiar to almost all car enthusiasts today. We even hear car collectors talking about Rat-Rodded GTOs, Rat-Rodded British sports cars and Rat-Rodded Caprice 9C1 cop cars. Machines of these genres are a far cry from real hot rods, but they take on the Rat Rod name when they are painted in primer and leave restoration shops with Navajo Indian blankets covering their once vinyl or leather seats.

By and large, those who restore cars professionally have mixed feelings about Rat Rods. The professionals can usually build one of these cars very easily and fast, but they make less money than they do turning out full-blown restorations. During an interview in January 2008, restorer and customizer Eddie Paul—who also manufactures special tools and machines for doing metal fabrication work—said he thought that hobbyists were losing interest in Rat Rods.

"I think the Rat Rod trend hurt sales of metal-finishing tools a bit, but that phase appears to be passing and the hot rod phase is coming back," Paul noted. "With such changes, the need for metal refinishing skills is returning to the marketplace and this helps the sale of the tools needed for this type of work."

While this may be the professional view of less-than-perfect Rat Rods, cars with old-school looks make car building more affordable for many regular folks. "We have a shop across the street that does very nice $75,000-and-up custom cars and I even do welding work on them," says Cowboy Bob Norris, the owner of Grade A Welding in North Fond du Lac, Wisconsin. "But when I took a Model A coupe body and turned it into a flat-black roadster, my aim was to do it the way we used to when I was in high school, which was a far cry from $75K."

Norris says he saved a considerable amount of money by going the Rat Rod route and still wound up with what I think is a cool car. His Rat Rod roadster sports a beautifully transferred '41 Ford instrument panel, but it has only a single bucket seat and the passenger door is held shut with a rubber bungee cord.

Building any type of collector car in Rat Rod style is certainly another valid approach to vintage vehicle restoration. If you decide to go this route, try to avoid going too downscale in designing your car. While Bob Norris' high school roadster really nailed the right kind of look with its nostalgic full-wheel discs and other touches, we have seen other rust-and-primer buggies that try to pass off road grime as patina. That type of thing really doesn't work well.

If you think seriously about it, you'll realize that building a top-notch Rat Rod takes more work and creativity than restoring a car to the way that the factory designed it and built it. The original car got its good looks from teams of people who styled it and engineered it years ago. The Rat Rod gets its character from a builder like you. He has to plan both its appearance and mechanicals and then make the whole thing look good and function properly. It's not simple.

Really cool Rat Rod–style cars always rely quite heavily on the selection of a good-looking base vehicle, a just right application of color accents, an interior that draws attention (for one reason or another), a thoughtful choice of tires and wheels and a sense of humor and drama. You can't just not fix the rust on your buggy or spray bomb the fenders with primer. Such actions won't do the trick.

Wild-looking customs like this radical Chevy pickup with a '61 Chrysler front end are part of the Rat Rod/Old Skool Rodz kulture. Though shocking in pink, the interior of this truck—built by Randy Sharpe at DeLuxe Automotive Interior Stylists—is a work of auto-trim art.

With early cars and trucks, classic designs like the '32 Ford and the '39–'40 Fords work very well. Oddballs like a shark-nose Graham or Willys American work great, too. Late '40s fastbacks like '46–'50 Buick Sedanettes are very cool. Rounded cars like '50 Oldsmobiles and '53–'54 Chevys also work quite well.

Since many Rat Rod builders favor stealthy black looks, it takes good use of color accents to make the cars look just right. In the early postwar era, it was popular to paint the edges of wheels red. This gave the wheel covers a red accent. It also looked cool to add color accents to the edges of things like body side moldings and Buick portholes. If you're very lucky, a swap meet will serve up some translucent red plastic accessory wings to add to your hood ornament.

Some interiors inside some Rat Rods draw

A performance choice restoration starts with a basic coupe or hardtop and makes it look like a super stock drag racer. Steve Bimbi of Nickey Chicago had this '65 Plymouth Belvedere SS clone in his muscle car inventory.

attention because they look very funky. For example, EZ Boy Rod Interior Products (www.rodinteriors.com) makes custom-made, do-it-yourself upholstery kits with two-tone colors and vertically pleated seat inserts that look very 1950-ish. On the other hand, some builders like Randy Sharpe, of DeLuxe Automotive Interior Stylists, favor a wild approach with leopard skin seat cover treatments or shiny Mylar door panels.

Choosing tire and wheel treatments is just as important on a Rat Rod as it is on a Classic Packard or a Pierce-Arrow. There are traditional styles of tires like gangster whitewalls. Olds Fiesta wheel covers are in great demand, too. There are hot rod-style tires, like fat drag slicks and Baby Moon hubcaps to dress them up with. The fun thing to remember is there's no right or wrong when it comes to picking Rat Rod parts. You can wind up with good-looking or you can wind up with ugly, but it's impossible to be factory incorrect. There's no such thing as standard equipment or factory-approved accessories for a modified car.

If you're interested in taking the Rat-Rod approach to building a collector car, chances are pretty good you're a dyed-in-the-wool do-it-yourselfer. If your love is hot rods of the old-school variety, than you'll probably want to build the car the way they did in the old days. That doesn't mean you'll never need a little outside help to take care of certain unit repairs. In fact, you'll find this book helpful in tracing down suppliers and service providers who can help you with your project.

Dave Glass of D & M Corvette Specialists started with a '65 Plymouth Belvedere post coupe and built it into a Match Race Stocker. It looks like the factory-backed, altered-wheelbase Plymouths raced in the '60s.

The Belvedere has authentic 1960s roof stripes that suggest it was raced back then. However, it was not originally a straight-axle car and was restored to its current beautiful state.

Performance Choice Approach

Another approach to automobile restoration that is becoming quite popular is what I call the performance choice. I'm not talking about restoring a true muscle car back to factory condition. I'm talking about taking a car of a similar style and restoring to look like a super stock drag racer. In the high-performance segment of the old-car hobby, such cars are known as clones or continuation cars and they are very much accepted by collectors, as long as someone isn't trying to perpetrate a fraud scheme by passing the copies off as the real thing.

Turning a base-level early-'60s Dodge into a copy of a Ramcharger drag racing car from that period or a '64 Fairlane into a 427 Thunderbolt clone is actually a very practical approach to restoration. The finished product—if done right—can be worth more than the cost of buying the car and restoring it. Dave Glass, of D & M Corvette Specialists in Downers Grove, Illinois, proves the point.

Glass started with a '65 Plymouth Belvedere post coupe and built it into a Match Race Stocker. It looks a lot like the factory-backed, altered-wheelbase Plymouths that drivers such as Lee Smith used to drag race back in the mid-'60s. Glass's red, white and blue '65 Belvedere could easily pass for a high-dollar, limited edition Super Stocker if it had the original torsion-bar front suspension.

Glass says that the car did not always look as nice as it does today. "My Plymouth was drop dead ugly when I first bought it," Dave explained. "The crew in the D & M restoration shop redid just about everything—except the roof."

The car's roof is painted a medium-blue color with multiple white stripes running front to rear. Believe it or not, the paint on that roof is completely original, Glass discovered. "While we don't know if the car was famous, we do know for sure that this Belvedere was an old racing car. We purchased it from a man in Indiana, but all the evidence suggests that it was drag raced in Kentucky."

When found, the car had no motor, but the four-speed gearbox was bolted in it and looked to be a 100-percent factory-installed item. The car was not converted to a four-speed, Dave feels. It had been tubbed and it carried a 6-point racing cage. "The guys at my Corvette store really got involved with this Plymouth build. Sometimes they think I'm a little eccentric or just plain nuts, to take on projects like the Belvedere, but they know that I really enjoy the cars."

The Belvedere was built about two years ago. All of the mechanical restoration procedures and bodywork were done right at the D & M Corvette facility. Dave's complex includes a fully equipped restoration shop, as well as a body shop and a service building. A man named Randy Ball was the only outside contractor to work on the Belvedere. He stitched up the red bucket seat interior. Fiberglass front fenders are fitted and mounted so they sit high off the ground.

The engine under the hood today is a 472 Hemi. The car goes to cruise nights in Downers Grove, but is not actually raced. "I got the racing out of my system years ago," says Glass. "But when I ran into a rep from Comp Cams at a car show, I asked him to get me a gnarly cam that made the same noises as a race car and he delivered in spades." The Plymouth has a sturdy Dana rear axle.

Also included in the performance choice approach to restoration is the Triumph owner who swaps his sports car's original SU carburetors for a pair of higher-performing Webers like these.

Glass loves how the Belvedere came out. It's a racing car, so it's cold-blooded until it gets up to 150 degrees, then it drives and runs good, he says. The only thing that could make life better is if he found out more about the car's early race history. He keeps hoping that someone will recognize the paint scheme on the roof and step up with documentation of the car's old drag racing career.

Dave's personal research shows that Plymouth built 11 acid-dipped Satellite coupes with 426 Hemi V-8 engines and four-speed gearboxes to race in the 1965–1966 season. "I grew up in that era and watched drivers like Dandy Dick Landy and Sox & Martin run cars like my Plymouth," Glass explained. "That's when I first raced my Willys, but it was also the onset of the funny car era. So I decided to build a car like the ones I used to see racing back then."

Restoring a car as a clone of a famous drag racer is not easy. Neither is building a continuation car. Both jobs call for gathering rare parts and doing lots of research to get the details right. Many of the enthusiasts who put such cars together collect the entire history of the vehicle and the men who drove it. And as I said earlier, such cars must be built the right way to have any real value. Just making a car look like a drag racer isn't enough. It also has to replicate the technology and high performance that went into the original car.

Though I have focused on drag racers in this section, it's important to point out that the performance choice approach to restoration is just as valid with other types of cars. At one end of the

spectrum, you have the collector of prewar cars who finds a chassis and engine from one of the more powerful early machines and then restores it with a speedster body. At another end, you have the British sports car fan who substitutes Weber carburetors for SUs or who turns his Austin-Healey frog-eyed Sprite into a vintage race car. If nicely done, such restorations can be worth lots of dough. The bottom line is that car collectors appreciate performance and are often willing to trade a few judging points for a couple of extra ponies under the hood.

The "Bitsa" Approach

Many vintage vehicle restorers don't really have a specific plan when they start their restoration. They may have a Pontiac body in the garage and find a Buick engine in the junkyard. They may put the two together to wind up with a working car and then add modern rims and tires they purchased at a garage sale. These folks are not trying to make a resto-mod or build a performance choice car—they are simply running what they brung to end up with a functional, good-looking vehicle. Some are motivated strictly by budget considerations, while others are simply being very practical or creative people.

Also included in the little bit of this and little bit of that class are restorers who are fixing vehicles that are virtually impossible to get parts for. People in this situation generally have two options: they can try to fabricate close-to-original parts by working from photos and attempting to make scale drawings of the needed components. Then, they make the parts or have them made. Other restorers may simply substitute a part that works, without worrying about how much it resembles the factory part. They might put a tractor muffler on a truck or a motorcycle muffler on a sports car.

Some enthusiasts go way beyond the fabrication or swapping of a few individual parts to restore a car. Instead, they scratch-build their own complete cars from parts of various vehicles. Lee Bestul, of Iola, Wisconsin, originally constructed his beautiful Bestul Roadster in the early 1950s, when he was a young man. He used flathead V-8 Ford running gear and modified the sheet metal panels from other cars to create a personalized sports car. Cut-down 1946–1948 Buick hoods were turned into fenders. They were mated with parts from other prewar and postwar cars.

Looking at the car today, you can sense that Lee took inspiration from cars like the Kaiser Darrin and the Nash-Healey, not to mention production models like the first Corvette. When the car was

The Bestul roadster that Lee Bestul of Iola, Wisconsin, built in the early '50s was made from parts of several cars and patterned after models like the Nash-Healey and early Corvette. It was featured in magazines of its era.

This Cadillac displayed in the Historic Auto Attractions museum in Roscoe, Illinois, is made up of non-matching parts and both sides of the car are different. A Johnny Cash song about an autoworker inspired it.

completed, it gained notoriety and was featured in a do-it-yourself type magazine. The beauty of Bestul's car was that it was his own one-of-a-kind creation and it caused a stir wherever he drove it.

Lee Bestul went on to a career as an aircraft mechanic, but he held onto the Bestul sports car and his passion for special automobiles. After retiring, Lee started to restore the car he had built many years earlier. Many advances in automotive technology had taken place since the early postwar era and Lee was able to incorporate a lot of improvements in his refurbished sports car.

Perhaps the ultimate expression of the A Little of This and a Little of That approach was a series of three promotional vehicles made for Manufacturers Hanover Trust, a New York City bank. They were called the Anycars (spelled three different ways over the years) and they were made up of parts of different vehicles. The idea behind them was to get across the point that Manufacturers Hanover Trust would write loans for the purchase on any car.

The first of these vehicles was called the Any Car I and it was built in 1970. It was originally called the ForChevAmChrysVagen, but the name Any Car was easier for people to remember it by. The car's main body section was a Volkswagen Beetle sunroof sedan, but the tail fins were from a Chrysler 300 Letter Car. Parts from over 22 different models were used to construct the vehicle.

Called AnyCar II, the second vehicle in the series was as distinctive as its predecessor. Again featuring something for everyone styling, it incorporated parts from 50 automobiles from prewar to modern models. The dominant component was a 1929 Hudson sedan body. Other pieces were from a

Cadillac Eldorado and a Valiant.

The third promotional car was built in 1974 and was called ANYCAR III. It was as visually dynamic as its two predecessors. In this case, customizer George Barris was hired to create the vehicle. It included parts from a Chrysler, Mercury Cougar, Lincoln Mark IV, Mercury, Olds Astra Cruiser, Cadillac El Dorado, Buick Riviera, Cadillac, Datsun, Buick, Toyota, Lincoln, Lincoln Continental, Peugeot, Alfa Romeo and a Ford Pinto. The main body was donated by a 1974 Volkswagen station wagon.

An unusual feature of this car, inspired by the 1973 Gas Crunch, was a Mini Anycar that fit under the hood. This 27-inch wide miniature version was battery powered and had four forward speeds. It could actually be used for short-range travel.

The idea of making a functioning car out of a bit of this and a bit of that is such a common one that the late Johnny Cash sang a comical country song about an autoworker who builds a car out of pieces that he sneaks out of a Cadillac factory in his lunch pail and a coworker's motor home. As the song describes it, the project started in 1949 and lasted into the '70s. The car wound up being built out of parts from so many different model years that its title was a mile long.

While it sounds almost impossible to actually take parts from different years of Cadillac and combine them to make a single car, someone did actually do this to promote the song. The car they put together was again used for promotional efforts and it wound up in Wayne Lensing's Historic Auto Attractions Museum in Roscoe, Illinois, where it is on display today.

Restoring a vintage racing car is fun. This '29 Chandler Indianapolis 500 racer is on exhibition at the Historic Auto Attractions museum in Roscoe, Illinois. Some people restore such cars to actually race them.

1929 Indianapolis Race Car

Though it's doubtful that any restorer would want to turn a pile of mismatched parts into a car to promote a bank or a song, a lot of hobbyists may do a little mixing and matching to get a car fixed up. This is especially true when they have to stick to a budget and using a little bit of this and a bunch of that can help them make the most of parts that they already have on hand.

If you want to build a car to take to a judged show like the Pebble Beach Concours d'Elegance or the Antique Automobile Club of America's Fall National Meet at Hershey, Pennsylvania, this approach to restoration probably won't do the trick. However, if the car is being built to wow your friends at a cruise night or drive to a Back to the '50s event, it's the visual impact that counts more than a 100-percent factory restoration so use the Frank Sinatra system and do it your way.

Special Purpose Restoration Approach

A good example of a special purpose car fix-up project might be the restoration of an old racing car or the rejuvenation of a vintage police car. In both of these cases, the reason the car is being restored will dictate many aspects of the job. For instance, will you be rebuilding the racing car to participate in vintage racing? Or is it being refurbished for exhibition in a racing car museum?

If the car is going to be taken on the racetrack, you'll want to make sure it has a roll bar. Many old racing cars didn't come with one, but in this case safety is far more important than historical correctness. In a similar manner, you shouldn't try

racing a car without fresh rubber, even if the original tires had a distinctive look that's missing from the replacements. You can't be racing on tires that are 60 years old.

However, if the car is being restored only for stationary display in a museum like the Indianapolis Motor Speedway Hall of Fame, then you will be more interested in giving it a just-right appearance. You can leave the roll bar off and stick with the original tires.

Many old trucks are restored for special purposes, often to promote the owner's business or type of work. Dave Pugh operates a business called Expert Towing & Recovery in Oshkosh and Omro, Wisconsin. He purchased a 1936 Dodge tow truck to promote the business and restored it as a part-time project.

With its low original miles, original drivetrain and original 6-volt electrical system, the Dodge proved to be in pretty good shape. Dave spent $300 to restore the paint and mechanical systems and $50 to rewire the electrical system. He stored the truck in Omro and worked on it Tuesday and Thursday evenings and one weekend afternoon. It was pizza, beer—sometimes a Green Bay Packers game—and a lot of spinning wrenches, he recalls.

Dave did the drivetrain repairs himself and farmed out the bodywork. He had the truck painted in the white and purple combination used on most of his modern trucks. When the cab was done, he dropped it on the chassis with a modern tow truck. The wrecker unit and box only took six months to restore. The rare Sasgen towing derrick

Dave Pugh operates a business called Expert Towing & Recovery in Oshkosh and Omro, Wisconsin. He purchased a 1936 Dodge tow truck to promote the business and restored it as a part-time project.

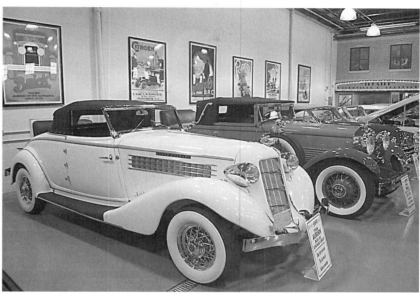

Looking for a job in the hobby? Some major private collections have full-time employees to maintain finished cars and restore new cars that are added to the collection. Many of these individuals work like general contractors.

was disassembled, sandblasted and reconditioned.

Dave Pugh enjoys taking his vintage Dodge to tow shows and antique car shows. While it doesn't go very fast, it gets lots of looks and lets people know about his towing and recovery services.

The General Contractor Approach

In the construction industry, the term general contractor refers to an individual or group that contracts with another person or organization to do the construction or renovation of a building, roadway or structure. The general contractor is an entity that has signed a prime construction contract, which spells out the details of the project.

The general contractor is responsible for the means and methods used in the execution of the contract and for completion of the project in accordance with the signed contract, which usually includes a budget, general and special conditions and the plans and specifications of the project. The general contractor usually takes care of the supply of the materials, labor, equipment and services needed to do the project. To get the job done, it is common for a general contractor to subcontract the work to specialized companies and individuals. He must hire the help in a managed way, so that all jobs required to do the project are completed on time, at a reasonable cost.

Many modern car collectors are starting to use the general contractor approach to get their cars restored. In most of these cases, the general contractor is a classic car owner himself. His role is to manage the restoration project, although he does not get directly involved in doing specialized hands-on work. Instead, the car owner may handle disassembly of the vehicle at the start of the project

and its reassembly later on, but individual unit repairs will be done by companies in locations that are remote from where the vehicle actually is.

There are also cases where large private collections, museums and restoration shops are hiring general managers who function like general contractors. Both the changes in the ways in which cars are restored and the fact that car collections are growing so sophisticated reflect the wisdom of restoring cars in a managed way. Auto restoration has become a very expensive undertaking and hiring a good manager or acting like a manager yourself can reduce the time and money it takes to build a car.

For the most part, auto restoration is no longer a pastime in which hobbyists spend 20 years restoring a Model T by the light of the moon and the warmth of the woodstove. Gone for the most part are the days of replacing worn bearings with pieces of shoe leather and machining your own cylinder head bolts on a belt-driven lathe. Today's restorers use computerized parts catalogs to order brand-new bearings and order their hardware from suppliers with CNC machines who supply bolt kits for different engines in a choice of black, cad-plated or chrome. It's a different world out there and it's changing more every day.

To most people, it makes common sense that hiring unit repairs out to specialists will shorten the time that it takes to restore a car, but restorers—especially those who fix cars up as a hobby—often

This '39 Studebaker pickup owned by Paul Katzke was the prototype of a turnkey hot rod built by Mark Wrobleski of Kreative Rodwerks in Phoenix, Arizona.

struggle with the idea that you can manage your cost if you're farming a lot of the work out to other people. If you're paying for labor that the car owner used to donate to the project, how can you possibly save money?

Labor is undoubtedly one of the more expensive elements of automotive restoration. Rejuvenating a car, truck or motorcycle is a labor-intensive endeavor and each year the cost of labor seems to shoot upwards.

Five or six years ago, one of my coworkers bought an early version of the '39 Studebaker pickup that Mark Wrobleski now builds at Kreative Rodwerks. Paul's truck was one of the first of the beautiful turnkey vehicles and since labor was less costly at the time, he paid noticeably less than what the latest version sells for. The '39 Studebaker pickup is one of today's best values in turnkey cars, but Kreative Rodwerks can't sell it for the same price it did six years ago. To keep its talent, the company has to pay higher labor costs.

If you use the general contractor method to restore your car, but pay for the labor at current rates, how can you manage your cost? I feel the economies here are in getting the job done by an

expert in that type of work the first time around. It is my experience that if you use talented vendors with a good reputation for doing the work quickly and properly (and a warranty they stand behind) you can wind up with a completely satisfactory experience that will cost you about the same or only slightly more than doing the work yourself.

Typically, the direct savings in using an outside contractor come in the form of job experience and not having to buy expensive parts two or three times. A simple case in point was a problem I had with the exhaust manifold on my 1948 Pontiac Streamliner Eight leaking carbon monoxide and making noise.

Since I restore cars strictly as a hobby and have no background in the field, there are times when I can't spot the cause of a problem instinctively. I took the manifold off and put it back on three times. Each time I had to spend about $50 for a gasket set and a few bucks for other things like a curved wrench, WD-40, hardware and a can of Eastwood manifold paint.

The third time I took it off, I sent it to a professional who knew immediately that it was slightly warped. (My first inclination was to think I had done something wrong in reinstalling it). The mechanic took the manifold to a machine shop and had it repaired for a total cost of about $75 for the machining and his work.

The bottom line was that I spent around $116 for a job that the professional would have done for $125. In addition, if I had gone to the mechanic in the first place, the job would have been completed sooner (though I doubt that he would have wanted to stop and repaint the manifold for me.) It's true that professional services will sometimes cost you a lot more than doing the job yourself, but if you are a good general contractor, I think you can strike a little balance and bring your project in on budget by actually getting other jobs done cheaper. And for many of us, if we can shave hours off a restoration by using professional services, we can use those hours to make extra money to help offset any slight cost overruns.

If you have to redo jobs on your car and buy new gaskets like these each time, you may find your costs running higher than subcontracting the work out to a specialist who knows all the ins and outs of the job.

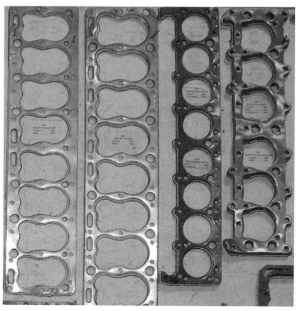

Chapter 2

The Elements of a Successful Restoration

Having a dedicated place to work and to keep your projects organized is an important factor for a successful restoration. This 40 x 72 ft. steel building is my workplace. It has a 20 x 20 ft. heated shop behind the larger overhead door.

Based on what I have seen over the years in professional restoration shops and learned in my own hobby shop, there are seven elements of a vehicle restoration. Planning and organization is the first thing to think about. If you go into a restoration without a vision of what you are going to accomplish, it is like shooting into the dark. A place to work is important. You will need more space than you think you do. Tools and equipment are the keys to success. You can't drive a square peg into a round hole without a square-peg driver (ha ha).

Finding or fixing parts is essential. Wage and price controls are important to maintain a controlled budget to handle restoration expenses. Time management is important. Most of us squeeze this hobby into already busy lives. Finally, hitting your goals gets the job done. Just check the cars-for-sale classified ads any issue of *Hemmings Motor News* to see how many project cars never get done.

Planning and Organization

Automobile restoration is not rocket science. Most jobs you'll encounter in your shop are a matter of taking the pieces apart, cleaning the pieces, painting the pieces, fixing or replacing broken pieces and putting the pieces back together again. Anyone can loosen or tighten a nut and almost anyone can spray paint.

So there are really only a few tricks involved in restoration. The one that requires the most talent seems to be the job of keeping things organized so you know where to find the cleaned-painted-fixed-replaced pieces prior to the bolt-them-back-together stage. Whether you restore on an amateur or

professional basis, keeping things organized is critical to the success of your project.

When you are at the taking-things-apart stage, get yourself an inexpensive wheeled shop cart with a parts tray on top and a parts shelf at the bottom. Typically, these cost under $25 at Wal-Mart and other department stores. Some have a sliding drawer under the top tray that holds a small socket set. They aren't industrial strength sockets, but they come in handy when you need a second socket of similar size to hold a nut while you're turning the head of the bolt with your good wrench. The tray on top of the cart may also include depressions that help you sort out different small parts. Bigger parts fit nicely on the bottom, small parts fit on the top and nothing gets dropped on the floor and stepped on.

A mechanic's seat on wheels is available in the same discount stores at about the same price. Sitting down while working on a car sure beats wearing out the knees of your jeans (not to mention your knees themselves). One style of mechanic's seat has a built-in tool drawer and a bottom tray. Another is like a round stool with a round parts tray at the bottom. Once you start using a mechanic's seat, you will use it all the time.

Plastic storage tubs come in real handy when disassembling units that have matching right-hand and left-hand assemblies. Just toss the pieces in the proper (left-hand or right-hand) tub. Nothing gets lost or mixed up or stepped on. The tubs come in a variety of sizes and, with the lids in place, are stackable. (Don't stack them too high if they're filled with heavy parts like starters.)

A $2.50 cupcake tin makes a great sorter/storer for small

This building in Fond du Lac, Wisconsin, is home to Hamilton Classics. Restorer Steve Hamilton has turned it into a neat, well-organized shop, with shelving and furniture needed to store supplies, equipment and parts.

A tool board made from plywood is a great way to keep both hand tools and power tools organized. Some mechanics draw outlines of each tool on the spot it hangs in, so they know exactly what goes on each nail or hook.

For sorting and keeping track of small auto parts, there's nothing better than a cupcake tin for the price of $2.50 or so. You can write notes directly on it with a felt pen and sand them off later on.

parts, like brake hardware or valvetrain components. You can immediately tell which return spring goes on which side if you arrange the pieces in the same relationship they had when on the car. You can write on the tin with a felt marker pen and then buff the writing off later.

The careful storage of nuts, bolts, screws and fasteners is very important. Use parts storage chests with those little plastic drawers. There should be a separate drawer for each size or thread style. Label them carefully and you'll know right where everything is. Another good way to store hardware or small parts is in shelf bin units available from discount tool suppliers like JC Whitney, Harbor Freight and Northern Tool. These have colorful molded plastic bins that lock into steel racks with gray baked enamel finish at an angle. Having the bins angled makes them easy to see into and reduces the amount of floor space these racks take up in your shop. Double-sided models are also available.

As far as shelves go, after trying many options from cheap gray-finished steel shelving units to wooden shelves, I have found sturdy chrome-plated wire shelves on wheels to be the best option. I purchase these on eBay at the lowest price I've found anywhere. Wire shelves do not collect a lot of dust and, since they're on wheels, I can move them out to sweep behind them. If I rearrange the shop, I do not have to empty the shelves—I just roll them to the new location.

When it comes to shop furniture like cabinets, shelves, tool chests and workbenches, modern hobbyists have a wide range of choices available. Hobby publications like *Old Cars Weekly* and AutoTrader's *Classic Cars & Parts* are filled with ads from companies that make nostalgic- or professional-looking shop furnishings for the home garage set. I have to admit that my workbench is an old retail store counter that I bought years ago at an estate auction for $11. It works, but it isn't the prettiest thing you ever saw or the most well designed workbench.

Small shelves that hold spools of different gauges of wire are nice to have in a home restoration shop. At a hardware store going-out-of-business sale, I also picked up one of those tin cabinets that hold spools of hose that pull out through different size holes in the front. Most old auto parts stores have them.

Having an old computer in your home restoration shop is a good way to track the progress of your work. Adding a photo scanner allows you to copy pages from old shop manuals so you don't get the originals greasy.

In addition to having room for cars you plan to work on, your home restoration shop should have a place to keep stuff. These tires, wheels and a spare engine are being stored at Classics Plus Ltd., in Fond du Lac, Wisconsin.

If the tool chest in your hobby shop is stuffed, you may want to consider building a tool board. "My tool board makes great use of air space by allowing me to hang tools on the wall from the floor to the ceiling," says Bill Kroseberg, the Automotive Technology instructor at Waupaca High School in Waupaca, Wisconsin. "Having a tool board is a big help in teaching students how to keep their tools organized and put them back in the right place. You can draw an outline of each tool on the board and then you know if one is missing. We used double sheets of oak paneling and anchored it to the cinder-block wall with metal inserts and lag bolts. It's strong enough for the heaviest tools."

I used Kroseberg's tool board as a model and built one for my shop. My son and I started with four sheets of plywood. We mounted two sheets side by side on the bottom of the wall and two more directly above them. We wound up with a tool board 8 feet tall and 16 feet wide that takes up most of one wall in my two-car-garage-sized shop. It holds every tool I need for most restoration jobs.

In addition to tools, a well-organized restoration shop needs a bookshelf for the storage of spec sheets and repair manuals. In addition, these days it doesn't hurt to have a computer with Internet access right in your shop. The last time I visited Wal-Mart, they were selling a very small Acer laptop with wi-fi capability for $338. There is a lot of technical and get-me-out-of-a-jam information available on the Internet and if you have DSL or wireless in your home, it will pick up a signal in your garage.

I recently visited a publicity-shy friend who has a very successful high-tech professional background and a genuine passion for old cars. Combining his talents, he tracks all restoration work and service work on his 140 vehicles by computer. He has programs that print out sheets that tell him when

each car requires service and what needs to be done to it. He also has every part and tool in his shop logged in on a computerized inventory. How's that for organization!

Any shop, large or small, can benefit from organizational techniques like those spotlighted in this section. You simply cannot put things back together again properly if you cannot find the pieces, tools and aids you need to accomplish the work. Many vintage cars have been taken apart, but only a fraction of them get put back together again. The secret to finishing a car is good organization.

Setting Up Shop

To work on a car you need a place with room, light, heat and security. I have seen cars that were nicely restored in places that weren't the best, but if you are going to restore a car using the general contractor approach, you are going to need a pretty good place to work so that you can stay organized and move your project along quickly. You are going to require storage for both the car and its restored parts, as well as room for shipping and receiving parts sent to rebuilders located in remote areas. You'll need to have your tools handy (like restorers always did), but you'll also need a place to keep your computer, which is becoming a big aid to today's restorers.

Space—The place you work will have to provide sufficient room for the project or projects that you have in mind. However, that doesn't always translate into lots of space. I once met a man who was doing a very nice restoration of a World War II Jeep in a one-car garage. He had the body suspended from the rafters and a loft for parts storage. Since the Jeep was a simple and small vehicle and since he was a super-organized person, his one-car garage was sufficient for his project.

Logic dictates that you need more room to work on multiple cars than to restore a single vehicle. Although this collector has abundant space, some hobbyists work their restoration magic very well in much smaller areas.

Having good light is extremely important when working on a car. To get things done, you have to be able to see what needs doing. Work lights and spotlights help a lot when trying to visualize how parts fit back together.

However, most of us need more space than that to do a car, truck or motorcycle.

Generally speaking, you need a disassembly area, an equal-size area to store removed parts, and a third area, of about the same size, to store your new and refurbished parts. When you start to reassemble the vehicle, your disassembly area can be used for assembly. If you were going to paint the car yourself, you'd need a fourth, specialized area for that purpose. The approach we're taking in this book assumes you'll be farming out the paintwork.

If you store your parts on the wheeled, wire

shelving units that I spoke of earlier, you can get by with a shop that is about 25 x 25 ft. to restore most single vehicles. This is about the size of a two-car garage and permits a disassembly area, a large parts storage area and room for two shelves (one for storing smaller removed parts and the other for storing your smaller new or rebuilt components).

Naturally, if you are going to be working on more than one car at a time, you'll need more room. The same is true in the case of a truck, because everything is larger on a truck. In contrast, a small car like an MG Midget can be restored in a smaller space. You can also restore a motorcycle in a smaller space, since almost everything on a motorcycle is smaller than it is on a car.

In addition to having sufficient space for the job you're planning, the room you are using for your restoration should be neat, clean and orderly. High ceilings are a definite plus, since they give you wall space for mounting shelves and hanging tools. Another advantage to a high ceiling is that you will be able to lift the car higher in the air if you have a vehicle lift in your shop.

Lighting—You can't work on a car in the dark. Good light is essential to do the job right. The more lights you have illuminating the work, the easier it will be to fit parts together and get your wrenches on the fasteners. If possible, use skylights or sidelights to fill the shop with natural illumination, since this will help lower your electric bill.

Having lights available in your shop requires that the shop be wired for electrical service. You will have to hire a licensed electrician for a proper and legal install. If you are building a new shop or remodeling an old one, leave the stud walls uncovered until the electrical wiring is installed. This will make the electrician's work go much easier and faster, which will save you money. Remember, if you plan to run a big compressor or other heavy-duty machines, conventional household wiring won't do. You'll need 220V service to your shop.

HVAC—In addition to light, your home restoration shop needs to be comfortable to work in. You can't work on a car if you're shivering. How big an issue this will be depends on where you live, of course. If you work on cars in Phoenix, Arizona, you will probably be more concerned about installing air conditioning than putting a heater in. Some restorers can work very well in rather low temperatures, especially when wearing a heavy insulated work shirt or lined coveralls. Other mechanics are warm-blooded and can't function in cold of any degree.

There are many options for heating a shop from

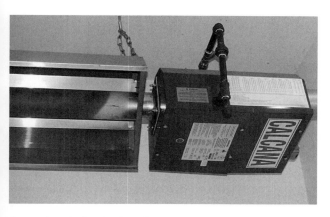

A popular choice for keeping home restoration shops toasty in winter is a radiant heating system like this one. Whatever type of system you use, have it installed by professionals and safety checked each heating season.

space heaters to sophisticated forced-air systems, radiant heating systems and heating coils in a concrete floor. Though old-fashioned woodstoves can raise safety issues, a professional restorer I know heats his entire shop with a very safe wood pellet stove. His stove throws off wonderful fireplace-like warmth and the cost is a fraction of heating with petroleum-based fuels. Many professional mechanics like waste-oil heaters and the latest models burn clean and save money.

When choosing a heating system, you can get a lot of information on the Internet and local heating and cooling contractors will be happy to tell you about the products they sell. Whatever system you use, make sure that it is installed correctly and has a good exhaust system for taking carbon monoxide out of your restoration building. Another thing to remember is that some systems can't be run down to the last drop of fuel. For instance, if you're using a propane fired radiant heater, you should refill the propane tank at or before the 10 percent level. If you let it go lower than that, your propane provider will have to pressure check the system.

If you're going to heat your restoration room, you'll also want to make sure that it is well-insulated and as weather-tight as possible. It is kind of senseless to pump heat into a space that doesn't do a good job of retaining it. That's kind of like pouring water into a bottomless glass.

Car buildings are often large and have many spots where heated air can escape. In my case, I have a 40 x 72-foot metal building with overhead doors. Insulating the entire building was cost prohibitive at the time I had it erected, but I had thought ahead and realized I planned to build a walled off shop in the east side front corner of the building. So I

originally had the entire roof insulated. Later, when I built the 25 x 25-foot shop, I had the walls insulated. Styrofoam panels line the back of the overhead door and the door has a rubber seal along the bottom. I still haven't insulated all the walls, but only the shop is heated and it is fully insulated to keep the heat inside. Wisconsin winters don't bother me.

Security—The place you restore cars also has to be secure and security measures range from keeping out thieves to keeping out varmints. Another part of security is keeping your work area safe and free of things you could step on or trip over.

Fire Safety—Naturally, fire safety is a big concern in any shop where gas, oil and other combustibles are stored. Personally, my biggest fire concerns are about my own human fallibility: Will I work until I'm very tired one night and leave a switch on when I close the shop? Will the night come that I forget to unplug a battery charger? I have seen human errors cause many disasters. You can contact your local fire department to create a preplan for your shop. This will give them an idea of your shop's layout and help them save it if a fire erupts.

A big way to avoid burning your own shop down is to have a checklist you use, before leaving the shop at night, to make sure you didn't forget to do something. Check to make sure all those oily rags were put in a special fire-resistant container. Check to make sure you unplugged everything you have to. Check that no flammables were left in the vicinity of the heater or furnace. (Ideally, they should all be stored in a special type of cabinet.) Make sure you turned off the lights and that you activated the security system if you have one.

Of course, many old car hobbyists do not have electronic security on their shops and have no intention of going that route because of the cost involved. One thing they can do is purchase dummy security cameras to mount on the building. These look like real cameras and sensors and can keep at least some thieves away. And there is

A friendly electrician had salvaged this antitheft and anti-fire security system from a commercial building and installed it in a hobbyist's restoration shop. The locking key case below it is a good place for spare keys.

You will want to have all the basic tools in your home restoration shop, including a full set of different types of screwdrivers including flat-blade, Phillips head, Torx drive, Prince head, Reed head and Allen head styles.

certainly no substitute for a good set of sturdy locks and chains, as long as you use them. Include a lock-up review on your nighttime checklist and go over it to make sure that all the locks are closed and fastened.

Tools and Equipment

A third element of car restorations is the tools and equipment needed to fix cars. You may already own some of the tools you need to do automotive work, so inventory what you have. Know how long your essential tool list is, the tool you need most is the one that gets the next job done. However, the more tools you have in your arsenal, the closer you'll be to owning every tool you'll ever need.

Basic Tool Kit—A basic tool kit should contain at least three screwdrivers with shaft lengths 1-1/2 to 8 inches. There are various types such as flat-blade, Phillips head, Reed head, Prince head, Torx drive, Allen head and clutch head. You can buy a kit with removable and interchangeable bits for your screwdriver.

Pliers is another basic tool. To start with you'll definitely need linesman pliers, needle-nose pliers, bent-nose pliers, locking-jaw pliers, interlocking pliers and special snap-ring pliers. As you build up your tool set, you'll want to add small pliers of each type, which come in very handy in tight spaces. I also like a small pliers I bought with inward-facing end that can get under nails and rivets to extract them. A good auto shop will have dozens of different types of pliers.

As far as wrenches go, you'll need open-end wrenches, box-end wrenches and adjustable wrenches and you'll need both SAE (inch-fractional) and Metric wrenches. Ratcheting box wrenches come in handy, as do shorties that can get you into tight spaces. A good ratchet wrench set with 1/4-, 3/8- and 1/2-inch drives is important. You'll want both regular and deep sockets, and as many adapters and extensions as you can afford. As you build your set of wrenches, you can add U-jointed swivel sockets, curved manifold wrenches, crow's foot wrenches and on and on. You will need a torque wrench.

Here are some other tools and equipment you should have in your shop:
• Flat files, half-round files and rattail files
• A hacksaw
• Chisels from small to large
• Punches from small to large
• Claw hammer, ball-peen hammer and mallet (to start with)
• Tin snips, compound cutters and wire cutters
• Trouble lights and floodlights
• Basic set of brake tools
• Basic set of battery service tools
• Basic set of tire changing and repair tools
• Basic set of bodywork tools
• Basic ignition system tools (from feeler gauge to timing light)
• Basic oil change tools (including filter wrench and oil drain pan)
• Jacks and jack stands
• A creeper and a mechanic's stool
• Test instruments: compression gauge, vacuum gauge, dwell-tach
• Workbench

Where to Buy Tools—Almost every estate auction has old tools. Business liquidation auctions are a good source, too. You can often buy high-quality automotive tools for a lot less. Some of these auctions are advertised in hobby publications. Inspect items before bidding; write down your top bid and stick to it. Auctioneers will work for higher prices once they see you buying.

Modern charity stores tend to compete with chain stores. They carry new closeout merchandise, like cheap tools made overseas. The prices are often the same as those for better tools sold elsewhere. For automotive work, some of the brushes, mirrors and magnet tools might be OK for your toolbox, but otherwise your money will be better spent somewhere else. Also check for shelves, racks and displays donated by businesses that can serve as shop furniture.

Warehouse outlets or liquidators sell tools like

This 20-ton bottle-jack-style hydraulic press was on sale at a Harbor Freight discount tool store when purchased. Though used only occasionally, it paid for itself within a few months by eliminating outside services.

This mobile engine test stand is actually designed for American V-8s, although an MG Magnette engine fits in it just fine. The rebuilt motor can be tested and tuned out of the car, thus saving you time and money.

those handled by charity stores or overstocks from name-brand manufacturers. Most liquidators are stocked with tools and equipment made in China, some of it heavy-duty in nature. A professional restorer purchased a sheet metal brake from a liquidator, but replaced all fasteners with American-made hardware. Stores of this type are often willing to bargain. The tools liquidators sell are generally OK, but avoid grinding stones and high-speed wire brushes. Name brand versions are safer.

You can get excellent buys on rather good-quality tools at Wal-Mart, Kmart, Lowe's, Home Depot and other such big box stores. They also stock large items like air compressors, air tools, parts washers, pressure washers and shelving. Prices are normally lower than manufacturer's suggested retail, but you can do even better if you're patient. These stores will sell 80 to 90 percent of their inventory at close to full price and then put drastic markdowns on the remaining items at the end of the season. You'll save up to 50 percent or more when they are reduced.

The best known department store tools are Craftsman products. Sears and Kmart sell them now. Sears has some very good sales promotions and you should be able to save money.

Automotive swap meets are a great place to purchase tools and equipment. Some vendors attend estate/liquidation auctions to build their inventories. They may have gone to the auction of a repair shop 1,000 miles away that it wouldn't pay for you to travel to. Most used tools purchased at swap meets sell for about one-third (or less) what they cost when new. You can find floor jacks, engine stands and engine dollies in the $10–$25 range. Be careful when buying electric or air tools a swap meets, as you have no way to test them.

Discount tool suppliers sell tools for lower-than-usual prices by mail order or even through retail stores. Harbor Freight of California and Northern Tool of Minnesota are two of the leaders in this category. Tools in the JC Whitney catalog also qualify. Most of the tools carried by discounters come from China or Japan, but they are sold with limited lifetime warranties.

Mechanics say that tools from discounters work well for home restoration work, but might not hold up in everyday professional use. A Harbor Freight 20-ton bottle-jack press I purchased for $179 has already paid for itself in savings. A $139 transmission jack, also from Harbor Freight, did a great job removing a transaxle. I also purchased a Mobile Engine Test Stand (METS) from Northern Tool for just over $400. It allows me to test run and tune rebuilt engines before going through the hassle of putting them back in the car. This piece of equipment should save me a lot of work and time, which is just like saving money in a way.

Many tools are sold with online auctions, particularly on eBay. Some satisfactory online tool purchases have included a used heat gun to help warm a plastic convertible window prior to installation, a nice rolling shelf to store parts on, stainless steel staples for trim work and a self-darkening welding helmet.

One trick in searching for tools on eBay is knowing what to call them. If you're looking for a crankshaft seal installer, do you search under that description or under the manufacturer's name, such as Kent-Moore #321567 seal installer? The more ways you search, the more you'll find. You can even try searching under possible misspellings, such as "seel" installer. This could turn up a real bargain. Warning: If you see tools on eBay listed with brand names like Pittsburgh Tool, Chicago Electric or Central Pneumatic, they are Harbor Freight

Restoration is a matter of removing old parts and replacing them with NOS, reproduction or reconditioned original parts. The damaged MG steering boot on the left was replaced with the reproduction part on the right.

There are still caches of new old stock parts around. Classic car dealer Jim Carlson, of Wisconsin, has a big inventory of NOS parts for 1950s and 1960s Chevrolets. He uses them when he restores Chevys to factory condition.

products, probably purchased on sale and marked up for resale on eBay.

Whether you set out to buy cheap tools or decide to go with the highest-quality tools that money can buy, it always pays to comparison shop, ask about shipping options and investigate other ways of saving money. You may be able to buy that 4-post vehicle lift used as a display model at a show near your home. You may be able to find a nearby tool supplier with perfectly good scratch-and-dent tools. If you put some thinking into buying tools for your shop, you'll have money left to get even more neat tools. Remember, he with the most tools wins!

Finding or Fixing Parts

Finding parts for a vintage car can be both challenging and rewarding. Some hobbyists spend years looking for a rare component needed to complete a restoration. When they find it, they get the same thrill that deep-sea divers feel when they find a sunken ship loaded with gold doubloons and pieces of eight.

The first step of a restoration is to remove those parts from a vehicle that are broken, bent, non-functioning, worn, rusted, dull, cracked, torn, scratched or otherwise altered from like-new condition. The goal is then to replace those parts with others that are in original, as-the-car-was-built condition.

The replacement components should be either new old stock (NOS) pieces, which are never-used factory-made parts, refurbished original parts that have been restored to like-new condition again, aftermarket parts of varying quality that date from the era of the vehicle or exact reproductions of the original parts (repros or repops). When all of the bad parts on a vehicle have been replaced with good parts, the car is considered to have been restored. This sounds pretty simple, but it isn't. Finding good parts is the important factor.

NOS Parts—NOS parts for classic cars are very desirable to collectors, but these are getting very hard to find. Years ago, automakers usually stopped

stocking parts for cars within ten years of a model going off the market. Now, thirty years have passed since old-car collecting boomed in the late 1970s. This creates a situation where supplies of no-longer-made parts are getting low. During the 1970s and '80s, as carmakers computerized their parts-supply systems, they instituted much tighter inventory control. This meant the parts disappeared even faster.

Several years ago, I fixed up four Pontiac Sunbird convertibles for my granddaughters and myself. The cars were only about eight years old, but some parts were impossible to get. General Motors considered the cars too old to make parts for. Conversely, the aftermarket parts suppliers considered the cars too new to tool parts for. We wound up essentially having to fabricate a few parts.

NOS parts are also known as OEM (original equipment manufacturer) parts. They are desirable because they look best and work best on old cars. Due to changes in production technology, it can be impossible to exactly reproduce some old parts. Modern manufacturers can get close, but collectors are tuned into spotting little differences. Original parts are often sturdier, too.

There are still caches of NOS car parts around the hobby. Just recently, I visited a dealer friend who has a large trailer filled with NOS parts for 1950s and 1960s. Of course, these parts are now worth a lot of money. A quick check of parts auctions on eBay will reveal some of the incredibly high prices being paid for NOS parts. Items that once cost a few dollars are now a few hundred dollars.

As far as NOS mechanical parts go, it is important to remember that few parts were made only for one car. Usually, the design engineer considered a vehicle's size, weight and horsepower

Many parts, like this GM intake manifold, are stamped with parts numbers, casting numbers and date codes. In some, but not all cases, the numbers can be used to identify the part or even tell when it was manufactured.

Some aftermarket or reproduction parts have improvements designed into them. This reproduction water pump for 1949–1962 Cadillacs from Kanter Auto Products is claimed to work better than an original pump.

and then looked for an existing part that fit such an application. Therefore, you may find that a single mechanical part was used on Buicks, Pontiacs and Oldsmobiles in certain years. This common use of a part means the component is interchangeable between different cars. Hollander Publishing and some other companies produced parts interchange manuals that are worth having in your restoration library to help you find parts.

In most cases, parts made by branches of General Motors may fit Buicks, Cadillacs, Chevys, Oldsmobiles or Pontiacs, but they are not going to interchange with a Ford or Chrysler. Of course, there is the same partial commonality between Ford, Edsel, Mercury and Lincoln and between the five makes in the Chrysler pentastar (Chrysler, De Soto, Dodge, Imperial and Plymouth). In England, many marques wound up under the Nuffield (later British Leyland) umbrella and shared mechanical parts.

Parts made by automakers usually have parts numbers cast into or stamped on them. Parts may have other numbers on them as well, such as manufacturing date codes or casting numbers. The automakers published parts books or Master Parts Catalogs. These books list all the part numbers according to year, make and model. When you look parts up in a book, you may see them organized by group numbers. The group number will tell you whether a part is for the engine, brake system, rear axle, interior, etc. The part number will tell you the specific year, make and model vehicle the part fits. These numbers only apply to factory parts; aftermarket parts will have different numbers.

As supplies of NOS parts have dwindled, refurbished original parts have become a growing branch of the old-car hobby. Many small companies today are thriving by specializing in the repair and refinishing of original parts. Both bright metal trim parts and hard mechanical parts are being restored and this whole cottage industry is a major element of the general contractor approach to restoring a classic car. Many hobbyists are contracting out to these companies to get individual parts restored. Later, we are going to cover many of these vendors and discuss the specific unit-repair services they offer.

The specialized restoration of specific, individual automotive subsystems evolved from the belief that the original factory parts are far superior to aftermarket parts or reproduction parts. That restorers accept this to be true is very apparent in the British sports car hobby, where the supply of reproduction parts is extremely good. There are a number of companies that sell reproduction British car parts via mail order catalogs and, with few exceptions, you can order just about any brand-new part for any of these cars via these catalogs.

Some of the parts are sourced from Great Britain and these are generally considered good parts. In other cases, the parts are made in India, China, Taiwan, Japan or other offshore locations. Professional restorers who install the reproduction parts will tell you that their quality varies. They all look just like the originals and some work that way, too. But others do not. And the last thing a professional restorer wants to do is put a flawed part in, say, a rebuilt engine and then have the car owner return with a broken engine in three months. In 2002, the British parts makers and restorers met to form the British Motor Trade Association so that they can work out these kinds of issues with repro parts.

Aftermarket Parts—Aftermarket parts also come in handy for restoration projects. These are service parts manufactured in the general era the car was built, but made by companies other than the automakers. However, some aftermarket companies may have actually produced parts for an automaker. Aftermarket parts may vary in both design and quality from factory parts. They may have a slightly

Restoration is costly. Jewel Meetz, of Brillion, Wisconsin, makes one of his $4,500-plus reproduction '55-'56 T-Bird convertible top mechanisms about every 10-14 days. Restoring the original parts could cost even more.

To help keep track of your restoration expenses, get a large plastic food storage bag and throw all your receipts into it. The plastic bag will help keep them clean and dry until you get the chance to organize them.

different appearance, even though they will fit. The quality will vary according to brand. If in doubt, ask an old-time auto mechanic which parts he preferred years ago. Note that some aftermarket parts include design improvements over factory parts. Even though they don't exactly match an OEM part, they may work better.

Reproduction parts are actually the same as aftermarket parts. The main difference is that they are aftermarket parts made specifically for restoring classic cars. As with any aftermarket part, they can vary in quality. Fred and Dan Kanter, who used to deal mainly in NOS Packard parts, have become one of the largest suppliers of reproduction parts. They run Kanter Auto Products in Boonton, New Jersey, and have reproduced enough general old-car parts to fill a thick catalog. Not long ago, Fred Kanter wrote a letter to *Old Cars Weekly* relating how he had to reject a shipment of parts he had made in China because they were not up to his company's standards. These parts looked like perfect reproductions of originals, but they were not of OEM quality.

If you are buying reproduction parts, the best advice is to deal with a reputable vendor who advertises, prints a catalog and backs their products with a warranty. Parts sold by such firms may cost a little bit more because you're helping to pay for the services they offer. However, if you find a part to be not as good as expected, you'll be glad you're dealing with companies that offer a money-back guarantee.

Wage and Price Controls

If you want to restore a vehicle, it is going to cost you some money. In fact, I will guarantee you that it is going to cost more money than you think. If you let things get out of control, it will cost you more money than you have to spend.

I have a friend who does every-nut-and-bolt restorations of 1950s and 1960s automobiles. The basic cost of his restorations (labor included) is about $125,000. My guess is that it would cost you or I (free labor) around $50,000 to do a home restoration of equal quality. The typical home restoration is of not-quite-every-nut-and-bolt quality (also free labor) and usually runs $25,000 today.

If you are wondering how a car could cost $125,000 to restore, let me point out that my friend spends a lot of time making sure that every car he does winds up with perfectly straight body seams. Cars did not come from the factory this way and to achieve his goal, he takes every car apart and puts it back together a minimum of five or six times, before final assembly. In most cases, the home restorer doesn't work to quite the same standard of perfection. Hobbyists like you and I are fairly happy if we just get the car back to its original factory condition and leave it at that.

When contractors are hired to do portions of the work, you would expect the cost to shoot up, since you have to pay for their labor. But, I have found the premium you pay for using outside experts to be very small and well worth the money. It costs you a little bit extra, but you can wind up with a much better job.

Of course, you must do a good job in the general contractor's role. This involves everything from the initial plan for the restoration to what I call the institution of wage and price controls. In other words, you have to manage the expenses involved in the project and spend every cent as wisely as possible. This doesn't mean that you shouldn't use the best carburetor rebuilder to do your carburetor. Instead, you should first check all of the available rebuilders and compare what they do and the prices they charge. Then, if you decide to go with a service that has the highest price, you must look for other areas in the restoration where you can save your money back.

Tracking Costs—To save money, you have to know what you are spending. This means keeping track of the expenses related to your restoration. Get a large plastic food storage bag and throw all receipts into it. The plastic bag will help keep them clean and dry. Staple an inexpensive index card to each receipt, number it (in sequence) and date it. Write pertinent information on the card (How? What? When? Why?) and throw the card in the bag. Later, you can take the bag in the house and list the expenses, according to date, in an accounting ledger or on your computer. As you make each entry, think about the wisdom of that expense and whether it can be reduced or eliminated in the future.

Reducing Costs—A great way to reduce restoration expenses is to minimize them by buying smart. You can avoid at least some expenses by purchasing a pretty good car, truck or motorcycle to begin with. Buying a vehicle that has all of its parts can lead to big savings. Buying a vehicle that isn't rusty eliminates a lot of expense. Buying a car that runs well and drives well is another sure road to savings. You do not have to buy a completely restored car, but if you can spend a little extra and get one that doesn't need these big jobs, you can save a lot.

One easy way to afford that expensive carburetor rebuilder or a better quality paint job is to roll your sleeves up and do some of the other jobs yourself. There's really nothing you can do to the carburetor—if you spend the time to clean it, the rebuilder will hot-tank it anyway. But maybe you can save for the carburetor job by getting a kit and rebuilding the fuel pump yourself. When it comes to paint, if you do the labor-intensive prep work, you'll be able to cut the direct cost of the paint job. If you want to have as much work as possible done by experts, perhaps you can use the time that rebuilding a fuel pump or prepping the body would take to work overtime at your job and earn extra money for your restoration project. On the other hand, don't contract a job out just out of laziness. You might actually enjoy doing some of the real basic jobs on your car.

When my friend does one of his every-nut-and-bolt restorations, 50 percent of his time is spent on

There is no reason to pay a restorer's shop rate to get your parts cleaned. You should plan on doing this job yourself or hiring local auto tech students to rid those parts of grease, oil and road grime.

removing rust, grease and road grime. Parts clean-up is time-consuming work and there's no reason to pay a professional $50-$75 to handle this aspect of your restoration. I have another friend who hires high school students to do such jobs for him on Saturday mornings. The students enjoy the work (not to mention the money) and my friend enjoys teaching them about restoration work. Another option is doing the clean-up yourself.

There are different types of restorations and you have to plan for a type that fits your budget. You may prefer the rolling restoration, where you start with a pretty good, operating vehicle and fix it job by job as you drive it. The goal here is to restore both the mechanicals and the cosmetics, but to do it a bit at a time. You may want to rebuild the mechanicals and leave the cosmetics pretty much as is. This would be a driver restoration because you're restoring mainly the vehicle's functionality. The next step up is the show restoration. This would make the car good enough to enter a car show. A variation on this is the concours restoration that brings the vehicle's condition to the level of perfection. A concours restoration definitely gets you into the six-figures price range.

Keep Emotions in Check—It's very easy to spend a ton of money when you start disassembling a car. Your enthusiasm typically runs high at this point as you learn about your new acquisition. Usually, you think that the vehicle is better than it is and needs only a few parts to be perfect. Naturally, you're anxious to get them because you think it is only going to cost what auctioneers call little money to

Make sure that the front fender ornament you're buying for your collector car is the proper one. This particular part fits the 1936 Oldsmobile Six, but there's no guarantee that it's also correct for a 1936 Oldsmobile Eight.

Salvage yard parts that cost practically nothing years ago are more valuable today, but you can still save money using them if they don't need extensive reconditioning. Some parts on this glass-top Ford Skyliner are rare.

wrap the project up.

Then, you buy books about the new vehicle and notice that the one you bought has the wrong front fender ornament. Too bad you just spend $80 for a reproduction of the incorrect ornament!

It is far better to start taking the vehicle apart first. List the parts that are damaged or missing. Purchase the books and manuals and make sure the parts were correct in the first place. Continue your disassembly work until there is nothing left to take off and you have thousands of parts all neatly organized on your workbench. That should leave you with about 10,000 individual parts and a long list of stuff that requires replacing. Now start your search for needed parts.

If you're lucky enough to own a vehicle that has one-stop parts sources available, contact all of the suppliers in that market niche and send them the complete list of parts you need. Ask for a total price on everything and let them know that they'll be bidding against the other suppliers. This is a good way to save money over buying parts one at a time at full retail. You'll get a discount the same way professional restorers do and your restoration costs will be lowered.

Another way to manage your costs on a restoration is to spread the job out over a planned period of time, but be careful never to stop all work. Once you put the project aside, there will be a tendency to keep doing that and you'll wind up with a partly restored vehicle. As the general contractor, you have to plan things so there is cost-free work to do (sanding, parts cleaning, shop cleanup) during the cash-poor periods that always come along. If you made a large, one-stop purchase of parts in the beginning, there will always be something to do.

Buy Used Parts—Buying good used parts is another way to save money on a restoration and hobby publications carry ads from salvage yards

offering such components. Purchasing used parts always comes with risks involved. The parts may be incorrect, they may not function correctly or the seller and buyer may have different views about their condition. The best policy is probably to stay away from spending lots of money on used parts unless you're taking them off a junkyard car yourself. Then, you can assess their condition and see if they are worth it. As a general contractor who wants to control costs, but also get the job done and finished on time, I would use only used parts that have been rebuilt or refurbished by a specialist. Such parts will cost more, but at least you can count on them to look and perform like new parts. The car will run when it's done.

Time Management

Time management is another factor you'll deal with, if you approach automobile restoration from the general contractor's perspective. Going in, your goal is to get the project done properly and to get it done on time. Managing the time spent on a project also affects the cost, since spending more time on a job usually boils down to higher cost. You might say, "How can this be important, since I'm not paying myself by the hour?" The answer is that you're probably paying someone (machinist, body man, painter, etc.) by the hour and also, the parts that cost $50 this week could be $60 next week.

A few years ago, I had the radiator in my '57 Buick recored. When I moaned about the $450 price, the man who did the work told me a story. He said that there was only one company left in the country that had the ability to supply original-style upper and lower tanks for old radiators. This company bought up all its competitors until it had a

A few years ago, the cost of rebuilding radiators, like the one in this '57 Chevy, virtually doubled overnight. Reproductions are available, but check to make sure they have the factory-style tanks if your goal is authenticity.

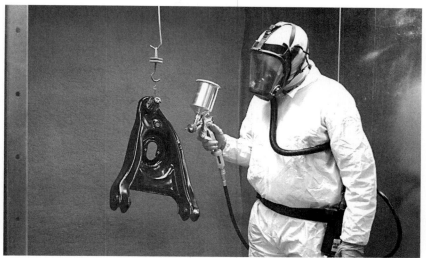

Painting parts sounds easy, but if you want them to look good, you have to remove them, clean them, paint them and reinstall them. The more steps you do, the longer you have to allow for your restoration. (Eastwood photo)

monopoly and then doubled the price of the tanks.

Another hobbyist had a '54 Chevy radiator repaired about a week before the company bought out its last competitor. The repair cost $225. Unfortunately, the Chevy owner didn't check the condition of his water pump when he installed the radiator. One week later, the old water pump fell apart and the cooling fan flew into the recently repaired radiator. The man took the car back to the shop and they fixed it. The man was more than a little unhappy about the price of the second radiator repair—$450!

In this case, dealing with the price increase was unavoidable, but imagine how you would feel if you had delayed buying parts for your restoration that week. Since prices on parts rarely, if ever, go down, you can see how planning your parts purchases early can save you considerable money. We all have budgets and limits on what we can part with at a given time, but if you have the buying power and know you'll be buying something anyway, why not get it at the earliest possible time?

It is important to plan the time you will be spending on a restoration, but this isn't quite as simple as setting aside a few hours each day or working on the car Wednesday evenings. Some jobs just don't fit neatly into preplanned time frames. Take painting parts, for instance. This job starts with buying primer and paint. Then there is cleaning, sanding and preparation of the parts. Spraying the paint usually takes just a couple of minutes. Later, there is drying time involved. You may want to apply a second color or a clearcoat.

After that, you need more drying time. In some cases, you may have to make repairs (fix drips, etc.) and buff the paint out. A final coat of wax never hurts, either.

It takes a bit of thinking about this process to make up your restoration plan and set aside the time needed to paint parts. In fact, a good general contractor will plan out the entire project against a set timeline. If things start falling behind schedule, adjustments can be made to bring the project in on time.

There are three main areas in which amateur restorers seem to have time management issues: 1) committing their own time to the project on a consistent basis, 2) back-ordered items on parts orders and 3) getting the guy at the body shop to complete the car on time. Any of these things can cause big delays and slow up progress on the restoration.

Each restorer has to find the best way to schedule his or her time for the project at hand. In my case, I work with a friend who comes to my home every Thursday night. I always have enough writing assignments to make excuses not to work on the cars, but when Vince shows up, I have to work on the cars.

The members of the Fondy Vintage Auto Club in Fond du Lac, Wisconsin, found another way to get everyone to donate time to the project. They made it educational and entertaining. Restorer Steve Hamilton taught them sheet metal fabrication. They met on a regular basis and socialized while working.

As these examples illustrate, restoration projects seem to move along best if there is a regular and

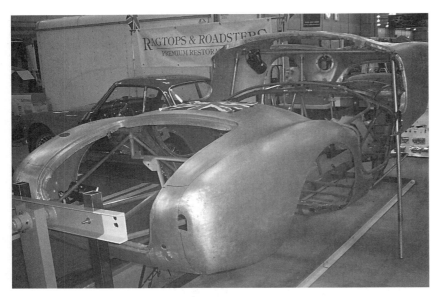

Dave Hutchison demonstrated a Cobra body fabricated by Ragtops & Roadsters at the Atlantic City Classic Car Auction. The metal body reflected the talent of the crew at the Perkasie, Pennsylvania, restoration shop.

consistent work schedule and if you do not work entirely alone. Committing specific time to a project is important and adding a social aspect makes the time fly.

If you are trying to restore a car and your parts vendor consistently says the parts you want have been back ordered, this is going to slow down your progress. It will also add to your parts shipping costs. Most hobby vendors are small businesses and can't keep an unlimited inventory on hand. This is totally understandable. One way to head off back order problems is to check availability when you are ordering. If a lot of parts are only available on back order, try another vendor.

Running into a problem getting the owner of a body shop to work on your classic car is fairly common. Hobbyists voice this complaint quite a bit. There are even stories of shops not working on a car for years. There is a simple reason for this—working on old cars, particularly obscure models, is often very labor intensive. Some shops think that working on a Marmon is the same as working on a Mustang. When they take it apart, they find things they're not familiar with and this slows their progress. It may even scare them away from working on your car at all. Instead, it will sit in the shop and they'll work around it.

Good communications and the proper selection of a shop are really the only stress-free way to deal with this type of situation. If you communicate well, the shop will understand what you want and when you want it. They can tell you honestly what

they can do and what they can't do. If you picked a shop with the talent needed to do a proper classic car restoration, you won't have to worry. Your cost may be higher, but there won't be any surprises down the road.

Generally, a shop that specializes in true restoration work will require you to sign a contact that clearly spells out the responsibilities and liabilities of each party. In rare cases, a shop may quote you a specific price for a job, but usually they work on a time and material basis. That means you will have to pay their shop rate for the hours they work on your vehicle, plus the cost of parts, supplies and your portion of shop overhead.

It is possible to come across local body shops that do excellent-quality work on old cars and these will generally charge a bit less than a shop in the restoration business. Most home restorers seem to prefer this type of arrangement, but communications are very important in this case, too. As I said earlier, body shops can make money faster on collision repair work and even the most honest, hardest working professional will prefer bringing income in via the most efficient method.

Hitting Your Goals

Since this chapter ends with a discussion of hitting your goals when you restore a vintage vehicle, let's go back and revisit something included in Chapter 1, placing special emphasis on one point. We noted: The general contractor is responsible for the means and methods used in the execution of the contract and for completion of the project in accordance with the signed contract, which usually includes a budget, general and special

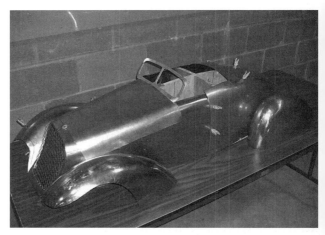

Under the guidance of professional restorer Steve Hamilton, members of the Fondy Vintage Auto Club got together once a week to fabricate this Auburn pedal car. They plan to use the finished toy to raise money for charity.

conditions and the plans and specification of the project. Getting the project finished is your primary goal.

One of the advantages of using the general contractor approach when you undertake an automobile restoration is the concept that hitting your goal (finishing the job) is part and parcel of the deal. The two can't be separated. In essence, you are making a contract with yourself to restore the car, truck or motorcycle and the project has to be completed if you want to enjoy the reward (a restored vehicle).

Though I don't have statistics to back up my point of view, after 35 years of bouncing around the old-car industry and talking to thousands of collectors, it is my personal belief that the majority of home restoration projects do not get finished. I'm talking about restorations done in the car owner's home garage, with he or she doing 100 percent of the work. For every vehicle in this category that you see at a car show, there are probably five more sitting in pieces in various garages. An automobile restoration is a difficult process and is hard to complete.

I do believe that more than 20 percent of hobbyists get their cars finished, but I do not think the people in this group do all of the work themselves. At car shows, they will talk about how they completely restored the vehicle, but in nine out of ten cases, you will find they took it to a body shop, a restoration shop and a trim shop, at some point in the process, to get various phases of the project done. In short, they did the general contractor thing, though they didn't know that they were doing it. From such observations, I began to realize that most completed show cars were done via farm-it-out method. That's when I started to formulate the concept of this book in my head.

Viewing a vehicle restoration as a process of complete disassembly, cleaning up rusty and dirty parts and sending the cleaned parts out to experts to be restored before you reassemble them may not be as romantic as the image of an old time hobbyist in bib overalls fashioning Model T parts on his bench lathe. However, if your goal is to have a nice, restored vehicle and complete it before you're eligible to collect Social Security, the general contractor approach to restoration is the one that gets you where you want to be in the most efficient way.

Put It Down on Paper—If you're already convinced that this is a good way to approach your vehicle restoration, there are several things you will need to do before lifting a crescent wrench or turning a Phillips head screw. Your first step is to draft a contract that you're going to sign with

These days, many professional restoration shops use the farm-it-out method to help get their projects completed. Jerry Kopecky played general contractor to get this '59 Dodge hardtop done years ago. Now, he owns the car.

yourself laying out the job requirements and details. Although this will be completely a mock contract, it will be this document that keeps you going if you feel the enthusiasm for the job starting to wane. Do not think that drafting an actual written contract with yourself is silly. If you were taking your vehicle to a professional restoration shop, the chances are pretty good that you would have to sign a contract with the shop owner. So why not make a contract with yourself?

The first things to put in writing in your contract are the plans and specifications for your project. The vision you have of this job and the numbers that relate to it (expense dollars, man-hours) should spell out what you plan to do. Are you thinking

After years of storing an Amphicar, Keith Matiowetz decided to put his general contractor hat on and take the car to a specialty shop in Illinois to have the body restored.

about a rolling restoration, a show car quality restoration or a pristine concours restoration? Your plan should spell out how you are going to accomplish your goal and the steps you'll be taking to get things done (disassembly, cleaning, r & r parts, reassembly). You should specify where you are going to do the work (in my home restoration shop) and what you hope to accomplish (a completely restored car, truck or motorcycle).

Your contract should include a complete budget for the project, and this is going to take a bit of figuring. You will need to create an written estimate just like the one a professional shop might give you. In it, you should project the cost of supplies (including solvents, paint, new tools, etc.), materials (car parts, upholstery and trim), outside services (machine shop work, chrome plating, powder coating and component restoration costs), utilities (like light and heat in your home restoration shop) and any other expenses that you expect to incur.

You should take a good stab at estimating the amount of time the restoration work will take you. Since you're not paying yourself an hourly wage rate, this won't translate directly into money, but it will be interesting to see how close you get to reality. I will bet you dollars to donuts that the actual time spent fixing the vehicle up will be a lot more than you think.

Finally, include special conditions in your contract. In the real world, the special conditions might cover any strange occurrences that could knock the project off schedule or increase the budget. For instance, if a restorer takes the vehicle apart and finds hidden rust that couldn't be seen when it was in one piece, he wants to be able to raise the cost to cover the extra restoration work the car needs. If you want to spell out such possibilities in your contract with yourself, that's fine. Even

better might be some type of bonus for getting the job done on schedule. For example: "If we finish early I'll take the whole family out for an expensive dinner." Perks like this can get your wife and kids excited about your project and help keep you motivated to get the job done.

Speaking of motivation, a sure way to lose enthusiasm is to make the restoration more work than play. If you come to feel that going out to the garage is like doing your chores, you are probably taking the job too seriously. Spending hours tinkering in your garage should be a pastime that relieves stress—not one that makes you stressed out. This is supposed to be your hobby, not a second occupation.

At the end of your restoration project, there may be a lot of loose ends to wrap up. As the general contractor, you're still in charge of handling all of the details. You should check your records to make sure that all bills for parts and services were taken care of. Perhaps all or part of the restoration can be deducted as a business expense, as in the case of restoring a vintage truck that will be a promotional item for your small business. If so, you'll have to check and file all of the documentation and pencil in check numbers and other payment information on each invoice.

As general contractor, you also have the responsibility of cleaning up the shop after the job is completed. Make sure that all the tools and equipment go back in their proper places. If you borrowed or rented any tools for special jobs, make certain they are properly returned. When everything is done, it's time to get the broom down off the hook and sweep the floor. You might be the boss—the general contractor—but you're also chief cook, bottle washer (and floor sweeper) in your own shop.

This Model A Ford 5-window coupe is one of those projects that never got finished. It was taken to John's Body Shop in LaCrosse, Wisconsin for restoration, but the owner lost interest and it's been sitting for years.

Chapter 3
Outsourcing: The Modern Restoration Method

The word "outsourcing" is not a dirty word, even though many diehard do-it-yourself purists may disagree. It describes the practice of transferring a job from an employee to workers at an outside company that contracts to do the same job for a set price. The outside company then uses its labor force to get the job done, usually at a lower cost. In many cases, the job winds up being done by workers in another country who are used to lower wages and the American worker who did the job originally winds up being laid off. For this reason, outsourcing is often spoken as if it is an obscenity and I can understand that.

In this book, we are talking about outsourcing restoration work to small American companies that specialize in restoring a carburetor, fuel pump, distributor or other vintage auto part. In fact, it is sometimes slightly more expensive than doing the work yourself and it probably has the potential to make the supplier (vendor) grow and add jobs. So, the kind of outsourcing we are talking about is definitely not a dirty word.

Years ago, when you read stories about someone restoring an antique automobile, it always seemed to be a backyard project that took the restorer 20 years to do with his own hands. Hobbyists would explain that they spotted a Model T in a farmer's field, snatched it out from under the nose of some raging bull, convinced a straw-hatted farmer to lower his shotgun and purchased the car for $25. They then dragged it home on a tow rope with help from a friend or relative, took it apart and put the body on sawhorses for a couple of decades. Apparently, some of these folks survived long enough to retire at 65 and then finally had the time to make the car look new again.

The modern old-car hobby isn't quite the same as the old-car hobby of years ago. Today's hobbyists are anxious to restore a car and not willing to wait 20 years before they can drive it. They have watched their everyday occupations work toward more and more efficiency and they've learned that doing everything yourself isn't the best way to get a job done. Some things have to be outsourced—farmed out to experts—to keep the progress moving. Sometimes it's better to hire the work done than to overload yourself with more than you can do properly. There's also the time factor. If you do a restoration job with your own free labor, but it takes you five times as long as an expert to do it, are you really saving? Maybe you could just give the work to the expert, get somewhat better results and use the time you save to make the money to pay for it!

The Old School Way: Years of Hard Labor

Things were different when the old-school way was the accepted method. Back then, people who collected old cars, trucks and motorcycles were often considered weirdos who accumulated old jalopies for no purpose.

Perhaps this view of the typical old-car hobbyist originated during World War II, when some early collectors did unusual things to save cars from the scrap drives that were staged to salvage old steel for the war effort. For example, Barney Pollard of Detroit, Michigan—a very well known collector—stood his cars on end inside steel sheds to keep them from being spotted. By the time the '50s rolled in, Pollard's cars (he had hundreds of them) were still being stored that way and were written up and pictured in several national magazines.

Car enthusiasts have long had a streak of eccentricity. The great metal fabricator Raymond Besasie, Sr., who built the first Excalibur body, created this X-3 Explorer in 1961. The dorsal-finned car was seen in many magazines.

The market for antique and classic cars was limited in the '50s and '60s, but development of the classic car auction industry and consignment auctions in the '70s greatly widened the marketplace and raised old-car values.

Many people who read the stories about Pollard thought it was weird to own hundred of cars with names that no one ever heard of and store them inside buildings with their noses pointing toward the ceiling. Each time the collection was publicized, it presented an image of a car collector that stuck in people's minds. It didn't matter that Barney Pollard was a successful businessman—all that most people remembered was his unusual car collection. And a lot of people then transferred that same image to car collectors in their own neighborhoods.

The truth is Pollard's cars didn't hold a great deal of value at that time. Many were rare marques, but most orphan cars weren't very desirable back then. The hobby was largely filled with Fords and large capital C Classic cars. There wasn't a big market for other old cars, so there was no motivation to restore any of the cars very quickly. The collection was impressive for the sheer number of cars it included, but the condition they were in didn't matter much at the time.

By the time Pollard died in the 1980s, there was an established marketplace for classic cars and the hobby was beginning to grow quite large. An auction was held to sell the Pollard cars and the results were reported in the trade publication *Old Cars Weekly*, which I worked for at the time. The prices paid for some of the cars were far higher than Pollard ever expected to see his cars sell for, since many of the vehicles were actually worth restoring by then.

As cars like Pollard's gained value in the market, people started restoring them to make money, rather than just to keep busy in the garage at night.

The old-car hobby changed from one in which people tinkered with the restoration of a car for years and years to a market in which people bought cars, rather quickly restored them and took them to a classic car venue to resell them. As more people got involved in collecting cars, the profit potential in selling went up.

In transitioning from a backyard hobby to a market-based hobby, the old-car industry went through some changes itself. Auctions had been used to sell cars for a long time, and early collectors like Cameron Peck of Chicago held auctions to get rid of excess inventory. However, the cars were usually sold at even money or maybe a loss. They were just extras from a big collection. The Harrah Automobile Collection in Reno, Nevada, also held several dispersal sales with Don Britt doing the auctioneering. As Dean Batchelor wrote in his book *Harrah's Automobile Collection* (GP Publishing, 1984), "There were very seldom any reserve prices and then, they were so modest as to be laughable."

Things changed in the mid-1970s when auctioneer Dean Kruse got together with local car wash owner Russ Jackson and classic car dealer Leo Gephart to hold a classic car consignment auction in Scottsdale, Arizona. After this auction was promoted in *Motor Trend* magazine, the sale got national publicity and drummed up a lot of interest in classic car collecting. It was a stepping-off point for the classic car auction industry as we know it today, with consignment sales of private vehicles and sometimes steep reserve prices.

Another sign of the growing commercialism sweeping the old-car hobby was the evolution of the Car Corral method of selling vintage vehicles, which is credited to the late Chip Miller and Bill Miller, the founders of Carlisle Productions. As the old-car hobby started to boom, these two collectors (who were not related despite having the same last name) launched an event called Postwar '74. It was a big hit and became an annual venue. In fact, it actually grew into a schedule of eleven different car and truck shows per year at its peak.

Chip Miller had been a Corvette collector and the Corvette Corral was a popular element of many Corvette shows. The corral was an area set aside to display only cars that were for sale. Prior to this, old cars had been sold along with parts in vendor spaces at swap meets. But a car corral was like a used car lot within a show. When the Car Corral became a big part of the Carlisle Flea Market's success, other event promoters picked it up and added it to shows across the U.S. This new emphasis on selling vehicles also changed the hobby.

A third sign of growing emphasis on the marketing of old cars was the growth of the large swap meet vendor and, along with it, the growth of the reproduction parts industry. Believe it or not, the formal roots of the old car hobby can be traced back to Antique Auto Derbies held in Philadelphia, Pennsylvania, in the early 1930s. A few years before that, the auto industry had celebrated its silver anniversary and some dealers started collecting older models of the brands they sold to show how durable the cars were. Many dealers at the time offered to trade new models for old ones. This could also be viewed as the start of the hobby,

Car Corrals, like this one in Wisconsin, were originated by the late Chip Miller, cofounder of Carlisle Productions. Chip adopted the term corral from Corvette events held at races.

because many dealers suddenly became collectors.

By 1936, the Antique Automobile Club of America was formed and by the 1940s, collectors like James Melton, Cameron Peck and Henry Austin Clark, Jr., were running museums and promoting car collecting nationally. The Hershey swap meet started in the early 1950s and hobbyists used it to swap parts they didn't need for others they wanted. Over the next decade, the swap meet became more of a selling market than a trading post. Some vendors who handled sales in a businesslike way began making livings selling old-car parts.

By the time the hobby boomed in the late '70s, old-car parts and service suppliers like Gaslight Auto Parts, Coker Tire, Bill Hirsch, J. C. Taylor and *Hemmings Motor News* (to name a few) were growing into large enterprises. A number of companies that started around that time including Classic Motorbooks, *Old Cars Weekly*, Eastwood, Carlisle Productions and the Atlantic City Classic Car Auction also grew by leaps and bounds. There were also several sales of companies that started small and enjoyed steady growth. By any yardstick, it was clear that the old-car hobby had matured and changed into a real marketplace.

As all of these changes occurred, the old-school image of a slow-paced hobby filled with people restoring antique autos just for fun underwent a slow, but natural, revision. Younger hobbyists who collected Dodge Chargers, Pontiac GTOs and Ford Mustangs joined the ranks of restorers and

The hobby boomed in the 1970s and several restoration market suppliers grew. Specialty tool supplier Eastwood, formed in 1978, prospered and today runs this factory outlet store in Pottstown, Pa., where bargains are offered.

Managing a project as general contractor involves assessing whether an expensive restoration should be done. This is a rare Mr. Norm Dodge from Steve Bimbi's Nickey Chicago shop.

This is not the generator for the Starship Enterprise! It's an electroluminescent instrument panel for a '61 Chrysler 300 that's been restored by JC Auto Restoration, a subcontractor shop from Lynnwood, Washington.

approached the job of rebuilding cars in a new way. Muscle car fans, especially, were used to tearing cars apart and rebuilding them right at the drag strip, in a single afternoon.

In many cases, the modern car collectors found that they were able to purchase reproduction parts and interior kits from mail-order catalogs and make a car look new again in months, rather than rebuilding it over several decades. Better yet, when they finished working on a vehicle, there was a real chance that they could actually make some money selling it, in a car corral or auction.

In the last decade or so, the changes in car collecting have moved toward greater sophistication in hobbyists' home garages. Old-car restorers are putting up roomy new buildings for their private museums and equipping them with professional-looking workbenches and cabinets, vehicle lifts, engine hoists, compressed air systems, sandblasters, tire changers, buffers, home powder coating systems, scanners and other devices that used to be seen only in professional repair shops. The restoration of a collector car is no longer your grandfather's hobby and has undergone drastic changes from the days of old.

The Old Gray Hobby: What It Used To Be

If the old gray hobby ain't what it used to be, perhaps we are better off for it in some ways. Today's managed method of treating a restoration project like a building contractor treats a construction job keeps hobbyists from spending $25,000 to restore a car that's only worth $7,500 in perfect condition.

Is that collector car really worth fixing up? This is the question you have to ask yourself at the start of the project. If you invest in a restoration, there should be a sound reason you're doing so. Televised classic car auctions have generated headlines that make people think the old Model T under the lean-to might actually be worth a fortune. Sadly, the headlines don't explain that the '59 De Soto convertible that brought $285,000 at an auction cost $150,000 to restore or that the same model sitting in a barn might cost $300,000 to fix up.

While some can't believe that a car costs hundreds of thousands of dollars to restore, that's the reality today. And those six-figure fix-ups aren't necessarily rip-offs. Try fixing the electroluminescent dashboard on an early '60s Chrysler. According to restorer Jerry Kopecky, used dash clusters cost over $800 on eBay. If you need a wiring harness to make it work, add over $2,000 for a reproduction harness! That's nearly three grand to enjoy paradise by the dashboard lights.

If you do any work on cars you know: 1) most repairs have to be done two or three times before things are right; 2) if you're going to do things right the first time, it may entail taking the entire car apart and replacing or restoring every part and 3) it will cost more buckets full of cash than you thought to fix the car.

You have to think seriously about sinking big bucks into an old car. First, consider if the year, make and model of car (as well as its combination of options) are of enough special interest to make a restoration worth doing. Then, ask yourself if the vehicle can really be restored properly or is it too far gone to benefit from an authentic restoration? Naturally, the market value of the finished car

Here's an example of how farming work out to experts saves money. A hobbyist bought three reproduction versions of this MG speedometer drum. None worked. He finally contacted Nissonger Instruments in New York. They are the former factory service center for this drum and still have the parts needed to restore the original speedometer. It was fixed and now works perfectly.

enters into the equation when considering if a car is worth fixing. "I learned a lot about the restoration business when I was doing cars for Jess Ruffalo (a collector who passed away in 2007)," says Jerry Kopecky. "We sold two cars that I did for Jess in the high six-figures range. Jess taught me that the market is very strong as long as you restore the right cars." Hardtops and convertibles are better restoration investments than sedans, and wagons are in between, Kopecky believes. The fancier station wagons with lots of accessories can bring really good money.

Whenever you restore a car, whether you are an amateur or a professional, it's important to keep in mind that you might want to sell it someday. So you have to know that you will be able to get most of the money you invested in the car back if you turn it over.

The thinking of younger restorers like Jerry Kopecky is different from the thinking of hobbyists back in the Barney Pollard era. Today's collectors are more practical and value-conscious—more concerned that they can get back the money they have to invest in a car. The work they do is better managed and geared to the goal of finishing the job that they start. They are putting the old gray mare before the cart and doing things the right way and more great cars are being brought back to life because of such commonsense thinking. For at-home restorers like you and me, using the general contractor approach to get the job done is also a commonsense way to get a car done.

The Modern Way:
Take This Job and Shop It

If you tackle a restoration the modern way and use what I sometimes call the "take this job and shop it" system, you'll still be doing a lot of work taking vehicles apart and putting them back together yourself. However, you'll also be farming out, or "outsourcing," as many jobs as you can to specialists who know all there is to know about a certain part or system. As I suggested earlier in the book, this might not add as much to your restoration costs as you think it will. In fact, I'm going to try to prove this with an actual example from my own restoration experiences.

Frenchman Andre DuBonnet invented Knee-Action Ride. The so-called DuBonnet suspension was used only on 1934–1936 Pontiac Deluxe Sixes and Eights and 1934-1938 Chevrolet Masters. The Knee-Action name was used later on a totally different type of suspension, but these did not have the DuBonnet system. My 1936 Pontiac Deluxe Six does have a Dubonnet front end.

A large housing on each side of the car houses the DuBonnet suspension. A support shaft resembling a bicycle pedal goes through the housing. The support shaft is splined in its center. It slides through and rides in circular bosses on each side of the housing. The pedal arm extending from the shaft has a wheel spindle on its remote end. This spindle passes through the brake backing plate and holds the brakes, the wheel bearings and the wheel on the car. A radius rod bolts to the brake backing plate and bottom of the Knee-Action unit.

A large spring inside the Knee-Action housing acts like a front coil spring. Two cylinders, each about six inches long, are bolted over two openings in the front of each housing. Inside the cylinders there are valves and strong springs that move a piston. These are actually the shock absorbers. The assembled Knee-Action housing is filled with oil that is supposed to be sealed in.

When new, the DuBonnet units worked well. The owner of one car with professionally rebuilt components told me that his Pontiac had a Cadillac-like ride. The weakness of the system is oil leakage and resultant wear. Many of the cars were driven with the system totally dry. This caused wear on the shafts and needles and more leakage. Without oil, rust would form in the housings. This in turn would lead to bent needle bearings, twisted splines and wear on the bosses.

Knee-Action units can be rebuilt. For most owners of these cars, the big question is whether to do the job themselves or send the units out to be rebuilt. There are two companies that rebuild these

Mechanic Vince Sauberlich helped rebuild my DuBonnet front suspension system. Vince did a great job, but outsourcing the work to a specialized subcontractor would have been faster and just slightly more costly.

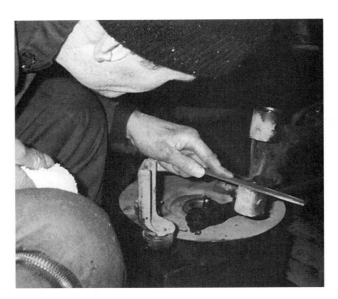

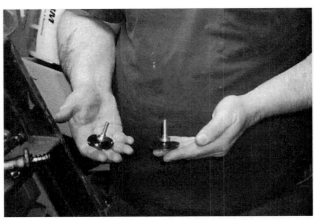

Joe Curto, of College Point, NY, started working on British cars in his driveway, in the '60s. Today he rebuilds SU carburetors for restorers all over the world and even manufacturers the parts needed to do this job.

units. They advertise set prices for the job and, in a best-case scenario, a pair of off-the-shelf units can be restored by the commercial rebuilder for about $800–$900. However, the amount of work and cost involved really depends on the amount of wear the old units have suffered. If the rare parts inside the DuBonnet suspension units have to be repaired or replaced, the price can as much as double.

Repair of DuBonnet units is addressed in shop manuals for each Chevy and Pontiac that the system was used on. If you're facing the job, you'll need such a book. Chilton and Motor manuals of the day also gave step-by-step directions. There was a useful article about do-it-yourself DuBonnet suspension repairs on the Internet at www.Antique AutoArchive.com. For many years, the Vintage Chevrolet Club of America's *Generator and Distributor* magazine also printed a monthly column on DuBonnet suspension systems. The column has carried a lot of information about them over the years.

The commercial rebuilders of DuBonnet units are Apple Hydraulics on the East Coast and Five Points Classic Auto Shocks of California. Depending on the model of car, these vendors either replace worn units with new ones they have already rebuilt or rebuild units that are sent to them by car owners. The companies also sell parts for do-it-yourselfers and supply the D-I-Y customers with photocopied instructions to help them do the complicated repair.

With the help of my mechanic friend Vince Sauberlich and a local machine shop, plus advice from restorer and author Matt Joseph, I decided to rebuild my DuBonnet units via the do-it-yourself route. My original thinking was that I would save money by going this route. Vince and I initially did the basic job for about $600–$700 (including new

king pins, brakes and radius rods). We saved at least $200—and probably more—over jobbing all of the work out.

Of course, we had to do a lot of grunt work and spend many hours on this dirty job. On top of that, after we had all the parts back together again, new leaks developed. The DuBonnet unit on one side of the car started to leak right away. The unit on the other side of the car initially seemed OK, but began to leak within a few weeks. In addition, we didn't know if we painted everything up correctly or whether everything would even work (it did work, but we literally didn't know what we were doing and probably had a pretty good chance of botching things up).

All things considered, if we could have gotten by just paying a commercial rebuilder $400–$450 per side to do the job it would have been the better way to go. The price of $800–$900 would have been higher, but the job would also have been done faster and been guaranteed. If the experts at Apple Hydraulics or Five Points Classic Auto Shocks had done the job in the first place, I doubt if there would have still been leaks. We had to deal with this problem by doing a major portion of the job over, not once, but twice! In addition to eating up time, we had to spend well over $125 for two additional shock sealing kits and other small parts.

As far as expenses go, I probably saved a little bit of money by going the do-it-yourself route with my Knee-Action repair, but after doing this job I have to admit that the cost of having the DuBonnet type units redone by commercial rebuilders like Apple Hydraulics or Five Points Classic Auto Shocks is a bargain. There is a lot of work involved in this repair and that adds up to a major investment of

James Ostrom, of Fondy Auto Electric, in Fond du Lac, Wisconsin, is seen rebuilding a 6-volt starter for a collector vehicle. Such companies rebuild your original parts so you end up with a matching numbers.

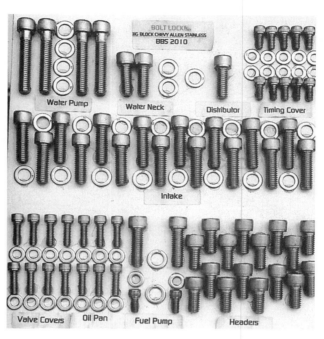

If you are a good general contractor you'll find ways to restore more efficiently. Bolt Locker—a company from Eau Claire, Wisconsin—sells this all-in-one bolt kit for Chevy big-block V-8s. It will save you time finding bolts.

time and energy. In addition, all of the hassle involved in painting the parts of the DuBonnet units and reassembling them again would have been avoided. When the rebuilt units arrived in the mail, all you'd do is install them.

Companies that rebuild the same components over and over also learn more about the workings of that part or system. They often learn about neat ways to make hidden improvements that will help your car run and drive better, without affecting its original looks. A carburetor rebuilder might know of a certain carburetor needle that will make your car idle smoother and run faster. A man who rebuilds distributors might be able to tune the distributor in your collector car for a choice of performance or economy. An expert in rear ends can possibly change the gearing to make your sports car quicker on the highway. All of these are other reasons that it pays to have an expert handle certain unit repairs.

Another important factor that arises when restoring vintage vehicles is the question of safety. Old cars, trucks and motorcycles are inherently less safe than modern cars. Using outside specialty shops to do individual unit repairs can be safer in at least two different ways. First of all, the specialty shop will usually have the equipment and tools needed to do a job safely. Secondly, since the specialist knows more about cars than most amateurs, the job will be done the proper way and the vehicle will be safer to drive when it's finished.

Most specialty restoration shops will guarantee their work for a year or so and that's a nice advantage of working with professionals who know

one thing pretty much inside out. In fact, this is particularly significant when you're buying a crate engine or transmission for a vintage car that you're building. If something goes wrong with one of these pricey components, it's nice to know that there's someone standing behind it with a money-back guarantee.

Another thing in favor of jobbing out restoration work is that the majority of specialists are set up to repair your car's original parts, rather than to replace them with reproduction or aftermarket parts. Since original factory parts tend to add to the value of most collectible automobiles, any parts that you wind up having rebuilt by specialists are probably adding to the value of your restoration. This is a very important factor today, because original parts are getting harder and harder to find and sell for lots of money at swap meets and in online auctions. Having such parts as the radio, clock, and gauges in an old car functioning properly is a great advantage when you put the car in a show.

Who's Got The Time Anymore?

Rare is the old-car hobbyist who brags about how much spare time he or she has to devote to the restoration of a car, truck or motorcycle. We live in a very busy world today and clearing the hours required to work on a back burner project like the restoration of a vintage vehicle is difficult at best. We really have to make time for our hobbies, particularly if they involve achieving a long-range goal such as the restoration of a vintage vehicle. So other than inventing a 30-hour day, how can we set aside the time we need to get our projects done?

These sports cars are parked outside the Fox Cities British Car Club's headquarters in Oshkosh, Wisconsin. In the winter, even more cars park inside and take advantage of the storage service that helps support the club.

Making the time you need to get your car projects done starts with a state of mind and the nice thing about using the general contractor approach is that it involves you playing the role of manager and having completion of the project as one of your job goals. If you were managing a team in a factory or a retail store and wanted to achieve a production or sales goal, the first thing you'd probably do is look for ways to motivate the team like a slogan, a theme or a symbol. To keep me motivated on my current restoration project (a 1957 MG Magnette sedan that she loves) my girlfriend bought me a T-Shirt that says I need my garage time. It may sound silly, but when I'm running out of steam on my project, I put that shirt on and it reminds me that I have a job to do.

A big help in keeping my project on track is working with a man who knows a lot more about cars than I do. My mechanic friend Vince Sauberlich usually comes by on Thursday night to spin wrenches with me and help me do the jobs that I'm not really skilled at. The really great thing about this is that it motivates me to do some work on my car at least once a week. Even if I cannot find the time to visit the garage any other time, you can count on me being out there on Thursday evenings. If you make working on a car as much of a social experience as a hobby project, you'll find yourself doing more needed work.

This idea of turning the restoration work into a social experience works big time for one club I belong to. The Fox Cities British Car Club started in 2002 and has grown to 150 members. This organization is now based in Oshkosh, Wisconsin, and is quite different than any other club I have ever belonged to.

Two members of FCBCC bought a former motorcycle dealership building and operate a car storage facility that also serves as club headquarters. To the average passerby, the metal building looks like a body shop or agricultural business, but inside

on any given weekend day—and most nights during the week—you'll find club president Jim Marks and other FCBCC members preserving British motoring heirlooms.

Inside the building is a two-bay shop area with lifts, tool benches, tools and equipment, a rec room, a meeting room, a library and even a British pub. A heated vehicle storage area holds dozens of restored automobiles from a Singer roadster to an Austin A90 Atlantic convertible. A second storage area has just been refurbished and more cars are located in an adjacent storage shed.

Jim Marks' commitment to his club is shared by its members. There aren't many rules, but the few guidelines FCBCC has are considered gospel. The first rule is based on the idea of members helping members. Marks sees FCBCC as a community in which members not only get access to a shop and storage, but to community parts. Spares are left out so members can take what they need in exchange for a donation to the club.

For a yearly fee, members storing cars at the clubhouse get a key to the shop, access to the community parts pool and space. Even better, they all chip in to work on their cars together and share their knowledge and expertise. The club's website (www.foxbrits.com) is also helpful in finding parts and tech tips. It carries advertising from members and gives them a calendar of events.

In the winter, the clubhouse is greatly appreciated by enthusiasts who don't have heated garages. They can work on vehicles in a well-equipped, heated shop and get their cars ready for the warm weather shows. To help them, the club presents tech session workshops where experts explain how to do difficult repairs. In some cases, a group of club members has gathered to help put a new engine in the car of a member who couldn't afford professional help. In one case, one member got his MGB repaired for cost and everyone had a good time working on her car as a group. It was also a learning experience for some.

Whether you do it yourself or via group dynamics, there are ways to clear time in your life to get your vintage vehicle restored. More and better tools and equipment, a well-equipped and efficient workplace, a good collection of technical manuals and books, how-to videos and DVDs and the use of a computer in your home restoration shop are all ways to streamline the time needed to get your project done. But, remember, none of these things will help unless you manage the job properly and maintain a commitment to getting the vehicle done. You're the one who's in control!

Chapter 4

Planning, Preparation & Training

After disassembling a vehicle, restoration is a matter of replacing or restoring all the parts and putting it back together. Chrysler restorer Jerry Kopecky starts by restoring the subframe and drivetrain as a unit.

If you were running a company that had a sales or production goal, one of the things you would want in your management arsenal are well-trained team members. Training can make a huge difference when it comes to getting a difficult job done on time and on budget. In restoring your vintage vehicle, you're essentially your own team. You might get a little help from friends or club members, but it's you that's in charge of getting the job done. Therefore, all of the training you can possibly get will come in handy.

As the general contractor, your main job in your car, truck or motorcycle restoration is going to be tearing your vehicle down and putting it back together again. If you think this is easy, you have another think coming. I'll admit that it is easier to take things apart than to put them back together, but usually that's only because we don't document the way things were put together in the first place and so we forget how the pieces fit together. But the documentation of a vehicle teardown is exactly what makes the systematic disassembly of a vehicle difficult when you plan on putting it back together. (Of course, if you're not putting it back together, taking a car apart is easy!)

Once you have the vehicle apart, the next phase will be fixing (or replacing) all the parts so the vehicle will run and look new again. As general contractor, this is where you are going to need to know who can fix the parts or where you can get replacements. You will also have to get a handle on the various outside restoration services that can restore some of your parts. Through all of this managing of the restoration job, you'll be using your head rather than your hands. You may find yourself spending more time at your library or your computer than in your shop.

If you're a good manager, you'll want to increase your own knowledge base through educational opportunities that are available to you. Believe it or not, a few hours spent in an adult education class might save you twice as many hours on your project. Though you are not planning to do all the work, you still need to take the vehicle apart and rebuild it. In addition, a basic understanding of the work that you're hiring out will insure that you're getting value for your money. And, of course, you have to know who you can send parts to for restoration.

Preparation for Disassembly

Tearing an older vehicle apart for the purpose of restoring it is a challenging experience. What you are doing is essentially destroying the vehicle while trying not to damage any parts. Even relatively new cars are difficult to disassemble, but with an older vehicle you usually must deal with added problems including larger-size parts, rust and possibly undoing some obsolete production techniques that are hard to reproduce for repair purposes today.

As an example of this third point, we thought we had a rear axle problem on my '36 Pontiac and I called a number of professional restorers to see how we could remove and replicate a giant rivet. Nobody knew. Luckily, the problem turned out to be something else and we got it fixed by conventional means.

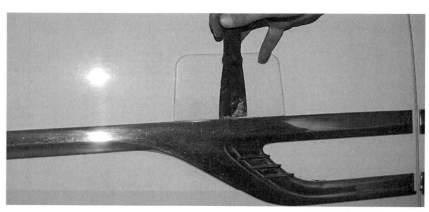

Take the car apart as carefully as possible. When removing stainless steel moldings, you can safely pry against a plastic body putty spreader with the thin blade of your paint scraper. The spreader will protect the fender.

When you are doing a restoration, you don't want to just tear the vehicle apart using brute force. Instead, it's important to preserve as many parts and fasteners as you can. Restored original parts are considered more valuable to restorers than replacements. So you must try to avoid bending, gouging, snapping, cracking or overheating parts as you struggle with their removal.

Before you start taking a car apart, have a notebook or voice recorder, a box of string tags, some wire twist closures, gummed stickers or labels, index cards, various size zipper-style plastic bags, felt-tip markers, an engraving tool, stamping punches, lots of rags and a digital camera handy. Do not use a film camera because you'll be concerned over the cost of making prints and you won't take as many photos. I personally resisted getting a digital camera for too long; I'm stubborn. But then I bought a digital camera that cost just over $100 and it helps so much. It has saved my butt more than once, when I was taking a car apart, by showing me how to put the parts assemblies back together again.

The notebook is for jotting down what you do in your own words. If you do this, it will usually mean a lot more to you than instructions in any repair manual. The voice recorder makes it easy to describe every step as you go along. If you like, you can use only the recorder during the actual work and later transcribe the commentary to your notebook. If you use a digital voice recorder, you can skip transcribing and just transfer the recording to your computer or a CD. Whatever you do, don't erase the file or tape until you have it permanently stored. You'll need it in the reassembly stage.

String tags, wire closures, stickers or labels, index cards, felt pens and an engraving tool can all be

used to mark parts with the year, make and model vehicle and other information. You may want to indicate whether the piece is a right-hand or left-hand part or its proper orientation when installed (up or down and so on). Stamping punches are used to number engine connecting rods so you know which order to install them in after they are reconditioned. After the machine shop reconditions the rods, the stampings can still be seen.

Small parts can be cleaned, repaired and stored in plastic zipper bags and information about them can be marked on an index card. Then, just toss the index card into the plastic bag and seal it. An engraving tool can be used to mark the backside of a part with information. Chrome shops use this technique to identify the owners of the parts that they have been sent for plating. Make sure that you engrave only on the backside of the part—not on the side that shows.

If you are working on just one car, you may feel that you can dispense with putting the year, make and model of the car on your cards, stickers or labels. I prefer always adding this information, in case you wind up with spare parts and try to sell them later. If the ID is there, you always know what you have.

Use at least a 2-gig memory card in your digital camera. If you shop for cards on sale, you can buy these for as little as $15. This card will hold at least 700–800 photos. And after you finish the job, you can put a record of the restoration on a CD and then erase the memory card so it can be reused. Take lots of pictures. When we rebuilt one engine, we forgot to note how some engine accessories were oriented and later we found digital photos that showed us how to properly position those components.

Specialty Tools for Disassembly—In addition to the tool recommendations discussed in Chapter 2, you will also need specialty tools and equipment to remove other parts and assemblies without damaging them. A set of brake tools will be necessary. You'll also need tools that can slide behind window cranks and door handles to release the attaching clips. These vary in design by manufacturer, but there are generic tools that can handle most types. A set of bead-filled fiberglass pry tools will come in very handy for prying off trim without damaging the trim pieces or body panels.

A set of dental picks can be used to get behind attaching clips and to snag and pull off small parts. Miniature needle-nose pliers are a godsend and one tool I have used over and over is a tiny pair of vise-grip pliers. When using pliers to remove any bright metal parts, tape the jaws so they don't scratch the part. Very tiny hammers and different sizes of mallets are great for tapping parts free without causing damage to them. Chrome trim can also be pried off by using a paint scraper levered against a body putty spreader. You place the plastic putty spreader against the body panel, then slip the blade of the scraper under the trim piece and pry against the plastic spreader, rather than the sheet metal.

For engine and transmission removal you'll need a chain hoist or an engine hoist. Most hobbyists prefer a cherry picker type engine hoist. An engine stand should be available to bolt the engine into once it's out of the car, but you will first have to separate the engine from the transmission. Many different types of pry tools from crowbars to U-joint removal tools will be used over and over again. You will definitely need both large and small pullers. My mechanic and I rely mostly on a set of reasonably priced pullers made overseas that come from a discount tool chain store. We have even connected the parts from several pullers to make a long-arm puller for yanking the front brake drums off my MG TF. So far, the pullers have worked fine, but we don't use them every day either.

One of the best budget tools I purchased from the same chain store is a 20-ton bottle jack press. Within the first month I had it, the press saved me money in removing and installing leaf spring bushings and a number of wheel bearings. A machine shop would have charged more for these services than the press cost me and it is still working fine.

Speaking of jacks, the more you have the merrier when it comes to taking a car apart. At various times, we have needed scissor jacks, multiple bottle jacks, a big hydraulic floor jack and old-fashioned screw jacks. Jack stands are another item that you can't have enough of. I have small ones, regular-size ones and giant ones in my shop. And I just purchased a Backyard Buddy Easy Access system, which is essentially four jack stands on wheels that a car can be rolled around on. We are going to use it to do some repairs on an MG TD this winter.

You will need a good set of flare wrenches for taking copper brake line fittings apart without destroying them. Of course, some of those rusty nuts will wind up getting distorted or rounded off. Some special tools may be required to remove them (or snap them off). Adjustable wrenches can sometimes be set to remove distorted nuts or you may need a nutcracker tool to cut the nut apart. In addition to such tools, various rust-busting lubricants are very helpful when taking apart rusty fasteners. Heat guns and propane torches are also handy for loosening up stuck nuts, but don't heat fasteners that have been soaked with flammable

A variety of hydraulic hoists are available for lifting the heavy engine out of a car. In most restorations, the transmission will remain attached to the engine and be removed for rebuilding at the same time.

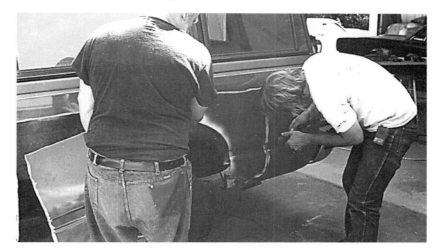

Body man Dave Stencil, of Scandinavia, Wisconsin, made use of a plasma cutter to remove rusty panels from a Chevy pickup, so a replacement rear quarter panel could be welded on. A helper holds the cut-off section.

lubricants or you could wind up with a fire. A friend of mine purchased a plasma cutter at a discount tool outlet and says it works great. He has used it to cut rusty panels out of several cars so they could be replaced with new metal.

Some parts removed from old cars may seem insignificant, but my advice is to save them all until the project is over. The fasteners used on many old cars—especially those made before World War II—may have the same thread patterns as later fasteners, but they sometimes have a different appearance. For instance, square-headed bolts were used in many applications, rather than hex-headed bolts. Also, some of the old bolts have meatier looking hex heads on them. Unless you save and restore the old hardware, your car won't have a factory look to it.

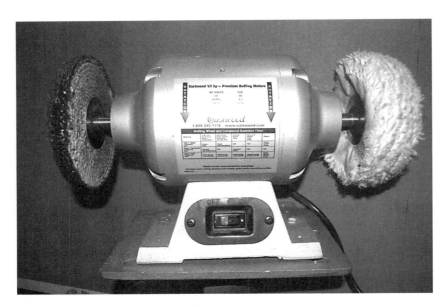

With a price that's well within the reach of most old-car hobbyists, this high-speed buffing motor gives the home restorer a way to polish up all the stainless steel trim on his old car. It is available from The Eastwood Co.

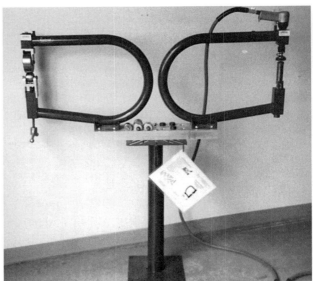

By combining an English wheel (right) and a planishing hammer (left) on a common frame, a supplier to Eastwood was able to develop this unit. The Pennsylvania tool company first marketed it for under $1,000 in 2003.

Old bolts can be cleaned of rust in tumblers, replated or reblackened and tapped out to restore their proper treads. Not every restorer goes through the trouble and expense of repairing old fasteners, but some do.

Specialty Restoration Products and Services

As the general contractor on your restoration project, part of your job is learning about the products available to the amateur restorer. From home powder coating systems to lifts capable of hoisting a small motor home, the old-car hobby has embraced the latest in technology and industrial strength hardware. The hobbyist willing to invest in some relatively modest-priced equipment can now fix leaky gas tanks, plate small parts to acceptable standards and buff stainless steel to make it look like new again.

Companies that supply hobby restorers have created their own market niche by finding and marketing products that help amateurs do what only professionals could offer years ago. Take the case of Eastwood, a Pennsylvania company that offers specialty tools, usually sold by no one else, that can help restorers, hot rodders and motorcycle enthusiasts get tough jobs done.

Familiar companies like Mid America Motorworks, Steele Rubber Products, Classic Industries, Custom Autosound, EMPI Inc., Year One and others also into the restoration marketplace. Classic Tube markets its stainless steel

fuel and brake lines, which are great to use in any restoration.

The largest car shows held throughout the country seem to feature many vendors selling the tools and restoration aids you'll want to have in your home restoration shop. You can get an extensive list of hobby events by visiting the website of *Old Cars Weekly*, the hobby's only newspaper. It will give you an online look at all car events that have been voluntarily sent to the weekly newsmagazine.

How can you tell which events have the biggest flea markets and swap meets with lots of vendors? I've noticed that the Bumper Boyz—a company that sells rechromed bumper parts—has been at all the big shows I've been to in the past year. I assume they get to even more big events than I do. They travel extensively across the country because their business plan includes car show delivery service. They have a website that contains a link for show dates and you can be pretty sure that most events they attend are large shows.

Located in the rear of this book, you will find an extensive listing of companies that sell restoration tools and supplies that you might be interested in contacting or looking up on the Internet.

Using Your Head Instead of Your Hands

In a lot of situations, the general contractor approach to auto restoration necessitates using your head instead of your hands. You are the manager of the project and that means that you have to decide

Bumper Boyz created a car show delivery program that cuts hobbyists' shipping costs. The company picks up a bumper at a show, takes it to California for replating and then delivers the replated bumper to another show.

Joe Curto of College Point, NY, restores SU carburetors for imported cars at a set price. Joe works on a repair-and-return basis. A short time after you send him your sad-looking SU carbs, they'll return looking like this.

whether the next phase of the work is something that you should do yourself or something that it's easier to farm out to an expert. In most cases, a restorer's decisions are guided by two goals. The first is to get the job done on time. The second is to get it done according to your budget for the particular project. In deciding whether or not to do a job yourself, you should consider how fast you can get it done versus the expert and how big the difference in cost will be.

I will give you a reverse example of a job that we did that we probably shouldn't have because it took us a couple of weeks to finish and we didn't save a whole lot going it ourselves, over the cost of jobbing it out. First, I will lay down a little background and explain that I'm factoring in cost of time when I talk about the cost of the job. If I spend an hour working on a car, that's an hour I can't spend working and making money. I use $20 an hour as an estimate of what my time might be worth on the job market.

In the fall of 2002, I purchased an MG TD roadster. I had wanted a T Series MG ever since my dad bought me a toy one when I was ten years old. I always thought I couldn't quite afford one. After 9/11, I realized life is short and vowed to buy the car I always wanted. My budget was still pretty tight, so I looked for a low-end MG TD and found one for $8,000. It had dual SU carburetors that leaked and worked terribly. I knew nothing about them at the time. After a few trips that smelled like I was riding in a gas can, I decided to take the carburetors off the car and send them to Joe Curto, in College Point, N.Y. Curto advertises a mail-order rebuild service for British carburetors. He does the basic rebuild for a set price, which was in the mid

$300 range at that time.

My carburetors were pretty bad, but Joe Curto did a fantastic job on them. A few weeks after I sent them off to New York, they came back looking like new. He had even brazed up some broken parts and put new brass overflow tubes on them (which a previous owner had cut off). I put the carbs back on the car following instructions that Curto sent me. After that, the TD drove much better. In fact, I drove it 8,000 miles in the summer of 2003.

In the fall of 2003, I purchased an MG TF. This car is geared differently than a TD and goes slightly faster. The TF also had signal lights, which the TD lacked. Since I drove the TD so much, a lot of driving was done after dark. I thought it might be safer with signal lights. I also thought that the TF was probably in better condition, but it turned out to be in much the same shape as the TD. That meant it also need the carburetors rebuilt.

This time I trusted the job to a member of an MG club I belong to. This man rebuilds SU carburetors on a part-time basis and he charged slightly less than the commercial rebuilders. If I recall correctly, the price was $325. And he did a great job. The carburetors looked like new and worked properly.

In 2006, I purchased an MG Magnette sedan in rough shape. This car needed everything and then some. I yanked the engine out of it and it turned out to be an MGA engine. I was lucky enough to find a true Magnette motor for sale on eBay and I bought it. This motor was supposedly rebuilt by a previous owner (not the seller), but it turned out to be a very poor quality job. Naturally, the SU carburetors need to be rebuilt. This time we decided to do the job in my shop.

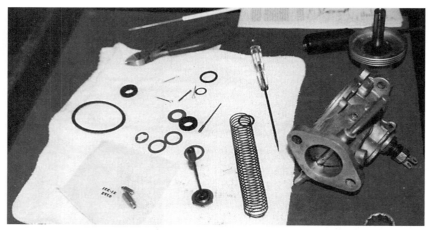

Armed with a carb kit from Joe Curto, instructions from an MG Magnette shop manual and few tools, you can try rebuilding SU carbs. If you value your time at $25 an hour, it may be cheaper to have Joe rebuild your carbs.

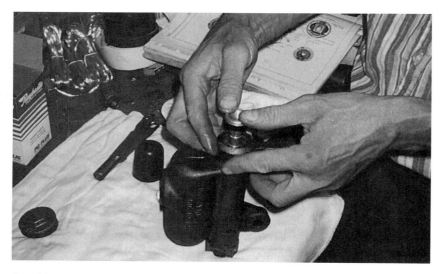

Consider what jobs you can tackle yourself. Mechanic Vince Sauberlich had little difficulty rebuilding this master cylinder, but what about you? Of course, there is no sense outsourcing jobs that you do know how to do well.

The first step was buying a rebuild kit from Joe Curto for about $75. We then spent the next three Thursday nights rebuilding the carburetors. We worked four hours each night, so that was 12 hours. And if my time is worth $20 an hour, we did $240 worth of work. Right there, we had $315 in the job. I also had to buy carburetor cleaner, new buffing pads and some paint, gaskets and hardware. In all, I ran up about $335 in costs and we weren't even sure the carburetors would work. We had never done this job before and had no experience with SU carbs other than tuning. As it turned out, they work fine, but if they quit in a few months, we

don't have the warranty that many commercial rebuilders offer.

Looking back on it, I have to admit that I failed to put my thinking cap on in this instance. It was fun to learn how to fix SU carburetors, but I really didn't manage this project well. If I had, I would have had a professional rebuild job backed by an expert for a lower cost and it would have been done faster, too.

What to do yourself and what to farm out is a big decision and the correct choice depends upon the job at hand, your own restoration skills and the equipment that you have available. You would not want to farm out an easy chore like changing spark plugs, but few home mechanics can repair a malfunctioning temperature gauge or resilver a headlight reflector. These are jobs that only a specialist will touch.

In some cases, your own level of restoration skills has to be considered. Rebuilding an old vacuum-operated fuel pump or rebuilding a brake master cylinder are jobs that many home restorers can handle, but both of these jobs can also be sub-contracted on a mail-order basis. Which direction you end up going in, as far as doing these jobs, depends on what work you're comfortable with handling yourself. Both jobs are fairly easy, unless you have absolutely no experience doing them.

Your ability to do certain jobs on a collector vehicle depends on what tools and equipment you have in your shop. If you own a HotCoat powder coating system from Eastwood, you can actually powder coat a subframe. I know a hobbyist who did a '69 Camaro this way in his home garage. He used the heat lamps Eastwood sells to cure the powder, doing a section at a time and then moving the lamps. However, if you don't have the equipment, you have to farm out the powder coating. So, tools and equipment definitely figure into the equation.

The great majority of professional restoration shops have to farm out three specialty tasks: machine shop work, chrome plating and upholstery. The chances are pretty good that, as an amateur restorer, you'll also be farming out these tasks to one degree or another. All three of these are fairly expensive jobs, so it may pay for you to put your thinking cap on before you decide to go whole hog into hiring the work done.

Do you have a lathe or drill press in your shop that you can use for part of the machine shop work? Are there places where you can buy a new part for less than the machining will cost you? Can you lap valves in by hand and save a couple of bucks? As the general contractor, you want to hire specialty help when you truly need it and benefit from it, but you

Most professional restoration shops use outside machine shops for jobs like crankshaft turning, which is being done here at Freedom Auto and Engine Rebuilders in Kaukauna, Wisconsin. Few restorers do it all these days.

A job that it is possible for amateur restorers to learn is convertible top installation. Mechanic Vince Sauberlich is seen applying glue to the quarter flaps of a new top he put on a GM J car convertible.

also want to hold your costs to a minimum.

Chrome plating can add a lot of cost to a restoration, so you'll also want to investigate how you can save money in this area. Your first reaction to this suggestion might be, "How can I cut my plating costs if it's not possible to have a real plating system at home?" According to Terry Meetz, of Custom Plating Specialists in Brillion, Wisconsin, the true expense in plating is in preparation of the piece.

"Two similar pieces can vary in plating cost if one has more pitting," Terry explained. "I don't count each pit. . .I inspect a piece and use 25 years of experience to set a price for plating it. However, if a customer has many identical parts in similar shape, they can all be prepped the same way and we can do the job faster. Therefore, I can give that customer a lower cost on doing each piece."

Most home restorers can't custom-stitch an automobile interior, but before going that route, you might want to check to see if someone reproduces the original factory upholstery in kit form. Quality-made interior kits are available for many vehicles. They fit like a glove and often require just minimal cutting or sewing. Nearly anyone who knows how to work carefully can stretch a precut kit over a seat and install it with hog rings and special hog ring pliers.

Another trim job that it is possible for an amateur restorer to learn is convertible top installations. Pre-cut top kits are available and there is plenty of good information on the Internet on how to install a rag top. A few special tools and supplies will be needed, but by your second top install you'll be paid back.

Educational Opportunities

It's not unusual to enjoy the restoration process so much that you want to learn more about it. At one point, I even instructed a class, organized through the Wisconsin technical college system, where I taught hobbyists about car collecting. Being limited to a regular classroom, it was not a hands-on class and we focused on automotive history, car values and other book learning. However, at times I arranged for restorers and hobby suppliers to lecture the class. The passion of the students to learn about old cars and old-car restoration was extremely strong. Attendance was never a problem.

A few years ago, I turned the tables and took a night school auto body class. I had wanted to do this for many years and it was great. The class was scheduled for four hours each Tuesday night between late January and mid-May. Of the 13 students in the class, more than half were old-car collectors. We learned so much more than basic bodywork, that four additional hours were needed to pack it all in.

Our instructor stressed safety right from the start. Students were told they needed eye protection, mechanic's gloves, a welding helmet and welder's gloves. The majority of students purchased welding helmets with self-darkening lenses, which are great for beginners.

Our bodywork project consisted of getting an old fender, cutting a hole or two in it, and then welding in a patch panel. The surface was leveled with plastic body filler, followed by lots of sanding and additional surface preparation. Once we had the surface repaired, we sprayed primer, did additional prep work and top coated. It was fun, but when I finished the class, I was not quite ready to paint my '36 Pontiac. However, I did learn a lot of things that would be handy to know if I was managing a restoration as general contractor. In other words, I didn't learn to do the job expertly, but I learned

Many old-car hobbyists find it worthwhile to go back to school, at night, to learn auto repair and bodywork skills that help in their at-home restorations. This class in Waupaca, Wisconsin, was called Bodywork Basics.

enough about it to spot expertise and know what questions to ask an expert.

We also learned quite a few general skills outside the realm of bodywork. We were taught how to use a machine that cleans fuel injectors and cylinder heads with a fluid that flows through the engine under pressure. This procedure cleans out carbon and increases fuel economy in many cases. I was able to use it to de-coke the head on my MG TD. That is a recommended service procedure for that car and using the machine made it possible to do that job without removing the head. That knowledge might come in handy someday and help me save time and money on a restoration.

Another machine in the shop flushed and changed automatic transmission fluid. You could watch the clear plastic lines as the dirty brownish fluid came out and the bright red fluid went in. The machine allowed a fluid change without dropping the pan and if you want to put in a new gasket and filter, you can drop the pan while it's empty and do the job with no muss or fuss.

There are several schools in the United States that teach auto restoration skills on a full-time basis and most amateur restorers that I know would have loved to have been able to enroll in these courses when they were younger. McPherson College, located in McPherson, Kansas, is the only four-year accredited college offering a degree in automotive restoration technology. Fortunately, the college offers an open-to-the-public summer program at its Automotive Restoration Institute.

These summer sessions give home restorers an

opportunity to learn auto restoration skills in convenient workshops. The same expert instructors and top-notch facility that have made McPherson College's Auto Restoration Program famous are available to hobbyists and professionals. Each of the five-day workshops concentrates on a specific skill area. Enrollees learn restoration through hands-on experience and working on actual cars.

Enrollments in each workshop are limited to a certain number, so that all participants can benefit from the personal attention of expert instructors and have ample time to use equipment. With this one-on-one approach, no matter what skill level a student is at, some restoration expertise will be gained through taking the workshop.

The curriculum includes valuable information on locating tools, materials and parts. In many cases, enrollees can bring parts from their current restoration projects to work on at McPherson College. Some of the workshops the school has presented for hobbyists include upholstery & trim; vintage bodywork; finishing touches (wood graining, pinstriping and stainless, brass and aluminum polishing); automotive painting; carburetion, ignition and tune-up, and engine rebabbitting.

For more information about the Automotive Restoration Institute's summer program, please contact the McPherson College Auto Restoration Department via email (martinb@mcpherson.edu). Anyone who is interested can also visit the restoration department's website at www.mcpherson.edu/technology.

Another school that offers programs in a variety of auto-related career fields is WyoTech. It has

This Model T was one of the cars being restored at McPherson College when I visited there about 12 years ago. Since then, Jay Leno and Hagerty Insurance have aided the school's Restoration Technology program.

Students at Wyoming Technical Institute learn a variety of skills for repairing or restoring cars, trucks and motorcycles. The students shown here are taking a class on automotive interior trim work. (Courtesy WyoTech)

For years, MG restoration guru John Twist conducted seminars for interested hobbyists at his University Motors shop in Ada, Michigan. Seminars on a range of topics were presented sequentially over two six-day weeks.

locations in California, Florida, Pennsylvania and Wyoming. WyoTech's goal is to prepare students with everything they need to forge a career in a variety of transportation technology fields.

Students in the automotive technology area work on engines. They learn how to diagnose engine problems how to get engines running right. This program covers engine rebuilding, engine maintenance, drivetrain systems and chassis repairs.

Other specialty areas addressed in the WyoTech automotive program include: Motorsports Chassis Fabrication; High-Performance Powertrain Engineering and Street Rod and Custom Fabrication. There is also a Collision & Refinishing Program and a Motorcycle Technology Program. The collision course includes instruction on Trim and Upholstery and Rod and Custom building. Information about WyoTech courses is available by visiting www.wyotech.edu/contact/live-call.

Car shows are getting in on the concept of teaching restoration skills. The 2008 Iola Old Car Show in Iola, Wisconsin, featured a Teamed to Learn education tent where retired high school teacher Fred Beyer talked about a program he created that's near and dear to his heart. Beyer's Hot Rod High program was aimed at teaching high school students how to restore classic cars. Beyer is now looking for ways to expand the program to help educate hobbyists as well.

The students who took part in Beyer's program learned machine shop skills, welding and sheet metal fabrication. They made parts for old cars in a high school's foundry and machine shop. They learned to fit body parts, form fluid lines, build engines and prep bodies for paint. Since the high

You can often get questions about your restoration project answered by the counterman at your favorite parts store. This is particularly true if he is Dave Glass at D & M Corvette Specialists, in Downers Grove, Illinois.

school did not have a body shop, final cosmetics were done by a local shop that worked in conjunction with the school.

In the program, the students helped restore cars for owners and the owners paid for the needed parts. No school or taxpayer funding was involved. A yellow Model A woodie was restored through the program. Shawano Community High School in Shawano, Wisconsin was the school that supported the original Hot Rod High Program.

Sources of Help & Information

When you take on the role of general contractor for the restoration of your own vehicle, chances are pretty good that you'll find yourself needing help

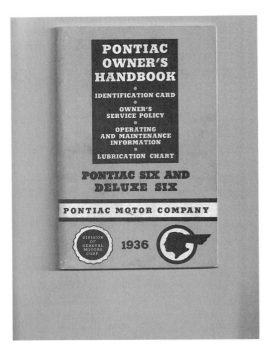

Automotive literature dealers sell sales catalogs and technical manuals for all types of old cars. Some, like this Pontiac Owner's Handbook, are pieces put out by the factory. Other literature was published in the aftermarket.

with the job of restoring a vehicle or with some skill your project demands. This book includes a very extensive listing of sources of specific types of help in its appendix, but in this chapter, I'm going to discuss some of general types of help and information that you'll find available locally, nationally and even internationally.

The counterman at your local parts store can give you invaluable help, especially experienced parts people who have been involved in the trade for years. When I started collecting cars I needed a carburetor kit for a '53 Pontiac straight-8. None were listed in the parts books, but after visiting several parts stores, I ran into a veteran counterman who recalled that the same carburetor was used on later-model Buicks and AMC V-8s with the linkage reversed. He looked up these applications and the kit was the same.

Old-car clubs are one of the biggest aids to vintage car restorers. Many clubs are national or international organizations, but most have chapters all across the country. One marque clubs help restorers most. They focus on one brand of car and generally have a panel of technical advisors who supply free restoration help. Most clubs publish newsletters that include tech tips and how-to-do-it information. Club websites with tech tips are getting more common. Some clubs reproduce hard-to-find parts as club projects. Sales of these parts go into the club's treasury. Many clubs conduct tech sessions at their monthly meetings.

The development of the Internet has given home restorers an instant source of information and a way to network with other old car nuts who may have worked on the same type of vehicle. Newsgroups have been set up to help enthusiasts share how-to information, as well as to pass on word-of-mouth advertising about good mail-order unit parts repair services. I belong to an MG T Series newsgroup and a man from Argentina was having fuel pump issues. He received over 25 suggestions from other owners to use a fuel pump rebuilding service in the Northwest. When a contractor gets that many recommendations, the general contractor—you—can feel pretty good about sending work to him.

The old car hobby supports an active auto literature trade that buys and sells original factory sales literature and technical manuals. Service or shop manuals are invaluable sources of information. A Master Parts Catalog will list all parts and part numbers for your car. If you're lucky enough to find a Factory Assembly Manual for your car, it will describe how it was built on the assembly line. Owner handbooks provide quite a bit of basic ownership information, including service data. Dealer service bulletins and training materials often cover fixes that the automakers worked out for field problems with their cars.

Each year dozens of different newsstand magazines and hundreds of books are produced by publishers who serve the old-car hobby. They often include how-to information. There are magazines such as *Auto Restorer, Old Cars Guide to Auto Restoration* and *Skinned Knuckles* that focus exclusively on technical articles that will help you plan and execute a restoration.

Many videos and CDs are available to teach different restoration skills from buffing bright metal trim to rebuilding engines. Sometimes you will receive free instructional CDs if you buy a kit of tools from companies such as Eastwood. Some CDs are available covering very specialized repairs. British car parts supplier Moss Motors sells a CD that tells you how to swap the tall gears out of an MG TD in place of MGA gears with a numerically lower ratio. People that I know have paid $750 to $1,250 to have this job done by a shop. The Moss Motors CD is priced very reasonably and can save MG T Series owners a bundle.

Car shows and trade shows are a final source of some great information that restorers can use. Trade shows almost always include seminars or workshops and these are starting to be incorporated into car shows, swap meets and auctions as well.

Although you can mail-order high-performance crate engines for American cars, there aren't many catalogs for complete, original MG TF 1250 engines like this one.

Chapter 5

Mechanical Restoration Tips

Now that I have laid down the basics of the general contractor approach to auto restoration, talked about the restoration process, discussed outsourcing and looked at training possibilities, it's time to dive into the process of actually executing a restoration with you functioning as the general contractor.

Cars, trucks and motorcycles are made up of different systems like powertrain, brakes, suspension, etc. A restoration can be well managed by restoring one system at a time. For each system you'll have to take things apart, decide what to do yourself, decide what to send out and put the restored parts together.

Since you will be using the general contractor approach, keep in mind that your goal is efficiency. You do not necessarily want to restore a vehicle at the lowest cost without considering the hours spent on the job. You also do not want to restore as fast as possible without any regard to cost. You want to manage the work and get the job done in the shortest possible time within your preset budget.

Restoration work can generally be divided into three main areas of repairs: mechanical, bodywork and interior. As you execute your project, you take care of each of these systems and you wind up with a car that looks like new again. There may be other minor things to deal with, but these are the Big Three.

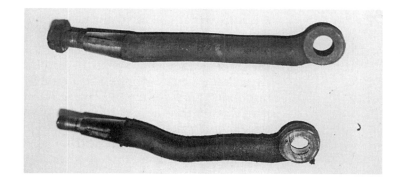

Replacing or restoring a mechanical part isn't as exciting as a cosmetic restoration, but sometimes it is absolutely necessary. These MG TD steering system swivel pins were identical before the bottom one got bent.

Unit-By-Unit Restoration

The first step of the restoration process starts with mechanical restoration. I have read books that state that the cosmetic aspects of a restoration—the bodywork and the upholstery—are the most difficult and important phases of a restoration, but I do not agree with that. There is nothing easy about dealing with your car's engine, drivetrain, chassis, electricals, cooling, etc.

Your car's nuts and bolts may not be as romantic as its red

Taking an engine out of a car and stripping it down requires five to eight hours. Typical shop rates would be $250–$400 for this job. Most general contractors can do this work themselves if they have an engine hoist.

This MGB engine was torn down and rebuilt by enthusiasts from the Fox Cities British Car Club as a group project to help a fellow club member. The lucky lady who owned the car got a rebuilt motor for the price of the parts.

paint or leather seats, but if the car doesn't function, it won't run. It makes sense to deal with the mechanicals first because they create the foundation that you build the rest of the car on. Also, if you get toward the end of a restoration and find that you're over budget, you can cut back by using, say, a vinyl convertible top, instead of a Hartz cloth top. Making a choice like that is much preferable to using cheap brakes rather than the best ones.

Engine, Transmission and Rear End

I think it is safe to say that true restorers are interested in rebuilding a car's original engine or a period-correct replacement. Usually, a restorer using the general contractor approach will yank the engine, disassemble it, take it to a machine shop for machining, find or order new parts, put the new parts in after the machine shop is done and reinstall the rebuilt engine in the vehicle.

There aren't many mail-order sources of authentic older engines, though there are exceptions to this rule. I have seen companies that catalog Model T and Model A Ford engines, you can mail order a rebuilt Ford flathead V-8 and I know several shops offer mail-order rebuilds of British sports car engines.

In 2001, Promar Precision Engines, based in Paterson, New Jersey, recognized a nationwide resurgence of classic car restorations. Promar started a program designed to meet the demand. The company sent representatives to car shows to promote the idea it could rebuild classic car engines shipped to it. Promar was already a remanufacturing company serving customers worldwide with a complete line of rebuilt and remanufactured engines, cylinder heads,

crankshafts, engine restoration services and components. It tried to create a mail-order business in doing older engines shipped to its New Jersey location.

Promar still offers the highly specialized service, but is not giving classic car engine rebuilding service the same promotional push it got eight years ago. Shipping engines is expensive and that is a big reason that most hobbyists wind up yanking their engine and relying on local machine shops and rebuilders.

Engine Removal—Yanking an engine is a job most DIYers can do with basic tools. It takes at least four to six hours to gain access to a powerplant, carefully detach its connections to a chassis and lift it out of a vehicle. At a $75 an hour, shops will charge $300–$450 to do this job and as much to put the engine back again. It is a job anyone can do and doing it yourself will save you a nice piece of change.

You'll remove the car's hood and any sheet metal that's in the way of the engine coming out. Then disconnect the wires, cables, fluid lines and linkages that go from car to engine. Your shop manual lists all steps to take an engine out. As you work, take lots of digital photos and keep a book handy to jot down notes. I have an old computer in my shop that I type every step into. Have food storage bags, index cards and a pen nearby. Each time you remove a part toss it in a bag, write it on the index card and put the card in the bag with the parts.

As you move along, more and more parts will come off and the remaining parts will get easier to see. Eventually, you'll see how the engine mountings work and figure out how to remove

This METS (Mobile Engine Test Station) was purchased from Northern Tool. It includes a full set of gauges so rebuilt engines can be test run and tuned up in it. Other companies have since started handling this product.

Gale Banks Engineering is a well-known supplier of high-performance crate engines. These brand-new motors are largely used to build hot rods and resto-mods. Car builders like the fact they come with a guarantee.

them. At this point, you can move in with your engine hoist and lift the powerplant out of the chassis. Some engines have lifting attachments to hook a hoist to, but often you'll have to put a sling around the block to lift it. Chains can cut into fresh engine paint, so think about a rope sling.

With the engine out, you must decide who'll tear it down. This is a job requiring skill and experience. It is easy to break things like head bolts and manifold studs. If you have done the job before, you shouldn't have a problem, but if it's your first time, get help. Special tools and equipment will be needed, starting with a stand to mount the engine on. If you take the engine to a professional rebuilder, they will do the teardown for you.

After the engine is torn down, take the pieces to the machine shop. Discuss what you need. They will know what's best. Do not cut any corners. For an obsolete motor, the shop may need help finding parts. The engine will be at the machine shop awhile, but you can keep very busy painting parts like the intake and exhaust manifolds, timing cover, air cleaner and valve cover(s) that didn't go to the machine shop. I like to rebuild everything while the engine is apart, so I send the carburetor(s), fuel pump, water pump and distributor out to specialists to be rebuilt. If it is going to be necessary to rebuild the instruments, I consider this part of the engine job. When the engine is done, you will need to have it hooked up to properly functioning gauges to test it.

When I do an MG engine, I send the SU carbs to Joe Curto in College Point, New York, for a standard rebuild. He also rebuilds water pumps.

E. Lawrie Rhoads, in Medfield, Massachusetts, and Jim Taylor in Bartlesville, Oklahoma, are equally good at fuel pump rebuilds. Other specialists are listed in the appendix.

Crate Motors—What about crate engines? According to the *New York Times* (October 25, 2006) high-performance replacement engines for cars—known as crate engines—have become important revenue generators for American automakers. In his article, "Instant Horsepower In a Box, Delivered Straight to Your Hot Rod," Joe Siano showed that sales are growing steadily. Crate engines are used in restoring modified muscle cars and in building turnkey hot rods.

Siano said Chrysler sold $2 million worth of crate engines in 2004, $4.5 million in 2005 and expected to do $5 million in 2006. Automakers sell crate engines priced from $1,400 up to about $17,000. A hot rodder interviewed for the article said he purchased a 435-hp GM crate engine with a two-year warranty for $4,500—about half what it would cost him to rebuild an old performance V-8.

Restorers who use crate engines feel they improve old cars and increase their values, too. With their reliability and warranties, crate engines have helped create a new type of vehicle called a resto-mod—a car with mostly original appearance features that has some styling and many technological updates. Crate engines are also used in so-called clone cars. Crate engines look great and can help create a very reliable car build. However, none are completely authentic as far as factory correctness goes.

Transmission—When you yank the engine out of your car, you might as well leave the transmission attached and take it out, too. Nearly all vintage car

Most transmission rebuilds involve parts replacement, rather than machining. MG restorer John Twist cut way parts of this transmission casing so he could use the old gearbox for demos at his annual restoration seminars.

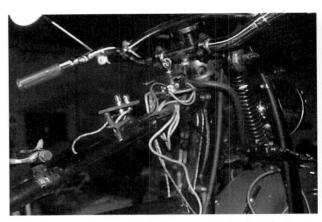

Cars, trucks and motorcycles have multiple electrical systems working in conjunction with each other. Curt Muller tore his 1948 Indian Chief apart so that he could check the condition of the wiring to the ignition switch.

transmissions need some work and you'll also want to clean the transmission housing and paint it up to make it look nice. Remove the engine and transmission as a single, bolted-together unit and then split the two apart once they are out of the car.

Restoring a transmission is a little different than engines in that they usually don't go to a machine shop to be rebuilt. You may be able to find a local transmission shop than can rebuild your vintage transmission if it's from the '60s or newer. If it is older than that, you may have to find a more specialized rebuilder who is familiar with older transmission technology. Of course, a lot will depend on whether the car has a standard transmission or an automatic.

In most cases, the big issue with restoring an older transmission will be finding the parts needed to make the repair. Most local shops understand the

Some hobby vendors will outsource the balancing of a driveshaft to smooth a car's operation. They'll also install new universal joints on the driveshaft to insure the smoothness and quietness of vehicle operation.

theory behind all types of transmissions, but have no idea where to find obsolete parts. It is true that some rare old cars have unusual gearboxes, but there always seems to be a specialist somewhere who can fix them. For example, the Alan Taylor Company of Escondido, California, is the only restoration shop in the world that rebuilds French-made Cotal transmissions commercially.

If the car you are restoring has a standard transmission, you will need to give the clutch attention too. At a minimum, you'll want to take the old clutch to the machine shop to have it faced. If more work is required, there are a number of companies throughout the country that you can send the clutch to in order to have it remanufactured to original equipment specifications. Heavy-duty options are also available from some of these vendors and several of them also rebuild driveshafts. They can balance a driveshaft and install new universal joints to ensure smooth, quiet operation.

Rear Axle—Most restorers do not do a total rebuild of a car's rear axle. Typically, a clean up and new paint is all that is needed. However, if repairs are needed, they usually require special skills and special tools. Shops that build racing cars deal quite a bit with rear axle technology and are a good source of help when it's required. There are specialists who focus on specific jobs, like changing the gear ratios in the MG TD so the car drives well on modern highways. When jobs like this are done, in addition to installing higher-speed gears, the shop has to recalibrate the car's speedometer.

Electrical System Restoration

Cars, trucks and motorcycles have multiple

The ignition system tucked under the hood of this rare 1931 Ihle-bodied BMW speedster is pretty basic. It includes a coil, a distributor and high-tension spark plug wires.

Collectors love to finish off their restorations with batteries and battery cases that carry the brand name of their favorite car, truck or motorcycle. Having the proper battery is a great way to win points at a judged show.

electrical systems that work in conjunction with each other. The starting system kicks the car to life. It includes the battery, the solenoid, switches and the starter. The ignition system fires the fuel/air charge in the combustion chambers. It includes the high-tension coil, the spark plug wires, the distributor, the condenser, the distributor cap, the rotor, the points (or electronic ignition parts) and the spark plugs.

The charging system includes a generator or alternator that converts mechanical energy to electrical energy to keep the battery fully charged. You will also need a voltage regulator to control the amount of electricity that flows to certain spots. Electrical accessories include lights, electric windshield wipers (if used), a radio, various power options and other electrically-operated equipment.

Electrical components can wear out or burn out. Many can be restored on an outsourcing basis. Restorable electrical parts include starters, generators, alternators, switches, distributors, heater motors, radios (and audio equipment), certain lights, electric gauges, solenoids and coils. Years ago, you could get electrical parts rebuilt locally, but today this is largely a specialty job because electrical parts on newer cars are usually replaced, rather than repaired.

Restorers also deal with electrical repair services such as conversions to electronic ignition system, lighting and radio upgrades, 6-volt to 12-volt system conversions and the complete replacement of a vehicle's old wiring harness with a new one. Batteries are another consideration. Some hobbyists want only name-brand batteries, some like the reproduction types that look like old-fashioned batteries and others prefer small Optima batteries that look almost like a six-pack of beer.

When I first started collecting cars, I could take a starter, generator or alternator to the local auto parts store and they'd rebuild it. If you check the factory shop manual for your 1930s–1960s car, you'll find instructions for rebuilding these parts. Today, there are fewer rebuilders who do this kind of work. *Hemmings Motor News* lists about a half-dozen companies that restore starters. There's probably a commercial rebuilder near you that can do starters, generators and alternators. Fondy Auto Electric, in Fond du Lac, Wisconsin is both a rebuilder and specialty retailer. About a year ago, I toured their facility.

Though it does restoration work, FAE is not strictly an old-car business. However, the number of obsolete parts it repairs dwarfs the amount done by many hobby-only shops. FAE started in 1968 as

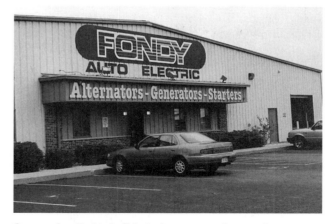

Companies that rebuild starters, generators and alternators can often be found locally. Fondy Auto Electric has three locations throughout Wisconsin, but also offers a nationwide ship-in rebuild-and-return service.

Fondy Auto Electric buys up old starters, generator and alternator cores to rebuild for off-the-shelf sales. These large shelving units hold the inventory of cores at the company's main location in Fond du Lac, Wisconsin.

a two-person shop serving the Fond du Lac area. Now, it has three facilities with more than 37,000 square feet of total floor space. Each facility houses complete remanufacturing operations and a giant inventory of completely rebuilt parts, including vintage items.

FAE told me the remanufacturing process starts with disassembly of the starter, alternator or generator. During the teardown, wearable parts such as brushes, bushings, bearings, starter drives and solenoids are discarded. Parts such as housings are reclaimed after thorough cleaning and inspection. New or remanufactured parts are substituted for bad ones as reassembly takes place.

The new, reconditioned and salvaged parts are installed following established procedures and specifications. After reassembly, all units are load tested in operating conditions similar to what will be experienced on a vehicle.

The rebuilding process is designed to make every unit look and perform better than new. The company feels its rebuilt parts will be installed in vehicles with batteries, cables, switches, engines, drive belts, flywheels and connections that have never been replaced and may even be old and worn. To operate efficiently and overcome conditions, the units are made tougher than new ones.

The company keeps an extensive stock of rebuilt units on hand that are ready to ship. In the rare instance a needed unit is not in stock (or if a customer wants the old unit rebuilt) a rebuild & return service is offered. You can send in your old starter (or alternator or generator) and have it rebuilt and sent back to you. This is very popular

with collectors who require matching numbers.

After many years of trying to cut corners and finding it to be false economy, I have come to the point with my cars that starters and generators get rebuilt any time the engine is stripped down or taken out of a car. It just makes sense to give electrical devices an overhaul when you have easy access to them. FAE will sometimes go through a unit, test it and do little more than minor work and bill me accordingly. I also recommend putting new belts on at the same time.

Distributors can also be overhauled on a outsourcing basis and Advance Distributors is one of few companies in the U.S. that will rebuild British car distributors on a mail-order basis. Actually, owner Jeff Schlemmer has been rebuilding both British and American car distributors for vintage cars. He does work for individual hobbyists, as well as for restoration shops across the country.

Jeff starts by degreasing the old distributors in an ultrasonic cleaner. He then media blasts them to get a nice, clean finish. The next step is installing new parts. After the distributor is reassembled, Jeff can redo the advance curve and fit the distributor with new advance springs. This will enhance the car's performance on modern fuels, improve throttle responsiveness and raise up performance.

There are a few vendors in the old car hobby who restore electric motors, electrical switches, electrical relays and solenoids (including overdrive transmission solenoids). A number of firms also specialize in rebuilding instruments and gauges, including those that use electric sending units.

For instance, Nisonger Instruments of New York specializes in fixing Smiths and Jaeger car, motorcycle and vintage racing gauges. This

Advance Distributors, of Shakopee, Minnesota, is one of few companies in the U.S. that rebuilds classic car distributors on a mail-in basis. They can rebuild a distributor to factory condition or make high-performance upgrades.

The busy desk of Bob Castagnetta, of Nisonger Instruments in Mamaroneck, N.Y., reflects his decades of experience repairing the Smith's and Jaeger gauges used in British cars, Shelby Cobras and many Shelby replicars.

This rare, unrestored Bonneville edition of the spring fork 1940 Indian Chief has an original magneto ignition. For old cars and motorcycles with such systems, a number of hobby vendors repair magnetos and rewind coils.

company started restoring Smiths gauges in 1949 and was once the U.S. service center for Smiths and Jaeger gauges. The staff has a total of over 120 years of experience.

Rebuilt instruments are calibrated to OEM specifications using very old, but extremely reliable factory calibration equipment and rebuilds are guaranteed. Most rebuilders, including Nisonger, give customers back the instruments they send in. Most rebuilding services are not exchange programs.

Some companies that rebuild electrical components can also supply devices to switch a car from 6-volt to 12-volt electrics. Nisonger craftsmen can even convert Smiths and Jaeger Instruments from positive to negative ground, which comes in handy if you put a modern radio into a positive earth British car. Electric tachometers can be set up for use with electronic ignition.

Many companies convert clocks to modern-day quartz movements. Nisonger also supplies factory-like Smith gauges for real and replica 427 Cobras. If you want your 427 Cobra to have a programmable electronic speedometer, Nisonger offers that too. It also develops new products like a faithful reproduction of the five-inch flat-faced chronometric/mechanical RC167 counterclockwise 8000 rpm tach used in many racing cars and sports cars of the '50s and '60s. The repro has modern electronic internals, so it is compatible with four-, six- or eight-cylinder engines and with electronic or points ignition.

For older cars and motorcycles with magneto ignition systems, there are a number of hobby service vendors who repair magnetos and rewind coils. Another vendor restores Delco lock-switch

ignition cables used on early General Motors cars. Countless specialists do all types of modifications to old tube-type car radios to make them play well. They can be transistorized and even converted to AM/FM radios without altering their original appearance. If your '70s car has an 8-track tape player, mail-order repair services are available. Electric windshield wiper motors can also be rebuilt to work like new again.

As far as a new wiring harness for a car you're restoring, these can be ordered from a number of different suppliers. In some cases, it will depend on what type of car you are repairing. British Wiring sells harnesses only for British cars, while other companies sell them for various American makes. Even reproduction harnesses for antique motorcycles are available. Harnesses cost several

To give your restored car the right look, there are companies that reproduce wiring that has the old-fashioned, braided cloth covering. These spark plug wires on a '36 Pontiac Six were sourced from Kanter Auto Products.

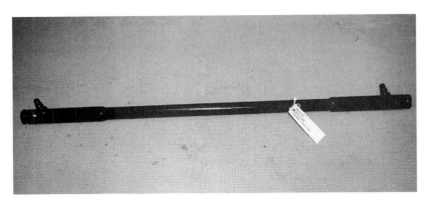

A Stockton, California, company named Rare Parts, Inc., builds steering and suspension parts for classic cars. It made this rare steering link for a 1939 Talbot-Lago. The car owner even asked for old-looking factory-like welds.

At each end of the solid bar stock used to make the Talbot drag link a hollow connector tube like this one had to be fabricated and threaded to accept the end plug. It was then slotted and threaded to accept a ball joint.

hundred dollars and up. Some use old-fashioned braided wire and some have the old-fashioned braided fabric covering over modern plastic wires. Although harnesses can be mail ordered, you will have to handle the installation. Of course, you could hire the job out to a local auto electrical technician.

If you are building a custom car, kit car, hot rod, resto-mod or any vehicle that you want to upgrade and modernize, aftermarket parts suppliers have some very slick custom wiring kits available. These kits incorporate color-coded wires, quick-connect attachments and other high-tech features for neat, convenient and safe wiring jobs. Some of the kits are even designed with a specific popular hot rod—say a '32 Highboy or '40 Ford Five-Window Coupe—in mind. You may find they also fit well in other cars of similar size and vintage.

Although the components of your car's electrical system can each be sent out and rebuilt individually, you are going to have to swap your general contractor's helmet for a mechanic's cap when it comes time to installing the pieces in the vehicle. Although you may see very simple illustrations of an electrical system in your factory shop manual, it is not something you can take right out of a box and bolt into your car. So, get out the wire strippers, black electrical tape and test light. You've got a little greasy fingernail stuff to do.

Steering

Where would you go to a replacement steering drag link for a 1939 Talbot-Lago Teardrop Coupe? If you think it's impossible, you haven't heard of an amazing company in Stockton, California. There are only 19 Teardrop Coupes known to exist in the world, but Rare Parts, Inc., helped make one steerable again.

Rare Parts manufactures and sells steering and suspension parts for all types of vehicles from the 1930s to current models. In 1957, company founder Lyle Burgess started a wheel-alignment service. By the late 1970s it was becoming clear that major suspension parts suppliers were no longer offering complete coverage on parts for older cars. This drove Burgess to start Rare Parts in 1981.

Burgess' concept was to specialize in steering and suspension parts and nothing else! He decided to sell one piece at a time, as needed, to the wholesale trade. This eliminated the need to stock slow-moving or obsolete parts at the warehouse, distributor or jobber levels. At the same time, repair shops could serve all of their customers quickly, regardless of the year, make and model of vehicle being repaired. Rare Parts was setup to deliver almost any suspension part fast. When needed, overnight delivery of catalog items is available.

Rare Parts has a full testing facility to conduct both destructive and cycle testing. That's why the quality of the parts being produced greatly surpasses OEM standards. Rare Parts also features a large wholesale inventory of over 1,000,000 steering and suspension components.

According to Rare Parts Special Project Coordinator Theodore Armendariz, building the 1939 Talbot drag link was a very unique project. He could have made that part from a straight tube and done it cheaper, but the owner of the car wanted it to be exactly like the original and insisted they make it from a solid piece of bar, no matter how much it cost. Theodore made a number of extra drag links, of course, in case another '39 Talbot owner needs another one.

The machine shop where Armendariz works can build practically any steering or suspension part. The shop is equipped with a CNC lathe, CNC

Wishbone-style lever-shock absorbers were used on U.S. cars through the early postwar period and on imports for many years thereafter. Worldwide Auto Parts, of Madison, Wisconsin, rebuilt these MG TF front units.

Working from under a Backyard Buddy lift, mechanic Vince Sauberlich loosens the U-bolts that fasten the leaf springs on an MG TF. As you can tell, this car is under slung with the leaf springs below the axle for lowness.

mill, presses, threaders, an induction heat treating machine, various welders and steel media tumblers. OEM drawings are used to help manufacture obsolete parts.

Enthusiasts or collectors looking for a custom piece or an obsolete OEM part can have it built. Rare Parts can make a steering drag link for Thomas-Flyer. Some parts are stocked and others are fabricated to order. Winter is probably the best time to have old-car parts custom made, as demand jumps in summer.

Front and Rear Suspension

As motor vehicles went from horseless carriages to high-performance cars, many changes were made in front and rear suspension systems. In the beginning, the automobile was little more than a wagon with a motor. Into the 1930s, many cars still used wagon-like beam axles and transverse leaf springs. A variety of independent front suspension systems with coil springs came out of Detroit in the mid-'30s. Some cars switched to coil springs at all four corners.

Shock absorber designs also underwent change. The first front shocks looked like large towers on the front of 1920s cars. Later, the lever-action shock gained favor. Airplane-style telescopic shock absorbers were found under most cars of the '50s–'70s, but McPherson strut front suspension became mainstream by the mid-'70s. In the early '60s, the always-innovative Corvette introduced an independent rear suspension to make it corner better on racetracks.

Restoring Springs—Collector car restorers using the general contractor system will find that leaf springs and coil springs can be restored. They may also find that going this route has advantages over reproduction springs. Restorers will also learn that some, but not all, shock absorbers can be restored by specialists. In addition, other front suspension parts like ball joints can be remanufactured by a California company that repairs and custom builds front-end parts for restorers.

One way to restore leaf springs is by re-arching them using the cold-setting method. Cold setting is done by bending spring steel back to original shape while cold. It is best done by a professional using a precisely controlled, electronically operated 150-ton press.

First, you must remove the springs. If you're working with rusty original parts, you'll want to spray everything with WD-40 and let it sit a few days. Then, get the car up in the air and make sure it's safely supported. The old nuts and bolts will come off easy with an air-powered impact wrench, but don't snap them. A spring shop may be able to find replacements, but don't count on it.

To remove the springs, jack up the rear end and support the chassis in front of the front spring anchor. Take the weight of the axle on a small jack. Remove the nuts from the U-bolts that go through the support plates to secure the spring to the axle. Slowly and carefully lower the jack and remove the U-bolts. Remove the rear shackle pin nuts and outer shackle plate. Remove the inner plate with the shackle pins on it. Lower the rear end to the

A technician at Accurate Alignment, in Appleton, Wisconsin, removes a rusty leaf from a spring pack fastened in a special fixture. Once removed, each spring leaf will be re-arched using the cold setting process.

Each individual leaf from a leaf spring pack is cold set by the expert use of a 150-ton hydraulic press to bend the stubborn spring steel. Cold setting is a rapid, rhythmic operation that takes a long time to learn how to do.

ground. Remove the pivot pin at the front spring eye. Lower the front of the spring down.

Accurate Alignment in Appleton, Wisconsin, is one of very few shops in my area that still has the equipment to re-arch a spring by cold setting. Each leaf is bent with a hydraulic press moving along it. The press should be of at least 50-ton capacity for a good job on car springs. In order to work the leaves in the press, you have to take the spring pack apart. Before taking it apart, the professional will check the shop manual specs and make some measurements to help him determine the proper arch. By sighting, measuring and other skills, a good spring man can figure almost precisely what a spring looked like when new.

After disassembly and cleaning, the re-arching process starts. The first leaf to be worked is the longest one on the bottom of the pack. It is measured up to determine a reference point near the center to work from. Then, the leaf is worked back and forth from center, a bit at a time, under the hydraulic press.

There is a rhythm to a spring bender's movements and just the right pressure has to be applied to the right point at the right time. If the pressure is too light, the spring steel will flex, rather than bend. If the pressure is too heavy, it will break. Working the leaf right to the end is difficult. Once the longest leaf is done correctly, the others are arched to conform to it. Each gets a little more arch than the last. Companies that do cold setting say that springs that bend back and forth, instead of cold setting, have lost temper. In this case, the only solution is making a new spring, but spring steel is no longer made in all old-car sizes.

Mike Eaton at Eaton Detroit Spring, Inc., in

Eaton Detroit is one of few companies equipped to offer restorers spring reshaping services. It can anneal a spring to take the memory out of it, reshape it and reheat treat it so that a new memory is put back in.

Detroit, Michigan, says that cold setting steel is a temporary repair. Spring steel never loses its temper unless it's heated, but it does lose it memory. According to Mike, the cold setting method of re-arching springs results in a short-term fix. Spring steel has a memory and unless this memory is erased, the spring will eventually return to the height it was at prior to being re-arched.

Mike Eaton says once a spring pack is re-arched, you can take a leaf out, lay it on the floor and chalk mark both ends. Go back in a year and the spring will be back to its flattened-out length, he says. Re-arching is a good quick fix, but if you have a car worth restoring the ultimate way, reshaping is best.

Eaton is one of few companies equipped to offer

Heavily rusted leaf springs, like the top one seen here, may not be repairable. New springs can be made, but some sizes of spring steel used on vintage cars are no longer available. This can create problems for restorers.

The techies at Accurate Alignment agree that re-arching leaf springs may appeal more to truckers than car collectors. It works best for driver-type cars.

restorers spring reshaping services. It can anneal a spring to take the memory out of it, reshape it and reheat treat it so that a new memory is put in. In order to anneal a spring, it must be taken apart and visually inspected for fatigue. Each leaf is blasted clean. After being re-inspected, it is heated to 1,650 degrees F. Then the leaf is placed on a pattern with the correct form and arch to reshape that leaf.

The reshaped leaf is quenched in special oil to cool it. This heating and quick cooling results in a leaf that is too hard or brittle to work well as a spring, so the leaf is heated again, for a set time, to 950 degrees. This process draws out some of the hardness. Once it cools, the leaf is shot-peened to relieve stress on it. The result is a spring that's retempered, reshaped and reheat-treated.

Reshaping a classic car spring costs more than manufacturing a new spring. The minimum charge is $225 per spring assembly and can be more—even a lot more. This doesn't include the cost of new bushings, spring liners, clips, reassembly and shipping. Eaton does not reuse old parts.

Not every spring can be restored by reshaping. The condition of the spring has to be considered. If there are broken leaves or if the leaves are separating at the ends, they probably can't be restored. Also, if there are pit marks on the flat sides of the springs or crazing, they may not be candidates for restoration.

In many cases, it's best to look for reproduction parts or even used parts, but if you are restoring a valuable straight-axle Corvette to concours standards, you will want original springs made out of no-longer-available grooved spring steel. In this case, the cost of reshaping probably makes economic sense.

As noted, there is debate over whether it's a good idea to re-arch leaf springs by the cold setting

method. Some say it gives a stiff ride. Another view is that the spring will loose its memory and settle back to its collapsed state in a short time. But, one website, for Jeep enthusiasts, points out that heavy truck suspension shops have re-arched springs for 50 years and wouldn't do it if it didn't work.

Mark Broehm of Accurate Alignment agrees, in a sense, that re-arching doesn't have as much appeal to classic-car restorers as to truckers. Truckers are looking to save costs, he says. If you're restoring an old car to drive, re-arching is probably suitable and affordable, but if you're restoring a classic as an investment, the cost of the job that Eaton can do might well be justified.

Brakes

If you want to do a brake job on your collector car, you can probably purchase the parts and do a standard, old-fashioned brake job without really outsourcing much of it except for machining. Though not as prevalent as in the past, you can probably find a shop not too far away that can turn your brake drums in a drum lathe or even attach rivet-on linings if that's all you're able to find. However, if you want to do the "last" brake job your classic car will ever need, you'll have to put your general contractor helmet on again.

Upgrading Brakes—I created the concept of the "last" brake job after I found myself having to do the brakes on one of my favorite old cars every other year. When cars aren't used much, the brake parts tend to fail more frequently. This is because brake fluid is hydroscopic, which means it absorbs moisture. If you do not use the car, the brakes don't warm up and dissipate this moisture. As a result, the moisture causes corrosion inside the master cylinder, wheel cylinders, brake lines and hoses. On the other

After a period of needing brake system rebuilds every two or three years, the author's '53 Pontiac got a total brake upgrade. This time it got stainless cylinders, stainless lines and silicone brake fluid.

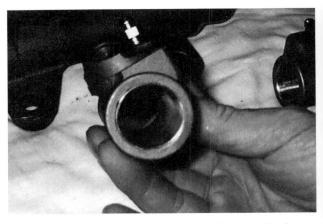

This '53 Pontiac wheel cylinder is one of many wheel cylinders and master cylinders that Brake & Equipment Warehouse, of Minneapolis, Minnesota, has resleeved with stainless steel. Other firms offer brass sleeving.

hand, when you do drive the car, it scrapes paint off brake drums and backing plates. Then, if the car sits a long time, these parts may rust.

When a collector car is stored for long periods of time or certain seasons, the solution is installing a set of stainless steel brake lines, sleeving the master cylinder and wheel cylinders with stainless steel or brass, and spraying parts with brake component paint. The first two aspects of the job can be farmed out.

A conventional steel reproduction brake line kit for my old car was priced at $155 and a stainless steel kit was only $24 more. Considering the advantages of stainless, it was worth the price. The supplier of the kit I used was Classic Tube, of Calverton, New York. Several other hobby companies also make stainless steel brake line kits. In most cases, the brake lines are bent to order, so you will have to wait until they make up a kit for your car, but it doesn't take long.

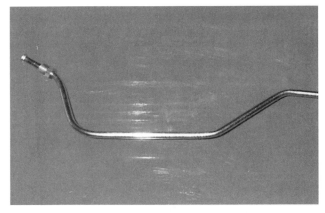

Classic Tube, of Calverton, New York, does a beautiful job of shaping stainless steel factory-replacement brake lines for vintage cars. For a rare car, they will do custom bending if you send them the old, rusty lines intact.

One nice thing about kits is that they are designed to match the factory parts perfectly. My car had six lines, but the kit had five. I checked a Master Parts Catalog and confirmed that five brake lines were correct. Someone had replaced a single long line with two shorter pieces. Later, I also found that the left rear brake line on my car was bent to fit a backwards-mounted right wheel cylinder. Apparently, whoever fixed it the last time could only find two right-hand rear wheel cylinders, so they bent new lines to work with what they had.

Stainless steel isn't the easiest material to bend, but my mechanic Vince Sauberlich carefully worked the shipping bends out by bracing the bent area against his knee and slowly spreading the two long ends of the tubing.

Vince and I sent the master cylinder and wheel cylinders out to be resleeved in stainless steel. Brake & Equipment Warehouse, of Minneapolis, did the work. They also offer wheel cylinder and master cylinder rebuilding services. If you want to rebuild these components yourself, they will sell you a kit. Brake & Equipment Warehouse also stocks thousands of other new brake parts that fit a wide range of applications for old vehicles. Brake parts are also available from many hobby vendors who sell NOS (factory) and NORS (aftermarket) old parts.

Brake hardware kits that include hold-down springs and the fasteners that hold the shoes to the backing plate can be found on eBay. You can actually find some of this stuff in your local NAPA store, since some hardware was used from the '30s straight through to the '90s. The parts store will not list applications for your vintage car. To find the

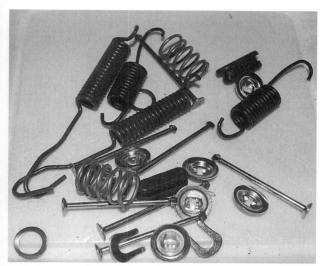

An old Pontiac Master Parts Catalog gave me a number for needed brake hardware. I then cross-referenced it with a modern number on a Pontiac dealer's computer. With this number, I visited NAPA and bought a kit.

Eastwood sells a special coating for brake drums that comes in several colors. We picked black. After wire brushing loose rust off the brake drum, we hung it from a twisted coat hanger and sprayed away.

parts, you have to check applications for late-model cars and trucks with rear-wheel drive and rear drum brakes. Compare your originals to the late-model hardware and you might find they match.

Since the engineers that designed our old cars years ago usually spec'd brake parts for them from a catalog showing existing parts, it is possible to find that many standard cylinders, switches and fittings that are still made today are correct for vintage cars. A good way to determine parts interchanges like this is to look for parts suppliers like www.rockauto.com that have searchable catalogs on the Internet. These catalogs will give you the modern part numbers and you can use then to

After installing a wheel cylinder kit in the stainless-sleeved wheel cylinder (Brake & Equipment Warehouse does this for slight extra cost), I bolted it to the backing plate and connected the brake line to the fitting on back.

make purchases from the online retailer or at local parts stores.

I had my car's drums turned at a local shop, then taped off the machined surfaces to paint the drums with Eastwood's black Brake Component Paint. After wire brushing the drums, I sprayed them. The surfaces were still pitted (you can't use body filler on drums), but they still came out looking very nice.

The factory recommended sanding linings. I used fine sandpaper and blew the dust off with compressed air (be sure to wear a respirator). A vixen file removed the grooves from the brake shoe ledges on the backing plates. Then, I dabbed a small amount of brake lubricant on them. I wire-brushed and graphited the cups and threads of all the adjusting screws and painted the screws. I also dabbed a very small amount of lubricant on the parking brake parts.

I mounted the front shoes by first assembling them at the bottom. Then, I passed the adjusting screw spring through holes in both shoes to pull them together. The slotted ends of the adjusting screws fit into notches below these holes, but don't install them yet. With the adjusting screw spring holding the shoes together at the bottom, spread the tops and fit them around the anchor pin. Place the anchor pin plate on the pin before putting the shoes against it. Notches on the top of both shoes go against the anchor pin. Below them are longer notches that the wheel cylinder links fit into. These are the short, slotted rods extending from both sides of the rubber wheel cylinder cups. Pull the shoes apart slightly at the upper (anchor pin) end and slip

Before installing the brake shoes and hardware to the backing plate, coat the bulges on back of the plate with a dab of grease so the brake shoes will move freely. Do not get any grease on the brake shoes.

Vince Sauberlich installed a spring to hold the shoes together at the bottom, then clam-shelled them around the anchor pin at the top. Note how the upper shoe plate fits into the slotted wheel cylinder extension rods.

Twist-to-lock nails at 4- and 8-o'clock positions pass through the backing plate and shoes to hold them. At the top, two strong springs hold the shoes to the anchor pin. These should be installed in their original relation.

the adjuster screw into place.

The hold-down pins that fasten the shoes to the backing plates must be passed, from the rear, through small holes in the backing plates. Place the hold-down spring and slotted cup over the outer end of each pin. Secure the pin on the backside and then use pliers or special brake tools to push the spring in, while rotating the slotted cup past the flat on the end of the pin. When the flat is crossways to the slot, the shoes will be locked in place. This takes practice.

Next install the anchor pin, then use special pliers, a large screwdriver or a brake return spring tool to install the return springs on the anchor pin in the same position they were originally. If the spring holding the front primary shoe was on the outside of the anchor pin, make sure it is attached that way again.

On most cars, the rear brakes will incorporate the parking or emergency brake actuating system. Designs vary from car to car, but it usually isn't difficult to figure out how to reattach all the parts if they are in decent shape. If the parking brakes are cable-activated and the cable is excessively rusted or stretched, you'll need to replace the cable.

If you find a vendor selling parking brake cables through ads, online auctions or swap meets, make absolutely sure it fits your exact year, make and series of car. In the pre-V-8 era, six-cylinder models often had shorter wheelbases than eight-cylinder models. As a result, the rear parking brake cables for eight-cylinder cars had to be longer.

Since it is getting hard to find some old parking brake cables, several suppliers are remanufacturing popular models on a commercial basis. This is a job that you probably never thought about outsourcing before, but the next time you do a restoration, you might find a rebuilt cable assembly is the way to go.

With the brake linings and hardware installed and everything checked, remount the drums. Follow your factory service manual as far as wheel bearing installation. If the drums do not slip easily over the brake shoes, back off the adjusting mechanism (often a star-shaped wheel) until they slide on.

Bleeding Brakes—Before you can adjust the brakes, you'll have to refill the system with brake fluid and bleed the air out of it. Disconnecting any part of the hydraulic system, allows air to enter the system. Air can also get in when brakes shoes are changed. This air has to be removed by burping or bleeding it out of the lines. This can be done manually or by using pressure equipment like an EZE Bleeder. This device pushes the air in the lines up to and out of the master cylinder.

The EZE Bleeder includes a powerful, hand-

Vince Sauberlich uses an EZE Bleeder to force brake fluid into the rear wheel cylinder under pressure. This pushes air bubbles in the fluid to the front of the lines and out the master cylinder.

Not all cars have identical brake systems. This MG design has a tiny wheel cylinder at 9 o'clock, two vertically mounted shoe retainer springs, a spacer at 3 o'clock and pine tree spring shoe-to-backing plate retainers.

U.S. cars have a star wheel adjuster that a special tool turns through slots in the backing plate. This MG TD wheel has a hole (at 2 o'clock here). If you match it up with a screw, you can adjust brakes with the wheel on.

operated, high-pressure pump, a hose to attach to the brake bleeder valve and various adaptors and fittings so that it can be used on different cars. Start at the right rear wheel cylinder (farthest from master cylinder). Attach the hose to the gun-barrel end of the hand pump and to the brake bleeder screw. Then push new fluid in so that any air bubbles in that line burp up to the master cylinder. When no bubbles can be seen burping up in the master cylinder, close the bleeder and move to the next wheel.

I like to use silicone brake fluid in my old cars. Some people swear by it and some swear against it. Many years ago, I obtained U.S. Army documents and photos that supported use of silicone fluid. I now have three cars using silicone fluid. They're driven regularly and we've never had a brake problem. We have heard that silicone fluid can ruin old brake light switches, but the use of a modern Harley-Davidson switch is a cure for many old cars.

Adjusting Brake Shoes—With the brakes bled, we were ready to adjust the shoes. To adjust the brakes, you need at least the drum you're working on jacked up off the ground. If you can put all four up, it's even better. Remove the rubber plugs from the adjusting slots in the brake backing plates. Insert a bent screwdriver or a brake-adjusting tool that can move the star wheel to turn the brake-adjusting screw. Move the outer end of the tool upward to push the star wheel down and expands the brake shoes closer to the drum. You want to get to where the drum can just be turned by hand, then back off as many notches a specified for your car.

There are cars that do not use star wheel adjusters. T series MGs, for example, have screws (one front,

two rear) that you tighten, through openings in the wheel discs, until you feel the proper drag. Other automakers used other designs. It's important to have a factory service manual. Some cars also require an anchor pin adjustment or adjustment of an eccentric. The manual will tell you how to adjust your car's brakes.

Once you have the adjustment set at one wheel, mount the wheel and tire securely. Continue around the car, adjusting one set of shoes at a time. If your car has self-adjusters, make the initial adjustment outlined in the service manual. Later, when you back up, the shoes will automatically adjust themselves.

After all four wheels are adjusted, put the rubber plugs back, lower the car, retorque the lug nuts at each wheel and top off the master cylinder if necessary. Road test the car. If it pulls to one side, more adjusting is needed. If it stops smoothly, in a straight line, you're done. For ultimate results, plan on redoing adjustments in a couple of weeks, after the car has some miles put on it.

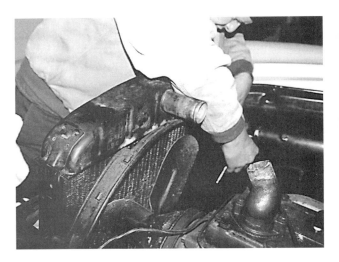

Vince Sauberlich wrestles a bulky old-fashioned radiator back into a '53 Pontiac. Treat your vintage radiator well. Often, a local radiator shop or auto air conditioning shop can help you with repairs.

Freeze plugs are designed to give before the engine block, if weak coolant mixtures start freezing. Some engines have only a couple of freeze plugs, while others have seven. Your machine shop will replace them.

Cooling

Two basic types of cooling systems are found on cars, trucks and motorcycles. Air-cooled engines are used in many motorcycles and in some cars like VW Beetles and Chevy Corvairs. Liquid cooling has always been more common and is starting to gain a foothold with motorcycle manufacturers today. In this book, we are going to focus on cars with liquid-cooled systems.

There are about ten main components of a liquid-cooled vehicle's cooling system. For a general contractor type project, five of them—the radiator, the upper and lower tanks, the water pump, the cylinder head (if cracked) and the heater core—can be sent to specialists for restoration. The other components are the fan, the thermostat, the bypass system, the freeze plugs and the hoses, all of which you can readily buy and install in your home restoration shop.

Most cooling systems rely on antifreeze flowing through hoses and passages in the engine and cylinder head(s) before entering the radiator. Air passing through the radiator cools the antifreeze. The cooling fan helps move air through the radiator. The radiator cap controls pressure created by the system that's used to lower the coolant's boiling point. The water pump forces coolant to flow through the system. A thermostat controls the temperature of the coolant by changing its rate of flow. The bypass system can send coolant back to the engine without it being cooled by the radiator if more heat is needed. Freeze plugs are designed to give before the engine block, if weak coolant mixtures start freezing.

Radiator Rebuilding—The radiator core usually has flat tubes. Aluminum fins carry the heat in the tubes into the air. The radiator has upper and lower tanks on each end. The tanks have the inlet and outlet hose connections designed into them. Brazing new brass tanks on an older radiator is a specialty job that's worth farming out. Today, there is only one company that sells old-fashioned brass tanks and this single-source situation has increased the price of having older radiators rebuilt.

Local radiator shops can do this work and there are also national specialists who advertise in *Hemmings*. Some old radiators can be repaired by a process known as rodding in which special rods are worked through the tubes to clean out crud and lime deposits. Don't count on rodding doing the trick for your next restoration project. Many years have now passed since most collector cars were new and often the amount of clogging is so bad that a new core and new tanks is the way to go.

Water Pumps—The cooling fan was connected to the front of the water pump on older cars. It would spin only when the engine was running,

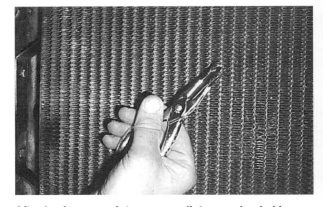

After having your vintage car radiator overhauled by a local shop or national vendor, you may still have to take care of small details like straightening fins bent in shipping. Eastwood sells this specialty tool designed to do just that.

Years ago, a car's cooling fan was connected to a pulley on the front of the water pump via a fan belt. The fan would turn only when the engine was running and the water pump was spinning the belt.

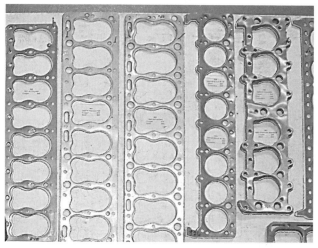

High-quality reproduction head gaskets are now being manufactured for many classic cars. Marx Parts, in Arpin, Wisconsin, sells a line of vintage head gaskets.

because it was driven by a fan belt instead. Years ago, if your car got stuck in traffic and started heating up, you could put the transmission in neutral and rev the engine. The water pump would spin faster and the fan would, too, and that would increase the cooling action. A water pump is a simple device that forces the coolant through the system as long as the engine is running.

The water pump has a metal housing with an impeller mounted on a spinning shaft. A pulley is mounted on the shaft outside the pump. A seal prevents water leaks. The impeller creates a centrifugal force that pulls coolant from the lower radiator hose and sends it, under pressure, into the engine. A gasket seals the pump body to the engine

Your car's water pump has a metal housing with an impeller mounted on a spinning shaft. A pulley is mounted on the shaft outside the pump. A seal prevents water leaks. Kanter now makes this reproduction Cadillac pump.

block. There are a half-dozen or more hobby vendors who rebuild or remanufacture water pumps for vintage cars.

Repairing Cylinder Heads—Although your cylinder heads are a mechanical engine part, they do have a critical role to play in the cooling, since the antifreeze flows through them and must stay inside them. There can be no coolant leakage due to cracks in the head or due to breaks in the gaskets that seal the head to the engine block. A blown head gasket will prevent the proper flow of coolant from passages in the block to passages in the cylinder heads. In addition, as the coolant escapes, it will eat into the metal and create channels through which the spark can jump. Eventually, this will contribute to a poor-running engine, due to damaged parts.

Cracked cylinder heads, especially in the valve seats, are big problems for car collectors, as are cracked engine blocks. I have run into hobbyists who had cracks welded up by local shops, but professional restorers often send their cracked engine parts to a handful of specialists who have been doing this work for many years. And at least one outside supplier is remanufacturing many vintage cylinder heads, although the cost of these —several thousand dollars—may not fit into everyone's hobby budget.

Head Gaskets—Head gaskets for many collector cars are getting fairly expensive, too, although the availability of rare head gaskets is increasing as more and more are reproduced. Head gaskets for Chevy and Ford small-block V-8s are still relatively inexpensive, due to the volume efficiencies of manufacturing a high-demand item. On the other

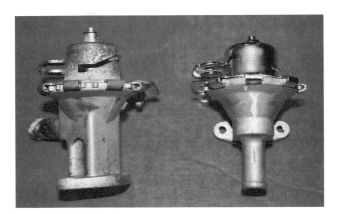

The left-hand heater control valve is for an MG Magnette. The other is for a Jaguar. The top sections are the same. Parts vendor Cecelia Bruce of Scarborough Faire said we could swap bottoms to repair the Magnette valve.

Coolant hoses are replaceable. Getting reproductions or making replacements for this '41 Ford V-8 is easy, but other old hoses might be very hard to replace unless you use non-original universal-fit flexible hoses.

hand, a Packard, Nash, Studebaker or Hudson gasket has to be found at a swap meet or ordered from sellers of high-quality reproductions and is generally priced accordingly. So, it really depends on what type of car you have. Head gaskets for my T Series MGs are available from several suppliers and fairly cheap, but a head gasket for one of my straight-8 Pontiacs is now well over $100 from any source. Of course, it's a part you can't do without.

Heating System—For interior heating, most cars use hot coolant that's directed inside the car. One hose carries hot coolant from the water pump to a miniature radiator called a heater core. The heater blower sends a portion of the heat into the car. A second hose returns coolant to the engine. A heater control valve turns the heat on and off. The system has ducting with doors that send the hot air

A thermostat is a valve that opens at a set temperature to allow coolant to flow through the radiator. A thermostat that fails probably can't be fixed. Get a new one or install a different type right in your radiator hose.

around. There are specialists who can repair old heater cores and heater control valves.

Thermostat—The thermostat is one of the regular service items in your cooling system. It may be possible to restore an old thermostat, but I'm not aware of any such service. A thermostat is actually a valve that opens at a set temperature to allow the coolant to flow through the radiator, rather than bypass it.

Thermostats are usually found at the front, upper part of the engine inside a housing that attaches to the engine and connects to the upper radiator hose. The housing bolts over an opening to the cooling system and a heavy paper gasket seals the connection. Most old cars use a 180-degree thermostat. Some old cars may also require a tin retainer that holds the thermostat in the housing.

Since thermostats can't be fixed—at least as far as I know—the trick with an old car may be finding a vendor who has a thermostat for your car. However, even this isn't super-critical as a modern thermostat can be positioned inside the upper radiator hose, rather than in the thermostat housing. Many owners of T Series MGs use a Chevy thermostat in the hose for better cooling.

A car can be operated without a thermostat, but this is not a great idea. It allows uncontrolled circulation of the coolant. It is possible for the circulation to speed up so much that the antifreeze doesn't have time to get cooled and overheating results. Or else, the engine will not get up to operating temperature.

The bypass system is another part you cannot send out for restoration. It is simply a cooling passage or hose that serves as a detour around the thermostat. The only problem can be total clogging

The MG TF blinker switch is electrical, but a vacuum switch in the unit shuts the blinkers off once they are turned on. It's a mechanical mechanism that holds vacuum for 15 seconds while the switch returns to off. I found a vendor in Dayton, Ohio, on eBay that fixes them. With a little creative searching you can find what you need for your restoration, whether it is expert advice or parts.

and that would be rare.

Freeze plugs are steel plugs used to fill holes left by sand casting the engine block. They come in standard sizes and are easy to find at any auto supply store. When you buy your old car it may have rusty freeze plugs that allow leakage, but when you restore the car and rebuild the engine, you'll install new freeze plugs and won't have to worry about them again. If you send your engine out to a machine shop or a rebuilder, they will put the freeze plugs in for you.

Coolant hoses are another replaceable item. With an old car being restored for show competition, the hard thing will be finding nice preformed upper and lower radiator hoses that give your car a factory-correct look. If you cannot find such hoses, flexible radiator hose will work, though it won't look as old-fashioned. You should be able to find reproduction style heater hoses, since they are being made for popular cars like '55–'57 Chevys and T-Birds.

It's The Little Things That Count

In addition to the major mechanical components like the engine, transmission, starter, generator, steering, suspensions, brakes and cooling system parts, there are smaller mechanical items to fix on cars and there are specialists out there who know how to restore them. Most of these craftspeople do this work as a sideline or a hobby and they may not have an established business set up. Finding them is often difficult. Sometimes you will find them running small advertisements in club publications.

In other cases, word of mouth advertising is the only way to locate them. As the Internet grows, many of these services can be tracked down through online searches. In some instances they have their own Websites. In others, they may pop up because they were mentioned in a newsgroup or listed a restored part for sale on eBay.

Electrical Switches—I encountered one such example of a small, unique service when I purchased my MG TF and discovered that the vacuum-operated signal light switch was not working. Of course, this type of part has an electrical element to it, but the vacuum switch in the unit, that turns the blinkers off once they are manually turned on, is a mechanical mechanism that holds vacuum for 15 seconds so the switch slowly returns to the off position.

I first took the car to a shop. The shop owner said that the original switch could not be repaired. Other sources in the New England MG T Register (the national club for these cars) said the same thing. So, we replaced the switch with a reproduction offered by a major mail-order supplier. The reproduction switch was installed and did not function at all. It was removed and returned for $150 credit. I then looked for NOS switches on eBay. I tried buying a switch from a man in Dayton, Ohio. I did not win the eBay auction, but I wound up emailing the seller. He said that he had figured out how to repair the vacuum switches, and could do mine in about an hour for $75.

I sent him my switch and he made the repairs for half the price of the reproduction switch, which didn't work. Later, I sent him a second switch and he repaired that one, too. Several years later, I had trouble with the signal lights again and removed the first switch he had fixed. I replaced it with the second one, which worked, but not properly. After a right-hand turn it did not fully switch off. On a left-hand turn, it switched off too fast.

My mechanic friend Vince Sauberlich and I took the first switch apart. We discovered that the vacuum switch that had been repaired still worked perfectly. The problem was purely electrical in nature. A U-shaped copper clip that makes the electrical connection had broken. We decided the best thing to do was take the second switch apart and pirate the U-shaped clip from it. Unfortunately, it didn't have one. The second switch—the one that did not work properly on the vacuum mode—was actually a reproduction switch. The moral of this whole story is that it seems better to use an original switch and to have it restored if it stops working correctly. It will work better and cost you less.

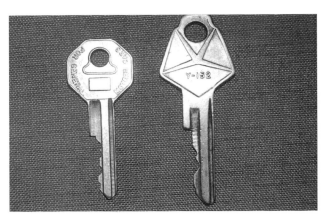

OEM (original equipment manufacturer) key blanks are best to use. On the left is a key blank for a 1930s–1960s General Motors car. The key blank on the right is for a 1963 Chrysler 300.

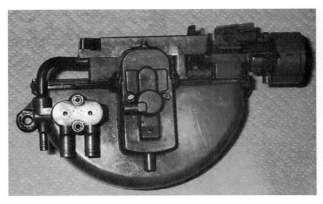

This '36 Pontiac vacuum wiper motor is a mystery to most modern mechanics. Repairs can be as simple as replacing dry grease in the vacuum chamber. If the vacuum motor needs rebuilding, you'll need a specialist.

Key Locks—Another good example of a small mechanical part that can cause problems during a vintage vehicle restoration is a key lock for the ignition, doors, glovebox or trunk. We take keys and locks for granted, until the day we break or lose one. Then we have a crisis. A HUGE crisis if the car is a classic. Gone are the days when you can stroll into your corner hardware store and get a key made for your MG TD or your '63 Chrysler 300J.

Mike Granlund, who runs Vintage Lock in Cambridge, Minnesota, makes hundreds of keys for car collectors and can fix or replace old locks. Mike is among a small number of suppliers of hard-to-find key and lock parts for classic cars, both American and foreign. Another such company, Key Men of Monroe, New York, also stocks keys and locks for antique buses, motorcycles and a few old airplanes. Some of the locks these companies work with are no longer manufactured anywhere. Vintage Lock has thousands of keys in their inventory. Key Men offers 31,000 keys to fit vehicles manufactured as far back as the '20s.

OEM (original equipment manufacturer) key blanks are the best to use. Both Vintage Lock and Key Men can supply them for classic cars. These are key blanks made by the company that made the keys originally supplied with the vehicle. Sometimes it's not easy to determine if a part is OEM. According to Key Men's website, Briggs & Stratton (now called Strattec) is still manufacturing key blanks that fit 75-year-old cars, but they aren't labeled the same as the originals.

Key Men points out that multiple vendors supplied keys and locks to automakers. Strattec, Yale and Hurd are among OEM suppliers for U.S. carmakers. Union, Sipea and Huff made keys for imported cars.

There are three types of key blanks. Replacements can be shaped like original keys, but aren't labeled the same. Look-alike key blanks are shaped and labeled to look identical to originals. Crest key blanks may have the carmaker's logo or some other promotional design.

There are a number of ways to go about identifying the right keys and locks for your car. You may see a code such as Y-152 on a Chrysler key or 8-50 over C on a GM key made by Curtis. These are called key codes. They tell locksmiths how to cut a key, without seeing the original key. The code may be stamped on the key or the lock cylinder or written in the original owner's manual if you have it.

There are three basic types of key codes: The Direct Code has numbers that correspond to cuts on the key and tell the locksmith how deep to make each cut. Some keys for older American cars and some foreign car keys use direct code. The Interpreted Code requires a locksmith to do some simple math. He or she may have to subtract something from the stamped number to get to the real code. Reference books tell locksmiths how to interpret codes. With a Book Code the number stamped on the key must be looked up in a code book. The code book index lists the numbers for the cuts that need to be made.

Once a key code is broken the locksmith refers to a guide that identifies the depth and spacing of the cuts to be made in the key blade. Key cutting machines are then set for a certain key. There are so many types of car keys that a setup for every key is not possible. A depth and space guide can be used. Each key code has a depth and space guide. Many codes share the same guide.

For peace of mind, you should have at least two sets of keys for every collector car you own. Take one set with you when you're driving the car and bring the other set along in case you lock the first set in the vehicle. Keys are inexpensive and it is not a bad idea to have a third set to keep at home.

Another small mechanical item that can cause difficulties are windshield wipers and windshield wiper motors. Last weekend, we visited a car collector to take photos of his 1936 Oldsmobile convertible. When the camera came out he wanted to put the right-hand windshield wiper on first. He explained that his car had windshield wipers that were unique to GM convertibles of that year. One of his windshield wipers broke and he has not been able to find a replacement.

If your car has electric windshield wipers and the motor stops working, that's probably an electrical problem that can be fixed. However, many old cars have vacuum wiper motors that modern mechanics have no experience fixing. A repair can be as simple as replacing dried out old grease inside the vacuum chamber. On the other hand, if the vacuum motor needs rebuilding—or if you need rare wiper arms that are hard to find—there are specialist vendors in the old car hobby who may have the parts and knowledge you need to get your windshield wipers slapping again.

There are also specialists who restore radio antennas, convertible top parts, clocks, motor mounts, springs and other unique parts for vintage vehicles. The amazing amount of experience and talent available to the home restorer (as well as the professional) also tends to grow in proportion to

This beautiful old clock was part of an option package for the 1936 Oldsmobile. Today, there are vendors who can completely restore it and fit it with a trouble-free quartz mechanism that will keep on ticking forever.

the collector-car industry. Also, as newer cars, trucks and motorcycles become collectible, new skills are being added to the talent pool. As the economy fosters more small business opportunities, it's likely that the number of people working in the vintage vehicle hobby on a full-time basis will continue to explode.

Chapter 6
Exterior Restoration Tips

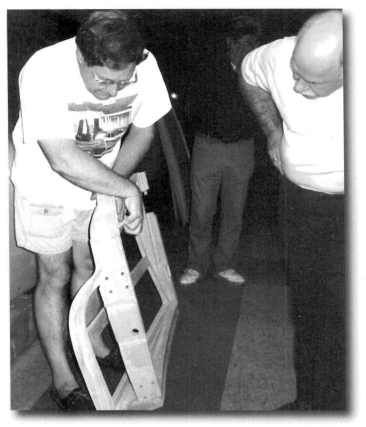

Dennis Bickford (l.) shows Ken Boulware a Chrysler Town & Country door panel, one of many wood-car parts he manufactures at his Vintage Woodworks shop in Iola, Wisconsin. Bickford also does upholstery and tops.

The general contractor approach to the restoration of a car, truck or motorcycle can come in just as handy for the restoration of exterior pieces as it does for the restoration of mechanical components. It is true that you cannot mail the whole body of your car to an outside restorer, but you may find any number of individuals and companies that restore specific sheet metal components, trim pieces, wooden parts for woodies, fiberglass hardtops, windshields and other so-called cosmetic items needed to make your car beautiful again.

Glass is an important cosmetic item, too. Old glass can cloud up or yellow. Bubbles can form between layers of old flat glass and look ugly. Glass that is chipped, cracked or broken must be replaced for appearance, as well as safety. Some restorers want tinted glass instead of clear glass. Certain repairs, such as wind wings on sports cars or police-style motorcycle windshields, use Plexiglas. Glasswork can also involve having etched letters or designs, such as on a vintage hearse or ambulance.

Lenses and lights factor into a restored vehicle's exterior appearance. Sometimes making lights look new again requires NOS parts. However, vintage parts are getting very hard to find, so there are specialists who restore lenses, gaslights for early cars and electric lights for later cars. Both glass and plastic light lenses can be polished to restore their appearances. Lights can be cosmetically restored and the reflectors on some can be resilvered.

Tires can't be restored, but there are a number of companies producing old-fashioned tires that restore the looks of your car. Since the appearance of tires on a correctly restored car is very important, I'll discuss some of the specialty suppliers. Also worth mentioning is the offering of tire customizing services that can change your black sidewall tires to whitewalls.

Painting, powder coating or polishing them can restore the wheels that your tires ride on and the wheel covers that decorate them. There are vendors that respoke the wooden artillery-style wheels used on early cars. Wire spoke wheels can be relaced to restore their looks, performance and safety.

Bodywork

Like most classic car restorers, you want your favorite ride to have a show-quality body. Straight sheet metal, flawless paint, smooth shiny chrome trim, crystal clear glass and eye-catching tires and wheels are elements that add up to good cosmetics.

You are not going to find a modern restorer who prefers

A number of hobby vendors manufacture new tires with old-fashioned looks and features. These all-white Firestone tires were seen on a Flanders 20 at the 2008 Masterpiece of Style & Speed in Milwaukee, Wisconsin.

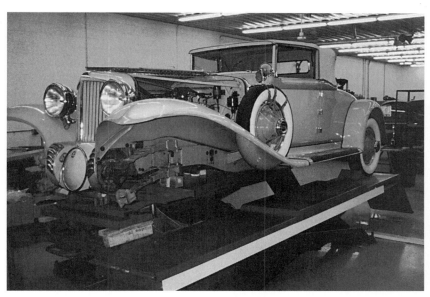

High-end restoration shops are likely to be selected for the restoration of classic cars like this Cord L-29. It was photographed at L'Cars, in Cameron, Wisconsin, a shop that focuses on Pebble Beach quality restorations.

the general contractor approach to vehicle restoration sanding body filler smooth or filling his Binks Model 7 spray gun with Duco lacquer. Instead, most enthusiasts I know take one of five routes to getting bodywork done on their collector vehicles.

High-End Restoration Shop—Restorers with large budgets or with very rare vehicles that gain tremendous value from a first-class restoration are

Among the unique jobs that hobbyists outsource to specialists to make their old cars look just right is the restoration of vintage license plates. Phoenix Restoration of Davenport, Iowa, restored these Iowa and Florida tags.

likely to go this route. High-end shops typically have $75–$150 per hour shop rates and specialize in every-nut-and-bolt restorations. Inside, the shop will look like a new car dealer service department or a set for Hot Rod TV. You can expect to spend a minimum of six figures for such a restoration.

High-end is a nice way to go if you can afford the hefty bills. The cost is high, but you do get good value. A good high-end restorer will be up front about the costs involved.

Craftsman Restoration Shop—The craftsman-type shop is run by a person who loves the restoration trade. He or she usually has a narrow specialty like brass-era cars or wood-bodied cars. Most of these restorers have been in business many years and operate in smaller facilities. Many of them live in or next door to their shop. The shop will look old fashioned and probably have a polished wooden floor. Some craftspeople are amazingly affordable, but their shop rates can vary from as low as $50 an hour up to $100 an hour. Getting a job done in such mom and pop shops may take a longer, but it will be beautiful.

Regular Restoration Shop—This type of shop is affordable, but not exactly cheap. These restorers offer driver-type restorations with partial vehicle disassembly, good bodywork for local car shows and probably a couple of non-stock mechanical upgrades to make the car run well. The facility will look like a body shop, but there will be only old cars inside. Shop rates are $45 to $65 per hour. Jobs

Although he specializes in restoring two-seat T-Birds, Jewel Meetz, of Brillion, Wisconsin, is currently doing this Model A Ford coupe. Being in a rural area allows Meetz to charge a relatively modest hourly shop rate.

Jewel manufactures this reproduction rear bumper guard from bronze. It fits 1955–1956 T-Birds. This one has been metal polished and is ready to be plated by his son, Terry Meetz, who runs Custom Plating Specialist.

get done relatively quickly, but never quite as fast as promised. The shop will be very busy and possibly a bit sloppy. Quality ranges from terrific value to just passable.

Local Body Shop—Many collectors use local body shops and today the shops are more willing to work on collector cars than in the past. Doing an old vehicle is more labor intensive than doing dent work, but insurance companies are scrapping new vehicles instead of fixing them. This means there is less collision repair work, and less revenue, so a lot of body shops simply need the work. Shop rates are probably $40-$50 per hour. Some cars like Mustangs and '55 Chevys get done fast because catalog parts can be used. Rarer cars can get hung up in these shops because parts are harder to find, or might take them longer to obtain since they don't work restoration work on a daily basis. A lot of hobbyists look for shops that will use old-car restoration work to fill in between regular jobs and charge less.

Retirees—Very popular with collectors are retired body men who worked on old cars when they were new. Some are extremely talented and love having the opportunity to stay busy and make a few bucks at the same time. They don't really have a shop rate, but most will work for $20-$30 per hour. If they do not have a shop at their house, they may only do bodywork and prime coating, but no painting. Some will come to your garage to work. These jobs usually move pretty slowly and can take a couple of years. The cost can be quite low, but sometimes these arrangements wind up in disputes. If you

want to go this route, check for other satisfied customers who used the same person.

Bob Lorkowski planned his L'Cars restoration shop in Cameron, Wisconsin, as a full-service, high-end shop that doesn't cut corners. While Lorkowski would love to work on Duesenbergs all day, he finds that isn't realistic. He says big car work tapered off following the 9/11 terrorist attacks. Fewer people wanted prewar classics restored or total restorations. L'Cars sees more demand for partial restorations, street rod builds and custom motorcycle tanks.

Restoration shops across the country are encountering the same situation and many are developing sidelines to supplement their business and help home restorers. Jewel Meetz, of Brillion, Wisconsin, has been restoring vintage cars since 1970. Back then he drove two-seat T-Birds, though he restored Pierce-Arrows and Model As. When he drove his T-Bird to the 1979 Iola Old Car Show, Pat Merrill and Jim Thibodeau admired his car and asked him about restoring T-Birds for them. Over the next three decades, Meetz became a T-Bird specialist. Meetz still restores all kinds of cars, but he also makes reproduction parts for '57–'59 Fords and '55–'63 T-Birds and it has become big business.

Rear bumper guards for '55–'56 T-Birds were made of stamped steel and used as exhaust exits. Like many through-the-bumper exhaust setups, the T-Bird's rusted. The answer was to cast the parts in bronze, machine them at Jewel's Body Shop and have his son Terry chrome them at his Custom

The fiberglass hardtops used on first- and second-generation Corvettes have over 60 different pieces of hardware. Matt Kokolis keeps a rack full of these parts ready to use in his business Glassworks, The Hardtop Shop.

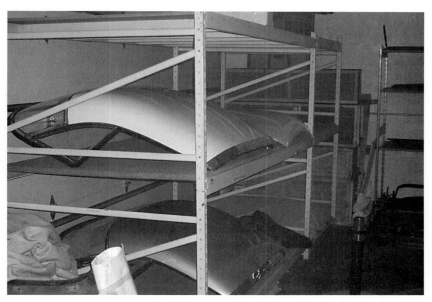

Corvette hardtops sent to Glassworks in Crescent, Pennsylvania, are stored on wooden racks until the time comes to strip them down and rebuild them. The workmanship on the finished tops is of show quality.

Plating Specialist shop. The '55–'56 T-Bird rear bumper guards that Jewel builds weigh 7.5 lbs.— more than three times the weight of the originals. However, they look just like the originals and will pass T-Bird club judging.

Jewel Meetz also manufactures a complete reproduction convertible top frame and mechanism for two-seat T-Birds, a glovebox grab handle for '61–'63 T-Bird Sport Roadster, the Q-shaped taillight doors for '61–'63 T-Birds, a chrome strip for the deck lid of '57–'56 Fords, sail panel plates for Ford Skyliner retractable hardtops and T-Bird bumpers ends.

As a kid, Matt Kokolis helped his father restore Corvettes. His dad launched a sideline business fixing 1956–1967 Corvette hardtops for people who wanted both tops. In 1999, Matt formed Glassworks, The Hardtop Shop and expanded from servicing Corvette hardtops to offering hardtop repair kits, as well as Corvette window glass. Glassworks also does stainless steel restoration.

Restoration of a Corvette hardtop starts with the disassembly of the hardtop frame. The top shell is sanded until it is smooth. Then, it is sent out for painting. Glassworks doesn't paint, but does do all the prep work.

Before the fiberglass shell of the Corvette hardtop is painted, all of the factory-installed stainless steel moldings are removed. The stainless steel parts are buffed to perfection. Fasteners and broken parts are replaced with NOS, used or reproduction parts. The liners and seals usually need to be replaced, too.

Glassworks replaces all rivets that hold the top together with new ones and installs new weather stripping manufactured expressly for Glassworks. The restored stainless steel moldings are reinstalled using correct-style retainers. According to Matt Kokolis, there are nearly 60 rivets, 50 screws and 40 nuts and fasteners used in a typical Corvette hardtop (the number varies from one year to the next). Glassworks carries all of them in inventory.

Glassworks sells kits that home restorers can use to do their own hardtops. The kit for a 1956–1962 hardtop includes: a dated or undated acrylic rear window, dated or undated side windows, bottom acrylic window retainers, a hardtop screw kit, a hardtop rivet kit, barrel nuts and short nuts. Kits for a 1963–1967 hardtop include a rear window, a cloth or vinyl headliner, a screw kit, headliner retainer clips and upper and lower molding clips.

If customers request an in-house mail-order restoration by Glassworks, the shop sends the customer a special damage-free box to ship the top in. When a top arrives, it is assigned a specific job number and a list of all required parts is made up so the cost of the restoration can be provided to the customer before any work begins. A sheet shows every part that will be used on the top and its cost. The tops are stored on special wooden racks until it's time to work on them.

Other restorers that supply exterior parts and services that home restorers can obtain by mail will

Glassworks, The Hardtop Shop, in Crescent, Pennsylvania, also restores early Corvette stainless steel windshield frames and installs new glass. In judged car shows, these windshields add points.

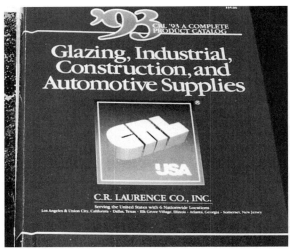

Professional auto glass installers use catalogs like this one to locate the supplies they need. Based in Los Angeles, C.R. Laurence Co., (www.crlaurence.com) is a leading supplier of automotive glass products and tools.

be found in the sources list beginning on page 107.

Auto Glass

As mentioned at the beginning of this chapter, vintage car and truck restorers often need new glass for their classic vehicles. Flying stones or gravel, a door that gets slammed too hard or even a rusty window sash that breaks off inside the door can lead to a broken windshield, rear backlight or side window. Many old vehicles that have been stored for a long time develop cloudy or discolored glass, even though no breakage takes place. Also common to find is a windshield that's been scraped up by worn out windshield wiper blades. On vintage motorcycles with police-style windshields, restorers may encounter cracked or yellowed Plexiglas.

As far as glass, there are basically two types for older cars: flat and curved. You don't have to worry about reflective glass, glass with electric coils, mirrors glued to the windshield and other high-tech options. However, as you get into cars of the '50s and '60s, you may have to decide between clear or tinted glass or use an epoxy to attach the inside rearview mirror to the windshield.

If there is any original glass used in pre-1930s vehicle that will be driven, consider replacing it with safety glass. My father always recalled the time that his head went through the windshield of an early '30s Oldsmobile that my grandmother was driving. Luckily, dad did not get severe glass cuts, but many people did back then. Laminated glass was an important safety improvement.

Most cars built prior to 1930 use flat glass (some older electric-powered coupes may be an exception). Most local shops can cut flat glass parts if they have a suitable pattern to work from. An old window can be used to make such a pattern. If you can't find a local shop willing to tackle such work, there are several national suppliers that specialize in supplying flat glass for classic cars.

Curved glass is another story. For years, salvage yards seemed to be the only place you could find curved glass for older cars, but things have changed in the last decade. Pilkington Classics began remanufacturing curved glass for many older cars under the name Glass Search in the early 2000s. Their prices were competitive and they could custom make hard-to-find windshields and backlights if they had sufficient (about 25) orders.

Pilkington Classics will make auto glass for classic, vintage, obsolete and exotic cars dating back to the early 1900s. It also produces date-coded glass for GM muscle cars. Shawn Megown, a sales representative for Pilkington, explained that there are many technical issues involved in manufacturing curved auto glass. He said that it may be impossible to make some curved-glass parts, but most glass can be produced in batches, at certain times, if there is sufficient demand.

Some restoration shops are remanufacturing windshield frames for specific cars and teaming up with glass manufacturers to also supply glass for the cars they service. As we told you earlier, Glassworks is supplying restored Corvette windshields. Another shop doing such specialty work is Ragtops & Roadsters, of Perkasie, Pennsylvania, which makes British car windshields.

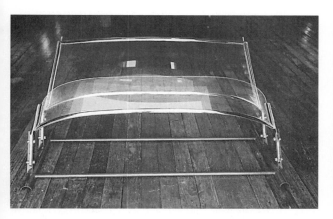

Ragtops & Roadsters restores chrome-framed British car windshields. It replates the frames, retaps screw holes in the windshield assembly plates and brackets and uses correct new glass and hardware.

This Lotus was getting some glasswork done at Ragtops & Roadsters in Perkasie, Pennsylvania. The yellow tape is holding pressure against the door window glass while a bonding agent sets up properly.

When he started Ragtops & Roadsters in 1990, Michael Engard was a former premed student at Temple University with a passion for aging MGs, Jaguars and Austin-Healeys. He opened Ragtops & Roadsters and created a specialty shop aimed at a nationwide market. Ragtops & Roadsters does both partial and show restorations in a quaint, 6,000-sq.-ft., bi-level secured building that was once the home of Dudley baseballs, which made balls for major league baseball.

Bob Malone operates McCluskey Auto Trim as a separate business-within-a-business in the same building. This widens Ragtops & Roadsters' customer base by giving the shop a professional upholstery specialist with years of experience. Malone installs custom concours interiors and does leather seat repairs, tops, tonneau covers, top boots, carpets and replacement door panels.

To tie in with the tops and upholstery services that Malone handles, Ragtops & Roadsters also sells restored British windscreens for cars with chrome-framed glass. It replates the windshield frames and stanchions and retaps screw holes in the windshield's assembly plates and brackets. The shop also uses correct new hardware to properly assemble the windshield frame.

Windshield frames can be assembled with the customer's own glass installed (if the glass is original and perfect) or with new glass or OEM Triplex glass. Bottom rubber seals, windscreen stanchions, body grommets and installation hardware are also available. Restored windscreens for Austin-Healey 100 and 3000 models, MG T Series cars and MGAs (standard and competition) are available on an exchange basis, with a $250 core charge.

Getting back to repairs of flat glass, there are some local glass repair companies that can do a

good job of helping the general contractor restorer. Some years back, Auto Glass Specialists—one of the big statewide services here in Wisconsin—helped take care of a pane on my '53 Pontiac Catalina. The car had been resting (and rusting a bit) all winter. On my first spring ride I hit a bump and the door glass fell to the bottom of the door. Luckily, the glass was OK, but it was no longer attached to the window riser.

Auto Glass Specialists removed the trim from the inside of the Pontiac's door. The window was

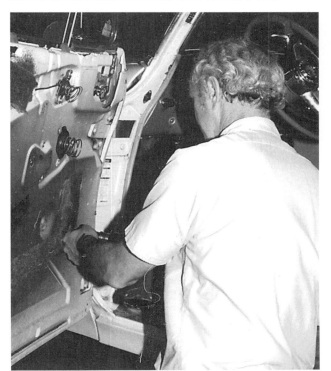

After the door window of this '53 Pontiac hardtop dropped into the door. Auto Glass Specialists, of Stevens Point, Wisconsin, removed the door panel to get at the glass and the parts of the window riser mechanism.

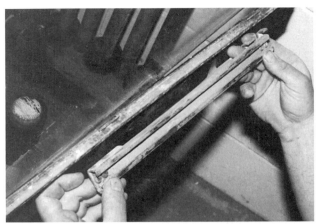

Spot welds on the gray sash had broken, due to rust. This caused the rusty channel on the bottom of the glass to separate from two metal tabs that normally hold the door glass to a channel that the sash slides in.

supposed to fit snuggly in a metal sash channel that had metal two tabs welded to the bottom of it. The screws that go through holes in the tabs fasten the sash channel to a cam track. The scissor-like part of the window regulator that raises the glass rides back and forth in the cam track.

Leaking water and condensation had corroded the sash channel. It was so badly weakened that 75 percent of the lower edge of the window had pulled out of the sash. In addition, the spot welds attaching the tabs to the sash were broken, leaving the window loose enough to hop out and fall into the door.

The inside door trim was removed to reveal the holes that allow access to the window riser. To reach some of the fasteners, the window sash has to be repositioned. The screws that hold the tabs on the sash to the cam track can then be removed. After loosening the sash channel, it can be removed. A new sash channel was not available, so the old one was repaired by spot welding.

Care has to be taken to weld the metal tabs back on the sash channel without welding them to the cam track. During reassembly, the cam track must first be attached to the window-riser mechanism, which is then attached to the sash channel via the tabs. If the tabs are inadvertently welded to the cam track, it would be impossible to remove it for the first step in the reassembly process.

After the welding was completed, the sash channel was prime coated to protect it from future corrosion. The bottom edge of the window glass was coated with glass primer and it was pressed back into the sash channel. A bonding agent was applied to ensure a tight fit. The bond was allowed to set up. Then, everything was reassembled by repeating each step in reverse.

As for Plexiglas motorcycle windshields used on vintage two-wheelers, these are actually made of a flat piece of crystal plastic that takes on a curve when fastened into a metal fixture. If your bike's windshield is cracked or yellowed, you don't have to drive to swap meets all over the country looking for a new one that costs several hundred dollars.

Careful welding was required to attach the metal tabs back on the sash channel without welding them to the cam track. During reassembly, the cam track is attached to the window riser mechanism before it's reinstalled.

The rust-weakened channel had to be removed from the bottom of the glass, cleaned and treated with a rust preventative to stop further corrosion. Here a technician applies an epoxy to bond the channel to the glass.

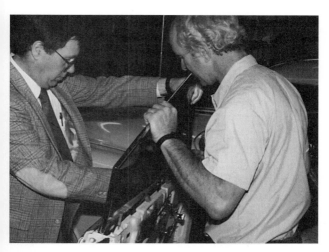

After the bonding agent set up properly, everything was put back together and reinstalled in the door of the car in the reverse order of disassembly. This fix worked perfectly and has lasted 15 years so far.

Vintage Headlamp Restoration restores and reproduces headlights for vintage automobiles. Many of its headlights are manufactured for early Rolls-Royce automobiles like this 1927 Phantom I Dietrich Cabriolet.

Just carefully disassemble the old one, loosen the fasteners and take it out of the metal fixture. Remove the slip-on beading attached around the edges. Find a local shop that cuts Plexiglas and use the old piece to make a new one. Mark holes and drill new ones in the same locations. Replace the edge beading (the metal fixture is designed to hold it in place). Finally, replace the metal fixture and reinstall all of the nuts and bolts.

Lenses and Lights

Vintage Headlamp Restoration is the name of a company that was established in Sheffield, England, in 1992. A silversmith named Peter Appleyard founded the firm. The company offers classic car collectors the highest quality headlight restoration and replication services. Vintage Headlamp Restoration claims to be the world leader in the restoration and reproduction of headlights for vintage automobiles. Many of its headlights are manufactured for early Rolls-Royce automobiles. Exports account for greater than 60 percent of Vintage Headlamp Restoration's sales. Over the years, the company has served enthusiasts from Europe, Australia, Japan, North America and the Middle East.

Vintage Headlamp Restoration is made up of a team of dedicated silversmiths who employ time-honored craftsmanship and unique skills to restore vintage headlights to their original state. Additionally, a range of reproduction headlights is available from the company. These headlights are handcrafted by specialists whose goal is to create headlights of concours restoration quality.

Vintage Headlamp Restoration also provides classic car restorers with the Marchal TP527 headlight unit, which is suitable for Ferrari, Porsche, Maserati, Alpha Romeo, Fiat and Frazer Nash cars from the 1955–1965 period. These headlamps are a standard seven-inch unit with silver plated brass reflectors and a chrome plated badge bar down the center. The glass is wrapped onto the reflector and has a detachable bulb holder. The Marchal TP527 lamps come complete with 12V 25/40W bulbs.

Classic Autopart Reproduction Service (CARS for short) located in Northern California also specializes in manufacturing top quality parts and accessories for antique brass-era automobiles. This company will fix or create new parts—including headlights—for all types of horseless carriages.

CARS designs and manufactures custom brass

Classic Autopart Reproduction Service (CARS) is a Northern California company that specializes in manufacturing top quality parts and accessories for antique brass-era automobiles like this Mercer Speedster.

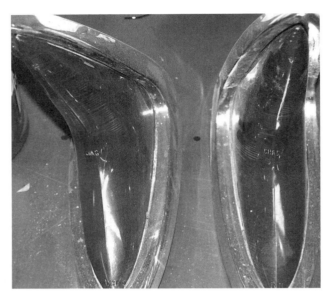

While you can find detailers on the Internet that restore plastic taillights, this is a job that most hobbyists can do themselves and save money. Many special polishes can be used to make taillights look like new again.

parts to restorers' specifications. The company is not just a lantern shop, machine shop or foundry, but a complete service supplier for brass-era automobile restorers. CARS will rebuild or recreate virtually any brass item found on automobiles manufactured between 1890–1915. Although brass is its specialty, CARS also makes bronze, aluminum, steel and stainless parts for pre-1916 cars. With the exception of a few generic aftermarket items, all parts are manufactured per customer order.

Steve's Auto Restorations of Portland, Oregon, is another American company that will restore classic car headlights (and taillights) on a mail-order basis. This company has been resilvering headlight, taillight and cowl light reflectors for 25 years. The resilvering process returns the lighting parts to their original factory condition and specifications.

Silver plating is the most effective way of restoring reflectors. This system is still in use today, because silver has reflective properties superior to those that result from putting chrome plating or other types of plating on a reflector.

Most original headlight, taillight and cowl light reflectors were made of brass. To determine if your car's reflectors are made of brass, do a magnet test. The magnet won't stick to brass. The process of re-silvering brass reflectors begins with a good chemical cleaning. This is followed by an initial polishing. The silver plating is done next. Finally, the parts are carefully finish polished.

Lights with steel reflectors can be more of a problem. The steel is often rusted and requires bead blasting. Steel reflectors cost more to resilver because they have to be nickel plated before being silver plated. The nickel plating is required to achieve proper adherence and shine. Sometimes very light pitting can be silvered over, but often the pits will still be visible if they are silvered over.

Reflectors that have dents, old gasket material or heavy coatings will required additional labor to prepare for resilvering. Steve's Auto Restorations can handle the disassembly and reassembly if the customer prefers. The restoration shop's hourly rate for these services is $70 and turnaround time is approximately four to six weeks from the time the reflectors arrive at the shop. Rush orders can sometimes be processed within three weeks for 25 percent extra.

To determine the cost for resilvering, measure the diameter of the headlight, taillight or cowl light from outer edge to outer edge. Steve's Auto Restorations charges so much per inch for each reflector that's resilvered.

Steve's Auto Restorations also stocks a wide selection of vintage headlight lenses, bulbs and gaskets. The company can also install 12-volt halogen conversion kits. Another of the shop's interesting products are precision-crafted glass reproduction lenses for the E & J Headlights used on some classic cars of the 1920s. To go with these, Steve's also stocks an E & J Headlight Gasket Set with exact fit replacements for original gaskets.

Plastic taillight lenses were commonly used during the 1950s and often require restoration to clean and brighten them so they look brand new. By the late 1980s, plastic headlight lenses were gaining popularity and they can get pretty sad-looking from environmental battering or too many trips through the coin-operated car wash. Some of these vehicles qualify as late-model special interest cars and may fall into the hands of collectors wanting to detail them out.

Restoring Plastic Lenses—The Internet is a good resource for professional detailers who restore plastic headlight lenses either by machine grinding them or polishing them. Message boards discussing the two processes suggest that grinding really can't make plastic look clear again and that polishes work better. It is not really necessary to use expensive detailing services for this job, as anyone can get a good polish and use it to make their plastic headlights look new again.

The Eastwood Company sells a $20 kit that includes AutoSol Paste, buffs and other supplies. Apply AutoSol by hand, using a small amount on a

You can rebuild your Corvette headlight motor with bronze gears like these, or send them out to vendors like Chicago Corvette to have the rebuilding done by an expert.

The well-known Max Baer Duesenberg, owned by Phil Kughn, wouldn't look quite right with non-skid tires or with raised white letter tires, but these gangster whitewalls have a very authentic appearance.

clean, dampened cloth and work it into the plastic. You can also put a four-inch loose buff on a wheel arbor and use your electric drill. Buff perpendicular to the lens and be careful not to generate enough heat to melt plastic. A quick final polish with a clean rag finishes the job. AutoSol can also be used on plastic grilles.

Although it borders on a mechanical repair, a stuck flip-up headlight door on a mid-year Corvette (or any other vintage car with hideaway headlights) has cosmetic implications, too. Your car just can't look very good with one eye open and one eye closed, so you're going to want to have that sticking or non-functioning headlight motor rebuilt. Several companies like D & M Restoration, Corvette Clocks by Roger and Corvette Specialties of Maryland offer Corvette headlight motor rebuilding on a repair-and-return basis.

Although many new replacement headlight motors are available for Corvettes through the marque's numerous specialty parts suppliers, the advantage to sending in the original motor, having it rebuilt and reinstalling it is that you then have a factory-quality motor that's like new again, plus you keep the car all original. In addition, a typical headlight motor rebuild by one of these vendors costs less than cost of buying a new aftermarket motor.

When a '63–'67 Corvette headlight motor is restored by such vendors, the motor is completely disassembled, thoroughly cleaned, lubricated and reassembled. All worn parts are replaced. Armatures are turned and cleaned, brushes are trued and bench-tested. Cosmetic issues can also be dealt with. You will get your original motor back, not a replacement. This is important if you want to have an all-matching-numbers car when the restoration is done.

D & M Restoration says it will also restore any

headlight motor for numerous makes and models of vintage, classic, antique or muscle cars including Chevrolet, Ford, Chrysler, Dodge, Pontiac, GM, Ferrari, BMW, Corvette, Firebird, Camaro, Chevelle, Corvair, Mustang and Thunderbird.

Replacement Tires

Installing the proper tires on a collector car can make a big difference in how the vehicle looks, rides and handles. I discovered this while doing a major fix-up on my 1936 Pontiac Deluxe Six Touring Sedan a few years ago and it's important for you to know if you're going to play general contractor on your own restoration. You can get tires for your old

These Lester tires have the correct fitment (size) and white sidewall width for a 1948 Pontiac Streamliner Eight or other cars of that era. Cars such as this one do not have tubeless wheels, so the use of tubes is a good idea.

This 1936 Oldsmobile convertible owned by Ralph Cornell has been fitted with Kelsey Tire's 6.00 x 16 Deluxe All-Weather models. These Goodyear Collector Series tires are part of Kelsey's Antique/Classic tire line.

Compare the tires on the 1936 Oldsmobile in the previous photograph to the ones on the LaSalle in this 1937 advertisement. As you can see, they look almost identical.

car at a local tire store. The salesperson will be happy to work out a size interchange on his tire calculator and sell you modern tires that fit. However, if you want the car to look right, ride right, sit right and gain value from the new tires, you should consider dealing with specialty suppliers that sell new old-style rubber.

No one brand of vintage tires carries the proper tires for all collector vehicles. I have had Universal bias-ply wide whites and Coker radial whitewalls on my '53 Pontiac Catalina and I just purchased a set of Lester tires from Wallace W. Wade for my '48 Pontiac. I try to select tires according to the design of a car and buy tires of any brand that suits the particular application best.

In the case of my '36 Pontiac, the tires I felt were just right for the car were Kelsey Tire's 6.00 x 16 Deluxe All-Weather models. These are Goodyear Collector Series tires in Kelsey's Antique/Classic line. They have 4-ply poly construction and a 3-1/2-in. whitewall. They also come in size 6.50 x 16.

John Kelsey says the following about these tires: "A pre-World War II restoration just isn't complete without these Goodyear tires. They were as much an industry standard of quality when new as they are today. This unique Goodyear diamond tread pattern continues to represent the discerning collector's tire of choice for total authenticity."

It was the diamond-tread pattern and the beveled look of the sidewalls that convinced me that a late-1930s car with Art Deco looks like my 1936

Pontiac needed these tires. Since tires are a major expense, I contemplated this purchase for several years before actually placing the order. When I saw the Kelsey Deluxe All-Weather tires at car shows, I knew I wanted them on the car.

What a great decision! With the old black sidewall tires, the car had always looked nice, but a little down on its luck. I had a local garage mount the Goodyear tires with tubes (also purchased from Kelsey Tire). After applying a nice coat of wax to the car's original 1936 Duco lacquer, the ceremonial removal of the blue protective coating on the tires' white sidewalls took place.

As the blue turned to white, it was like some kind of magic restoration potion had been applied to the old Pontiac. With the combination of a coat of wax and the old-fashioned tires, the car visually popped to life. There were still nicks and dull spots in the 80-year-old paint, but the appearance of the car was so much improved by the tires that the flaws became almost invisible.

When I tried to buy similar tires for my '48 Pontiac, John Kelsey said they would not look right on a postwar car. In fact, he said that he didn't really have a 16-inch tire for that application, but he gave us a list of all his competitors who did carry what we wanted. That's what's great about hobby businessmen.

I wound up buying Lester tires from Wallace W. Wade. I had known Tom Lester and thought it would be great to have his name on my car. Lester

Some old car hobbyists save on shipping costs by ordering their vintage tires and picking them up in person from the manufacturers, like Kelsey Tire, at swap meets, flea markets, car shows and trade shows.

High-wheel cars like this 1909 Economy Model G touring owned by Brady and Emily Mann, of Roanoke, Illinois, have wheels and tires that are very similar to those used on wagons and buggies.

was involved with Lincoln Highway Tires, the first company to reproduce antique car tires and I liked having this tidbit of hobby history reflected in my choice of tires.

The trick of turning black sidewall tires into whitewalls has been the high-demand service in the tire customizing industry for years. In the late 1980s, a method of adding white letters to tires was added to the array of available services. The development of new paints and other products greatly expanded the things that a tire customizer can do to enhance the appearance of tires.

Custom Tire FX, located in Cleveland, Ohio, has developed a system that makes it possible to attach rubber letters to tires, which they have done to more than a million tires since they've been in businees. The process can replicate some of the tire graphics seen in antique tire ads.

Thanks to Internet advertising, Custom Tire FX is now making some tire customizing products and services available to the public. For example, it has put together a kit to help people customize tires at home. The company also developed a specially formulated whitewall paint to replace a commercial product that became obsolete in 2001. The new paint is said to last the life of the tire.

The hard rubber tires used on very early trucks are a bit different than the wagon style used on high-wheeler automobiles. The truck-type hard rubber tires are much thicker and wider. A Connecticut company that has experience with replacing the hard rubber tires used on early trucks

is Pfahl's Mack & Antique Truck Restorations of Bethlehem.

Matt Pfahl started restoring antique trucks in 1992. When he did a total frame-up restoration on a 1924 Mack AB owned by Bill Kirby, of North Carolina, he had to restore the hard rubber truck tires. According to Pfahl this was not as easy then as it is today. Matt cut a cross-section of the old tire as

This hard rubber tire Mack Bulldog truck has been working in the circus industry since it was new. You can clearly see the effects of hard use on the rear tire. A few hobby vendors offer repairs for hard rubber truck tires.

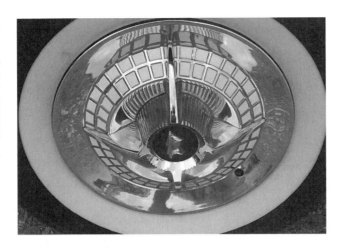

Most hubcaps and full wheel covers, including this 1959 Dodge wheel cover, can be restored by shops that do stainless steel buffing and polishing and/or chrome plating.

a model, then heated the steel rim to remove it from the spokes. He then sent the steel rims and the cross-section to a tire manufacturer so that new tires could be custom-fitted to the rim size. The hard rubber tires and steel rims were then pressed back onto the spokes with a 50-ton press with beautiful results.

Wheels and Wheel Covers

Wheels and wheel covers play into the cosmetics of any collector car and there are companies around the old-car hobby that specialize in the restoration of different types of wheels. As far as restoring hubcaps and wheel covers, most of them can be restored by shops that do stainless steel restoration work and/or chrome plating. In at least one case, the original manufacturer—Dayton Wire Wheel Company of Ohio—offers restoration services to car collectors. There are also shops and vendors who restore all types of specialty wheels from the wood-spoke wheels used under pioneer automobiles to the beautiful 8-lug aluminum wheels that high-performance Pontiacs offered in the '60s.

Companies such as Viking Wheel Service of Wilmington, Delaware, offer a range of wheel services including: straightening, paint stripping and refinishing (including powder coating), certified wheel welding, CNC face machining, polishing, chrome plating or custom finishing and custom work like wheel widening. If you need a specific type of wheel, a wheel locator service can help.

Viking Wheel Service uses specially designed hydraulic equipment manufactured and patented by Atlantic Machine Company. This machine can take a curb-pranged wheel and make it true again. Wheels to be repaired are mounted in the machine and trued to within at least twenty thousandths of an inch TIP (Total Indicator Reading). Ten thousandths of an inch TIP is the norm.

Viking Wheel Service relies on a wide selection of hub-centric spacers to ensure that they can accommodate any wheel in their machine. The hub-centric spacer increases the hold on the wheel to control hub flex and center locating.

Dayton Wire Wheel Company is approaching its 100th anniversary. It was formed in 1916 in Dayton, Ohio, and became the premier designer and manufacturer of wire wheels for the 92 years. From the beginning, Dayton Wire Wheel set a high quality standard for the automotive industry. The Wright Brothers, Henry Ford and Charles Lindbergh chose Dayton wire wheels. The mighty Duesenberg also rode on Daytons, along with nearly 30 other makes. Dayton Wire Wheels were used in more than 30 Indianapolis 500 races.

Dayton has perfected a restoration process that transforms even the most worn wire wheel to its former glory. The wire wheel first gets a complete wheel analysis in which the degree of rim straightness, hub wear and metal deterioration are noted. Dayton then advises the customer of its findings before any work is done. Sometimes it is impossible to restore a wheel to original specifications. In other cases, the wheel may require more than normal work and extra costs will be involved.

If the customer agrees, wheel information such as type, size, spoke pattern, offset, spoke size and nipple size are recorded. All parts are then labeled to ensure proper identification throughout the restoration process.

A stripping process removes all paint, chrome and fillers found on the old wire wheel. Then, the wheel is completely disassembled and examined for

Dayton Wire Wheel Company's manager Brad Crutchleo was at the 2007 SEMA show with this custom pickup truck. Dayton has perfected a restoration process that transforms even a worn wire wheel into a work of art.

In preparation for painting, Dayton Wire Wheel achieves a 180-grit finish on rims like this one exhibited at the annual SEMA trade show in Las Vegas. Show quality wheels even get additional polishing that gives them a 100-point appearance.

If you're restoring an antique car like this Oakland with wood-spoke artillery style wheels, Calimer's Wheel Shop in Waynesboro, Pennsylvania, is an acknowledged specialist in this particular area.

further flaws and to see if metal fatigue has occurred over the years.

Cracked or thin areas on the rim are welded. Pits from rust and corrosion are filled and sanded. Finally, bent or dented portions of the rim are straightened.

Dayton's restoration craftsmen actually manufacture spokes as close to the original specification as possible. Spokes are made in Dayton's own plant and in plain or chrome plated carbon steel or polished stainless steel.

Brad said the rim, hub, lock rings, nuts and weight covers are hand polished to a mirror bright finish. In preparation for painting, a 180-grit finish is achieved. Show quality wheels get extra polishing for a 100-point appearance.

An enhanced plating process applies four layers of nickel and chrome to the wheel components for a bright durable finish, even in recessed areas. All plated parts meet accepted auto industry exterior specifications.

According to Crutchleo, the new spokes are then carefully laced by hand and inspected for quality. Then, the wheel is checked for perfect alignment in both lateral and radial directions. Finally, all of the newly manufactured spokes are precision-tightened to a uniform tension.

Wheels to be painted are hand sanded and several coats of primer are applied. The wheel is then painted with four coats of enamel that contains an advanced hardener to protect against stone chips and corrosion. Wheels requiring a show finish receive additional attention to achieve a glass-like finish. The final step consists of a final inspection

and cleaning before shipment.

If you're restoring an antique car with wood-spoke artillery style wheels, Calimer's Wheel Shop in Waynesboro, Pennsylvania, is a specialist in this area. Bill and Bob Calimer belong to a family with a long history of repairing carriages. People began bringing automobile wheels to the shop for restoration in the early 1970s.

In order to be successful, Calimer's Wheel Shop had to build an automobile wheel that was accurate and strong and would last a long time. This has been the businesses goal for 28 years. Every attempt is made to make wheels that are duplicates of originals. This requires much handwork and the knowledge that comes from experience. Calimer's does not specialize in one make or model. It has made wheels for Model T Fords and early Mercedes cars. The company has several hundred spoke patterns in its collection.

The wood of choice for auto wheels in America was hickory, which is strong and flexible. Its combination of strength, toughness and flexibility can't be matched by any other hardwood. Oak auto wheels could shatter across the grain. Calimer's uses wood from local mills that is stacked and air dried. The spokes and felloes (wood rim) are kiln dried. The wheel is built using dry parts. This ensures that the wheel will stay tight for many years and last a long time.

To make a wooden wheel the hub hole is center bored so that the weight of the car rests on it. Then, all joints are machine cut and fit together by hand. The joints are then hand filed and sanded. Most wood felloe wheels require a metal rim to be hot shrunk onto them. Steel felloe wheels will be pressed together using hydraulic pressure. All wheels are trued to the hub (they should not be

A ventilated cotton buff is used for final buffing on stainless. Use white rouge for less aggressive work. To create a high-sheen finish, use white rouge or jeweler's rouge. Loose section buffs get in hard-to-reach spots.

Companies like Classics Plus, Ltd., offer stainless steel restoration services that can make old hubcaps and wheel covers look new. Here, Mike Freund applies more rogue buffing compound) to the piece of stainless steel trim. Stainless steel wheel covers can also be buffed up well.

interchanged). The wheels are not refinished during the restoration process, so the car owners can paint them any color.

Calimer's asks its customers to clean the grease off the hubs and send in: 1) A few old spokes from a front and rear wheel; 2) A half section of felloe when required; 3) Hubs, bolts, brake drums, felloe plates, T shaped rivets and other miscellaneous metal fasteners that need to be installed; 4) Felloe bands, clincher rims or steel felloes; 5) On rare occasions a demountable rim and lugs for wood felloe wheels and 6) Pictures for help, but in special cases only.

Moving from wood to stainless steel, the many hobby companies that offer stainless steel restoration services can often make your old hubcaps and wheel covers look like new again. I visited Mike Freund of Classics Plus Ltd., in North Fond du Lac, Wisconsin, to learn how he buffs stainless parts like hubcaps.

Mike uses a high-speed buffing motor. Different compounds or rogues are used for different metals. His buffs are made of sewn-together cloth. He pointed out that the tighter the stitching is, the harder and more aggressive the buff is. According to Mike, a Sisal buff is used on a hard metal like stainless steel. It has spiral-sewn construction and is made of woven-rope fiber covered with cotton cloth. The red treated Sisal buff gives an even faster cut and lasts longer.

Restorers like Mike generally use an emery buffing rouge for fast cutting on stainless. A light to medium gray stainless compound is good for medium cutting. It can be used on a Sisal or ventilated buff. The ventilated buff has pleated, biased cloth to keep the buffed piece cool and prevent streaking.

When Mike buffs, he lets his wheel run off the edge of the hubcap or trim piece. He works on the lower part of the buffing wheel, just below its center axis. The stainless steel buffing compound is applied sparingly. Mike takes the compound in his gloved hand and carefully rubs it on the spinning buffing wheel.

While buffing, Mike avoids using too much pressure. He works in stages, sometimes changing wheels and compounds that he keeps nearby. He begins his course work using a spiral sewn buff with stainless steel emery. Later, he might use a cotton ventilated buff with stainless steel or white rouge for less aggressive buffing. To create a high-sheen finish, Mike uses white rouge or jeweler's rouge. A loose section buff can get into hard-to-reach areas.

On aluminum wheel covers, Mike starts with a spiral sewn buff and Tripoli compound. He then goes to a ventilated buff with Tripoli. A second buff with white rouge is nearby for finer polishing. Then, a loose section buff is used with white rouge and jeweler's rouge to create a high-shine on the nearly finished piece and to get into hard-to-reach areas.

Chapter 7

Interior Restoration Tips

A nice but incorrect interior was fitted to a 1936 Pontiac that appeared in events for the company's 75th anniversary. Later, Pontiac Motor Division had this interior done correctly using the author's car as its model.

As general contractor on your own restoration, you'll be dealing with the question of soft trim as you get near the end of your restoration. Motorcycles don't have much in the way of upholstery and usually don't need a convertible top or interior work, though you may want to find vendors who can build an original seat. With old trucks, interior trim and top work is also not usually a big issue. Most vintage commercial vehicles are fairly basic vehicles. In the case of cars, of course, the restoration of soft trim can be a pretty intricate and costly process.

The Pontiac Historical Vehicle Collection owns a 1936 Pontiac like one I own. In fact, it is the very car that I saw on the cover of *Cars & Parts* magazine in 1976 and decided I wanted to own one day. (At that time it belonged to a man in Florida). The car owned by Pontiac had an incorrect interior. In 2001, Pontiac took the car to several events celebrating the company's 75th anniversary and heard criticisms of the interior. The company decided to have it redone by a trim shop in Detroit and the shop contacted me for a set of pictures of my '36 Pontiac's tattered, but all-original interior.

In the course of talking to the shop, I learned they were going to pattern an original-style interior for Pontiac. I figured I could save some money and asked what the price would be to make a duplicate copy for me. The estimate

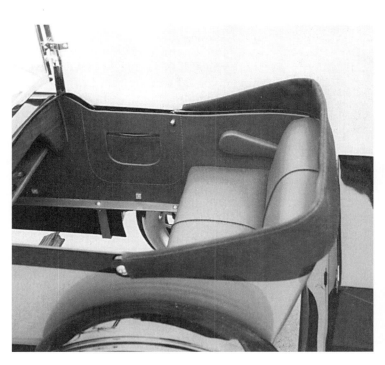

Even miniature auto interiors have their price. Dennis and Kathy Bickford of Vintage Woodworks, in Iola, Wisconsin, spent a total of 20 hours—at their full shop rate—making trim parts for this toy Cadillac Phaeton.

This Eastwood interior kit is being installed on an MG TD owned by Curt Strohacker, Eastwood's founder. Although this interior kit is readily available, it can cost over $1,000.

Mid America Motorworks, of Effingham, Illinois, sells do-it-yourself seat cover kits with clear step-by-step installation instructions.

came back at $4,800 and that did not include materials or installation. The trimmer said I would have to buy all the material separately and install the interior myself or hire someone else to put it in the car. It didn't take long to calculate that my money-saving idea was not going to work. A few years later, I ran into an old friend who had a '57 Buick convertible. To get his interior restored, he shipped his car back and forth to another state and spent $25,000 to have it trimmed!

As you might have guessed by now, interior restoration is an expensive process. Getting your interior redone for a reasonable cost is going to challenge your general contracting skills. On top of that, you can't put your car in an envelope and send it to a trim shop. If you are going to farm out trim work, you will have to deal with getting the car to the place where the work can be done.

One reason for the high cost of auto trimming is that it is not an easy job. This book doesn't preach the do-it-yourself approach to restoration and I will point out that catalogers like Moss Motors Ltd., that sell complete leather trim kits for British sports cars, always include wording in their catalogs that recommends using a professional trimmer to install the kits. This is done because so many of these kits—which carry prices over $1,000 with shipping and tax—are ruined by hobbyists who think they can handle the job of installing an upholstery kit.

The source guide beginning on page 107 lists

many trim shops from across the country that do upholstery work for classic car restorers. In this chapter, I'll discuss some innovative ways that several companies have tried to make dressing your car up a little easier on your wallet. In regard to convertible top installs, I'll discuss my own experience with this job and explain why I'll probably farm it out the next time. Some advice on dashboards, consoles, trunk trimmings and options for the inside of your car will round out this section.

Upholstery

I am going to recommend playing general contractor again and hiring a pro to restore your car's interior. I have seen interior installs done by even relatively experienced restorers and noticed

Al Knoch sells Corvette trim and upholstery products and offers hobbyists an at-the-show install program. The customer orders a top or interior kit, then visits the Al Knoch booth at a scheduled show to get the install done.

Gilbert Barraza, of Al Knoch, installs a Corvette convertible top at the Bloomington Gold Corvette show in St. Charles, Illinois. Carraza says that he can install two complete soft tops in a normal working day.

things like loose stitching, crooked seams and impossible-to-get-out creases and wrinkles. In many of these cases, the interiors looked pretty good. However, when you think about how much upholstery kits cost and how they weigh on a collector car's value, professional help is the way that 95 percent of us should go.

As general contractor, you want to hold down costs and stick to a schedule, but you don't want substandard quality either. Therefore, your job becomes a quest of getting the best value for the money spent. You can look for a trimmer that has found ways to cut overhead so jobs can be done cheaper or you can turn to companies that sell interior kits that are trying to "Henry Ford" their installs. By this, I mean that they are trying to apply mass-production methods to the installation of interior kits so that they can offer this service at an attractive price.

A new trend at vintage auto shows sees manufacturers of soft trim items like convertible top kits and seat upholstery kits doing installs during the events they travel to each year. The at–the-show interior and top installs take place at Carlisle, Bloomington Gold and Corvette Funfest, just to name a few events.

A tent is erected, tables are set up and a portable trim shop is set up right in the swap meet. It's like going to a Wal-Mart Supercenter, except instead of getting a haircut while your wife shops and the optician makes up new eyeglasses for your kids, at auto shows you get your collector car spruced up by professionals who know what they're doing while you shop for parts.

It works like this: You check the supplier's national ads to see their product line and to

determine if they are coming to a show in your area, then, you contact them and arrange a specific time slot for your car's install. You buy the top kit or the seat covers from them and set up an appointment. You usually pay for the kit in advance, but you will normally save the standard shipping costs.

Gilbert Barraza installs Al Knoch Corvette tops and interiors at shows. I talked to him while he was installing a convertible top on a red '62 Corvette. He told me this is a five-hour install and would cost the car owner about $500. Gilbert finessed two new top pads into position under the car's soft top and reached up, without looking, to feel his way through the installation process. It was obvious that he knew the ins and outs of a Corvette convertible top install. Due to his efficient way of working, Al Knoch can offer at-show installs for more or less set prices. Gilbert can do two tops or even more seat cover installs a day.

While Gilbert put the top on, Javier Torrez was busy stretching a bright blue seat kit over a Corvette back rest. Like his coworker, Javier dispatched the work quickly and professionally. It wasn't very long before he had the late-'60s style Corvette seat looking like new and was ready to start a second seat.

Companies that sell trim parts and accessories for collector cars through a mail-order catalog realize that many enthusiasts may not have the skills needed to install a new seat cover. Most customers in the I-can't-do-it-myself category are going to order the parts by mail order and take them to local independent shops to have the installation done.

For at-the-show Corvette convertible top installs like this one, a tent is set up right at the event and becomes a portable trim shop. In 2007, installing a '62 'Vette top like this was a five-hour job that cost about $500.

Most hobbyists dealing with upholstery that looks like this realize that they might not be able to restore the seat and turn to professional trim shops for help. This makes sense if you chose the proper shop.

This is the Mid America Motorworks Installation and Styling Center at company headquarters in Effingham, Illinois.

This makes good sense because trim shops and repair shops nationwide have the skills needed to do quality installs.

Still, a certain percentage of customers will ask if factory installation services are available. They prefer the "we service what we sell" approach and want to have the retailer or manufacturer put the product in their car. In 2006, Corvette parts supplier Mid America Motorworks, of Effingham, Ill., decided to test the waters in this area by opening an upholstery install center.

The company organized a Performance Choice team that offered product installation services. By July 2006, the new program was going so well construction of an Installation and Styling Center at the company's corporate campus began. Company founder Mike Yager had sponsored and appeared in a cable TV program that featured installs of many of his Corvette soft trim products. He decided that the interior of the new Installation and Styling Center should have the attractive look of the TV set seen on how-to-do-it type shows.

The Corvette Styling and Installation Center was officially opened in September 2006. Since that time, Mid America Motorworks has offered set-price installation services on a select group of its hottest-selling interior styling and accessory parts including C4 and C5 Corvette seat covers. Installs for other models are also available on a custom basis.

The Installation Center team has handcrafted unique interiors and installs regularly stocked interior kits. Mid America Motorwork's website provides a list of services and costs. The flat prices for most installs are based on average installation times. Customers who wish to have their purchases installed can call a toll-free number for a custom

quote and get the installation scheduled.

McCloskey Auto Trim, Al Knoch and Mid America Motorworks have tried to find more efficient ways to offer auto upholstery services at affordable rates. Innovative approaches like these will probably be seen more in the future and will be very helpful to restorers who function as their own general contractor.

Other things to keep in mind when dealing with other trimmers on the list in the source guide include how far away the shop is from you, their hourly shop rate and whether they will install a kit or materials that you ordered yourself (some shops will and others won't). If you are buying an interior kit, keep in mind that most suppliers see sales go up drastically in the warmer months and drop during the winter. Therefore, many will discount prices or

The Mid America Motorworks Installation Center team offers handcrafted unique interiors and installations of all regularly stocked interior kits. The Mid America Motorworks website provides a full list of services and costs.

Measuring sticks help set proper rear bow height—a critical measurement for a top install. Vintage Woodworks has made sticks for Town & Country cars. The manufacturer of a top kit will usually supply the measurements.

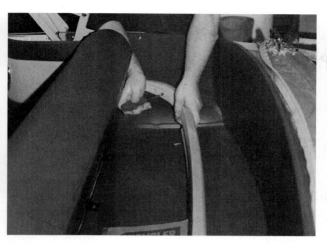

A screw is tightened to install a rear bow that has been wrapped with a fabric called bow drill.

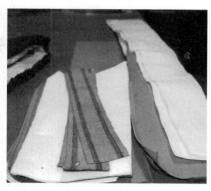

Tan fabric, lining material and webbing are the materials needed to construct the stay pads or bow pads for a classic car.

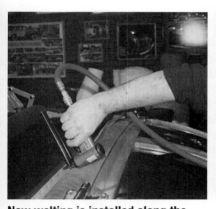

New welting is installed along the edge of the body tub. The welting provides a transition between the car body and the convertible top.

The job starts by aligning the top frame to the car's side windows. The first step is to line up the windows the way you want them and adjust the top frame to match. The side rails are the suspension bridge.

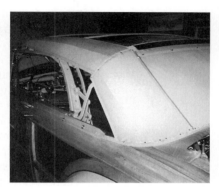

The Chrysler Town & Country convertible has vertical zippers at the edge of the bow pads to hold the curtain window in place. Along its top edge, the curtain window snaps onto a covered metal bar.

put their kits on sale during certain seasons. If this is their practice, buy during the sale season and you'll be able to save 10 to 15 percent off regular prices.

Convertible Tops

When it comes to doing a convertible top, the only way to outsource the job is to take the car someplace to have a top installed. You cannot send the top frame someplace, have a top put on it and reattach it to the car with a new top on it. This won't work. The top really has to be custom fit to the car's body. What follows is an illustration of how one custom shop does their convertible tops so you'll have an idea how it is done.

Custom cutting and sewing a convertible top may be the only way to go if you're trimming a classic.

Dennis Bickford has practiced this almost lost art for 32 years on Chrysler Town & Country woody convertibles. He works only at his Vintage Woodworks shop in Iola, Wisconsin. Bickford learned by intuition and picked up some tricks. He says making a top from scratch is always rewarding.

Dennis starts by aligning the top frame to the car's side windows. He lines the windows up the way he wants them. Then he adjusts the convertible top frame to match. The side rails are a suspension bridge. An adjustable inner arm lowers and puts tension across the windows to prevent a sagging top. A center adjustment keeps the top level. The front header adjusts by sliding the side rails.

The top bows are wrapped in bowdrill for a nice appearance. On Town & Country cars, the rear bow

The lower edge of the quarter panels is marked with chalk to match up with chalk line on the lower edge of the curtain. The bottom edge is then tacked in place as shown. On modern cars, staples are used for tacking.

The top is then latched to the windshield, and the fabric is gently pulled over the No. 1 bow. The position is marked, then the fabric is pulled a quarter inch past the reference mark. Then it is secured to to the bow with screws, staples and glue.

has a metal strip to hold the rear curtain. The rear bows have a specific bow height setting. Measuring sticks help set the bow height. Then bow pads are made to ride on the back radius of the bows and hide the seams. They also support the top structure and hold the bows in position. To make bow pads, a trimmer must know where seams are going to be. On Town & Country cars, bow pads are screwed to the second bow and tacked to the others.

After constructing bow pads, the next step is to build the curtain that will hold the rear window. Some curtains have a horseshoe zipper and others have a vertical zipper on each side. With a third type the curtain is tacked in place. Bickford's top had zippers down both sides and five snaps with cinch studs that go through eyelets in a metal bar along the top of the curtain to hold the curtain up and keep it in place against the rear convertible top bow.

A convertible top is made of three pieces: driver's side quarter panel, passenger side quarter panel and top deck. The quarter panels are constructed first by laying the material on the top frame. Dennis pulls the panels from front to back. If the bow pad is lined up, he can pull them tight and get all wrinkles out. A yardstick helps draw a straight line in chalk from the back bow to the front bow. If the quarter panel is taken off, you will see that the straight line turns into an arched line. Once the lines are established, the quarter panels can be cut out.

Measuring seam to seam across the front bow and the back bow establishes the size of the top decking. In simple terms, the next step is to remove the three pieces and sew them together. Of course, it takes a

single-needle walking-foot sewing machine with a guide do the sewing properly. The next step is to waterproof the seams with a sealer made for this job.

After sewing the top, Dennis places the assembly on the top frame and pre-tacks it with trimmer's tacks—not staples. He then trims the fabric over the top of the windows allowing marginal clearance for the doors to open and for the windows to clear the convertible top. The rear quarter panel may need trimming.

Dennis binds the edges using facings under the binding. Welting is used on the windshield header and bow as transition trim between the bow and top. Dennis installs it, then puts the top back on and tacks it down with stainless steel and galvanized

Bickford trims excess material off the rear quarter panel sections and the bottom of the curtain window panel.

For installing a Sunbird or Cavalier convertible top, a different type of spacer stick can be used to set bow height. The factory service manual gives specific directions on how to fabricate the proper spacer sticks.

staples. He then measures for the rear window, which must be carefully centered side to side, but placed slightly above top center for proper appearance. After the window is completed, decorative chrome tips and wire-on coverings are installed to give the top a fully trimmed, finished look.

DIY Convertible Top Kits—You can install a kit top yourself. By using good quality kits, asking questions and reading a factory manual, I learned to do this job and did three tops. I'm going to run through the steps and then, at the end of the instructions, I'll talk about why I would farm this work out if I had to do it again.

Top kits can be found in magazine ads, mail-order catalogs or on the Internet. Check the correct year and model of the car. Specify your color. Decide whether you want single-, double-, or triple-texture fabric. Some customers want canvas, but canvas can stain, fade and wear fast. Vinyl-coated fabrics are best.

New pads are recommended if the old top has the starved-cow look. A curtain window is not included in many kits. You may need new cables, tacking strip, hardware, wire-on and a front roll. You will need an upholstery stapler, stainless steel staples, cement, trim adhesive, razor blades and a yardstick.

Installation—Installation techniques vary. Our manual said to make spacer sticks to hold the top rails in alignment. This eliminated measuring bow height. What follows are step-by-step tips based on our kit:

Start by removing moldings from the body well. Cover the deck lid, remove the molding fasteners and store in plastic baggies, along with slips of paper with reinstallation notes. Use a grease pen to mark where screws and moldings hit the old top.

Lift the top and remove the roll strip at the front.

Take out all staples and screws. Save screws and other hardware. Remove the rubber weather-stripping from side rails, the glued-on quarter flaps and one end of each cable. If the top is attached to the middle bows, remove the attaching screws and the listings.

Latch the top to the windshield header. Remove the wire-on from the rear bow. Remove all staples so they don't poke through your new top. Remove or pull back the well cover to get at the fasteners below it. On some cars removing the fasteners loosens a removable metal tacking rail. My car had a plastic tacking strip. It was bolted on the outer edge of the body well and didn't come off. Loosen everything enough to remove the old top. If the tacking strip is damaged, replace it.

If you are installing new pads without spacer sticks, remove one pad and use your yardstick to measure bow height. You should be able to check the measurement with the top maker. Staple your first new pad to the roof bows. It will hold the frame in alignment as you install the second pad.

Remove the rear curtain. Mark the center of the rear bow. The new curtain will have a notch to line up with your mark. Staple the curtain to the bow from the center, pulling wrinkles as you move toward the edges. Unlatch the top and prop it up. Fasten the bottom of the curtain and window to the tacking strip with the tacking rail or other retainer. Close and latch the front and make adjustments.

Before installing the new top, lay it on a clean floor under the old top. Transfer reference marks like bolt holes and tacking strip locations to the new top. Now put the new top over the old one and compare reference marks. If you see differences, use half the distance between the two marks as your reference.

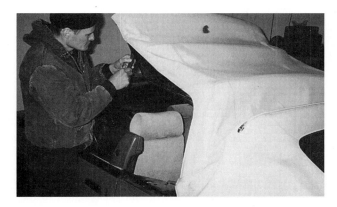

Mechanic Vince Sauberlich removes one end from the metal cable that threads through a lengthwise pocket sewn into the top. These cables are sometimes broken or rusted and, if so, must be replaced with new ones.

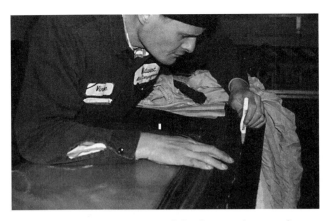

Before installing new top panel, lay it on a clean surface under the old top. Transfer reference marks like bolt holes and tacking strip locations to the new top. Put the new top over the old one and compare reference marks.

Position the top over the framework until it sits right. Secure the top to the No. 2 and No. 3 roof bows with listings. Raise the top off the windshield header and attach all cables. Center the top valance over the No. 4 bow and staple it on, working from the center out. Pull out fullness and wrinkles. Using screws and contact cement, fasten the quarter flaps in position. Reinstall weather stripping along the side rails, using screws and trim adhesive to hold it in place.

Latch the top to the windshield. Pull the fabric gently over the No. 1 bow and mark its position. Pull the fabric a quarter inch past the reference mark. Secure it to the bow with screws, staples and glue. Check proper top appearance and operation. Install the roll at the front that overlaps the windshield header.

With top latched, staple the new fabric to the tacking strip. Start at the front of the tacking strip and move to the rear. Use only a few staples so you can make pulls and adjustments as you move around the curved sections. Try to eliminate wrinkles. Avoid excessive stretching. Keep the top material flat.

Install wire over the staples in the No. 4 bow. Install end caps on the wire-on. Use a silicone sealer for waterproofing. Make holes for the belt molding studs in the bottom edges of the top and backlight and line them up with the holes in the tacking strip. Install fasteners on the studs where they protrude inside the body well. Reinstall the well cover. Leave the top up several days to set.

Although you can handle an install like this one, as general contractor of your restoration, do you want to? It depends on your goals. I was doing these cars for my granddaughters and wanted them to have decent looking convertibles with tops that didn't leak. The job of installing a top took a long time. Vince and I had to buy many expensive new things like an upholstery stapler and stainless steel staples that we may never use much again. When it came to parts like tacking strips and supplies like glues and sealers, we could not get exactly what the factory used and had to run all over for replacements.

On the first two cars we installed bone white tops that came out looking good, but for various reasons like a change in tacking strips and inexperience, the rear curtain windows did not lay as flat and smooth as you would like them to on a show car. On the last car we did, with a black top, we got the rear window perfect, but we positioned the top slightly off the rear bow and the wire-on did not cover the seams. Again, it was not what you'd want on your show car.

After latching the top to the windshield, Vince Sauberlich pulled the fabric gently over the No. 1 bow and marked its position. He stretched it a quarter inch past the reference mark and secured it to the bow with staples.

On the car with the black top, the rear curtain window fit the tightest and looked the smoothest of all three tops. This was the result of cranking the heat in the shop up to about 90 degrees for a few hours.

Chrysler fin car restorer Jerry Kopecky will use a subcontractor named JC Auto Restoration to get this fishbowl Chrysler instrument panel restored. It uses the electroluminescent lighting system developed by Sylvania.

All in all, we saved money doing the top installs ourselves, but in the long run the savings were not what you'd expect. For the money we saved, we got installs that looked good and worked good, but weren't as nice as you'd want for show. And another important thing to think about is we owned what we got. There was no taking the job back to a shop to get little problems set right. All in all, if you're doing a show car, you might want to farm this job out, but pick a good shop and go over the install with them in detail to make sure it's done right.

Dashes, Consoles, Trunks

For advice on dashboard restoration, I turned once again to Jerry Kopecky.

Kopecky agrees with me that modern car restoration involves a lot of subcontracting with outside suppliers. Many trim parts for Mopar models aren't reproduced and have to be rebuilt by

specialists. Kopecky can get interior kits for most cars he restores from Gary Goers, but other bulk soft trim materials like fabrics come from S and S Custom. Most Chrysler cars of these years came with padded dashboards and many dashboards are available from Just Dashes.

One unique aspect of restoring the Chrysler 300F is its Buck Rogers–type instrument panel, which has all of the engine monitoring gauges housed in a semi-globular display bubble with electro-luminescent lighting. At first glance, the restoration of one of these instrument panels seems to be on a par with building your own space shuttle, but Kopecky located a company named JC Auto Restoration that restores them. Another supplier from Canada manufactures replacement wiring harnesses for that dash.

To make the dashboard restoration work easier, Jerry designed his own dashboard rotisserie. After sending the display bubble off to JC Restoration, he mounted the rest of the entire assembly in his dashboard rotisserie, so he could flip the unit over to work at different angles. The dash has a lot of bright metal trim bits that he sent out to Iverson Automotive, in Minnesota, to be replated or buffed.

The dashboard was taken completely apart, and every piece was sandblasted and refinished. The old brittle and spliced wiring was replaced with a new harness. All chrome trim parts were replated and all gauges were sent out to be rebuilt.

Kopecky keeps a visual record of all work done

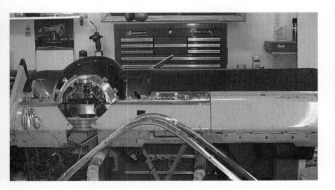

This dashboard rotisserie fabricated by Kopecky's Klassics holds the unit securely and aids in removal of the fishbowl instrument panel. A supplier in Canada makes wiring harnesses for Chrysler 300s.

This is an instrument panel for a '60 Chrysler 300F after restoration by JC Auto Restoration. The Lynnwood, Washington, subcontractor is a four-person shop with two full-time instrument panel and gauge restorers.

To restore this rare '38 Packard radio delete, subcontractor John Berry of Phoenix Restoration hand-hammered new circular brass parts, glazed them and photographed an original to match the lettering style.

with digital photos and videos. I would highly recommend this to any restorer.

John Berry is another subcontractor who offers special services needed to restore a dashboard. He started by painting and printing reproduction faces for motorcycles because the Antique Motorcycle Club of America's national meet is held near his home in Davenport, Iowa. In 1997, a Jaguar owner told him that the skills he used to restore gauge faces were in demand by car collectors. Today, John's Phoenix Restoration restores gauge faces, trimplates and body tags.

While there are many stick-on overlays for popular antique auto gauges, John Berry works from scratch. Many overlays are the wrong color. Some reproductions are too glossy while others are simply not done well. After disassembling a gauge, John makes new artwork to match the original. This can be as simple as setting type to match the original, but many letter styles can't be matched. To duplicate these, Berry uses sign painting experience to hand-paint masters. Later, he converts these to silk screens and reprints the same faces.

Berry carefully matches original paint on the gauge face. Then, he strips off all of the old paint. Some gauge faces are made of brass and have transparent glazes. New glazes are mixed prior to stripping the old ones off. John straightens the face, if needed, and makes sure it's free of rust. He warns that some gauge faces can't be repaired and must be remade of aluminum or brass.

Restoration is a case of priming and repainting or reglazing. Additional silk screens are made so the

faces can be reprinted and remounted to the gauges. The needles are painted the proper color and the gauges are reinstalled.

Berry recently restored a '38 Packard radio delete plate that had been hit with a hammer. The glass was completely gone and the brass inner panels were badly bent up. Since Packards were upscale cars, many had radios and this makes radio delete plates hard to find. Berry located a man with a still-boxed NOS plate, plus another still in a car. The man would not sell either one, but he did let John photograph the one that was in the vehicle.

John hand-hammered new circular brass parts and glazed them to match the originals. He then took his photo of the original piece and used it to match the lettering style on the inner glass face. Berry drew on his 40-plus years as a sign painter and screen printer to hand paint a master to match the lettering. He then made a silk screen and printed the lettering on the backside of new glass.

Berry replaced the curved glass outer face, cutting a piece from the center of a 12-inch curved-glass clock face. He replicated the plastic disk and hand-built and polished an aluminum trim ring. He mounted the refurbished original emblem and affixed everything to the center of the new delete panel. The original chrome bezel was fully intact and needed only a good cleaning.

D & M Restoration, which was mentioned earlier in this book for its clock and gauge restorations, also serves as a subcontracting shop for the restoration of instrument clusters, glovebox doors and center convenience consoles for antique, classic, vintage and muscle cars. You can send your parts

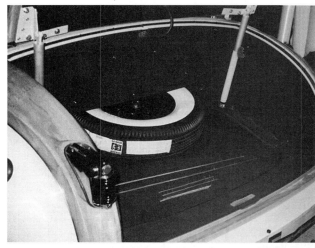

Trimmer Dennis Bickford says they make a lot of little trunk trim parts and Jenkins Restorations of North Wilkesboro, N.C., has trunk lining material for 1937-up cars, but a trunk is done as part of restoring the vehicle.

into the Greenville, South Carolina, company to be restored and returned to you. D & M will send you back the same unit you sent in, but it will look quite a bit shinier and newer.

Vintage Woodworks manufactures a lot of little parts that people need to restore their trunks properly. And Jenkins Restorations of North Wilkesboro, N.C., has the correct trunk lining material for 1937–2002 GM cars, but you have to trim a trunk as part of restoring the vehicle. (I checked the Jenkins Restoration website and they also carry Trax trunk lining material for late 1940s–1950s Mopar models and the cross-stitch and chain-link types that are correct for certain Buicks and Cadillacs). Other vendors in the sources list carry do-it-yourself trunk trim kits for popular collector cars.

Adding Optional Equipment

Selling car buyers optional equipment was a way for factory dealers to increase their profits on auto sales. Options also raise the value of used cars. Many collectors like to load up their vintage cars with as many extras as they can find. It's true that you could lose points for an incorrect option in a judged car show, so some people ask, "Why add something that could cost you judging points?" On the other hand, people who started collecting cars in more recent years seem to love options. In many cases, this is because they are used to driving newer cars with a lot of them. They are used to having such features.

In one way or another, options make a car more pleasant to use. They warm it in the winter, cool it in the summer and make it easier to steer. There is little doubt that a collector car today is more valuable if it has lots of options. The one exception might be the car with too many options. There is a difference between a car that's loaded and one that's overloaded. No one has set down a rule on how many options are too many, but good taste will tell you that.

Although an original old car may come with some options, it wasn't until the 1980s that most cars sold in America came with options bundled on them like computer software packages are sold today. In the early '50s, even very basic equipment like signal lights and rearview mirrors were extra-cost options. Directional lights were mandated for all cars in 1953. In the mid-'60s, safety items like seat belts, headrests and collapsible steering wheels were changed from options to government-required standard equipment. As late as the 1960s, most cars did not have air conditioning. It was largely standardized in the '70s by AMC.

The interior of this '47 Chevrolet owned by Ralph Cornell, of Lodi, Wisconsin, has had many factory options and period-correct aftermarket accessories added to its interior to dress the restored car up for shows.

Collectors often want to add options to their cars when they restore them. This changes the car from its original showroom-new state, but car show judging standards allow the addition of options as long as they were originally available for the year, make and model of car from the factory. As mentioned, an option could cost you points if it's not right for your car. It could also cause point deductions if it is not in good condition, if it doesn't function properly or—in the case of French-style beauty judging—if it detracts from the car's clean styling.

The nicest way to add an option to a collector car is to find a new, never-used NOS option in the factory packaging with the original instructions included. Many car dealers wound up with options on the shelf that never sold and these have trickled down to old-car parts vendors over the years. Today, these once-cheap extras have become relatively pricey items. Most NOS options selling on eBay bring hundreds of dollars and some wind up with prices in the thousands.

While I was wrapping up this book, I ran down to the Kopecky's Klassics restoration shop to shoot a few last-minute photos. Jerry Kopecky had just taken delivery on a 1960 Chrysler parts car from Texas that had a completely intact factory air conditioning system. The plan was to put this option in a 1960 Chrysler 300F convertible he was

This beautiful old factory radio and clock option package seen on the dashboard of Ralph Cornell's 1936 Oldsmobile convertible is a rare sight today. Authentic options like these can add thousands of dollars to a car's value.

restoring. Jerry paid $4,000 for the parts car to get the A/C and was then facing the cost of restoring the whole system to look and work like new. Sometimes adding options to a collector car is not for the weak of wallet, but as Jerry knows, it pays off when it comes time to sell the car today.

With the rising demand and values, some hobby suppliers are rebuilding certain interior options on a subcontractor basis. Dozens of companies rebuild vintage radios and other audio equipment like eight-track tape players. Radios can also be upgraded with AM/FM capabilities. Vendors who operate steering wheel restoration services can redo optional deluxe steering wheels —such as banjo style wheels for 1930s cars—that enhance the inside appearance of cars. Muscle car collectors will pay hundreds for an optional wood-grained steering wheel that other companies restore to look like new. Several outfits remanufacture tachometers, another hot muscle car extra. Seat belts are another popular accessory and a number of suppliers repair these using the old hardware with new webbing. Most motorized options can be repaired by electrical part rebuilders (see list of electrical component restorers in the mechanical section).

Most shops bill for time and materials. The time charge is the shop labor rate times hours. This shop has a sign that jokes about the labor rate, but $50 an hour is low. Materials are the parts and products used for the job.

Chapter 8

Purchasing Parts & Services

The bywords of vintage automobile restoration are time and materials. After you own a car, these are the things you'll need to purchase to get the vehicle done. Time is labor. Materials include parts and supplies. As general contractor, your job is to procure these things at prices within your budget.

When you buy things for your project, you have to take off your yellow general contractor helmet and put on your green-brimmed accountant's eyeshade. You're working in the Purchasing Department now and your job is to find parts sources, compare their prices (as well as quality), place the orders, track the shipments, log in the goods or services, pay the bills and keep all necessary records of the work completed and how much it costs you.

You say that your father and grandfather restored old cars and never kept records, so why should you? The answer is that times have changed. Years ago, hobbyists didn't restore cars to the standards that prevail today. Due to this and other factors, restoration was a much less expensive hobby. Dad and grandpa probably worked on cars as a pastime and then sold them for little or no profit so they could start another project and enjoy more of their hobby. Today, even an at-home restoration can cost what you make in a year. However, the restored car has value and there's an active collector car marketplace. You can take it to an auction, sell

it and turn a good-to-excellent profit. However, if you don't know what you have into a car, how can you figure out what price to ask for it?

For some modern restorers, the expense of a restoration is a cost of doing business. They may be restoring the vehicle to use as a promotional item in their regular business. The car or truck may become part of an advertising campaign for their career. Other collectors restore cars specifically to sell them for a profit. An accountant or tax professional can tell you if this applies to you. If the restoration is a business expense, you need to keep good records of all of the costs involved. Match up those check stubs with the correct invoices and keep them in a safe place. Don't risk taking a deduction without documentation.

Another good reason to keep track of restoration expenses is that the old-car hobby is addictive—and I'm not kidding about this. Americans love cars and easily get swept up in the mystique that surrounds classic cars, trucks and motorcycles. I have seen people come into the hobby and within a year or two, they have as much invested in a show car as they do in their home. Not only do they restore the vehicle—they also buy a trailer to tow it around on and a pickup or Suburban to tow the trailer. Keeping a record of expenses is a good way to stay sober (as far as the car addiction goes) and prevent over-enthusiasm.

Today a restored classic car has value and there's an active collector car marketplace. This '41 Cadillac convertible was taken to the 2008 Atlantic City Classic Car Auction where its owner hoped to sell it for a profit.

In this chapter, I'll lay down some tips that will help you save money and hassles when purchasing old-car parts. Like any good teacher, I have made some of the mistakes (luckily no huge ones) and learned from the experiences I have gone through. There are cheap parts and there are good parts. There is no such thing as cheap, good parts, but there are sometimes ways to shave your costs a bit when buying the best parts out there.

I'll also talk about shop rates and what kind of time investment a good restoration takes. The old adage that time is money applies very strongly to auto restoration. Labor rates at professional restoration shops can cause a lot more sticker shock than the latest showroom prices of new cars. As your own general contractor, you'll want to find the lowest rates for quality work when it comes to setting up the jobs that you subcontract to outside specialists.

A very efficient tool for the classic car restorer of today is the Internet. This window on the world has made it possible for you and I to network with people anywhere in the world who can help us get our car restored. The Internet has made it easier to find old-car parts and it has brought down prices on some parts by increasing seller competition for your dollars. That doesn't mean every part being sold on the Internet is a bargain. The Internet is simply a tool, but if you use it wisely, there are ways it can cut your costs and help you save money.

Finally, this chapter will wind up re-emphasizing why record-keeping is an important part of a well-planned and well-executed restoration. I'll talk about practical ways to record your costs, your progress and your success.

Parts Buying Tips

Being a smart purchaser of old-car parts has two elements to it. First, you have to find the best sources of the parts. Second, you want to try to get them at the best price you can. Of course, the best price isn't necessarily the lowest price, unless you want to try to stop a 4,000-lb. piece of iron with $5 brake shoes.

Here are ten tips on ways to find parts, check quality and get the best price:

1. Always remember that many mechanical parts were not made specifically for one car. The design engineer took the car's size and weight and looked in a book of available parts to spec the best one for the application. Publishers like Hollander put out books that list the different cars a certain part fits. If you can buy a Hollander Interchange Manual or use one at a salvage yard, you'll be able to find all of the cars that used the same part.

2. Modern suppliers have worked out parts interchanges of currently available parts that fit older cars. For instance, www.rockauto.com has extensive applications listed in its online catalog. You can go there, enter the year, make, model and some specifications for your car and you'll find a list of current part numbers that fit your vintage postwar vehicle.

3. When searching for parts on auction sites like eBay, try to think of all the different ways sellers

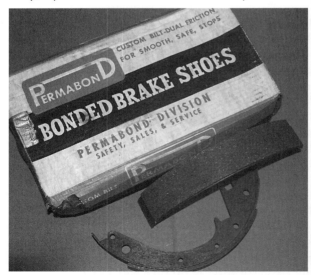

The best parts aren't always the lowest priced ones. Do you want to stop a 4,000-lb. car with $5 brake shoes? These NORS (new old replacement stock) shoes from Northwestern Auto Parts are hefty and American made.

might spell a car's name or describe a part. For example, Camero is a very common misspelling of Camaro. You may find the part you need with no bids if you search under Camero. Along the same lines, different folks use the terms spoiler, wing, and airfoil to describe aerodynamic options that bolt on the edge of the trunk.

4. Parts last for years, but sometimes their part numbers change. I once found some much-needed brake hardware by looking in a 1955 Pontiac Master Parts Catalog and taking the number I found to a modern GM dealer. His computer was able to tell me that the original number had become obsolete, but the same parts were still being manufactured under another part number and were still available at GM dealers and NAPA parts stores.

5. Sometimes parts were slightly redesigned over the years, but the internal components needed to rebuild them remained the same. The Carter WCD two-barrel carburetor was used on Buicks and Pontiacs in the early 1950s and on AMC cars in the 1960s. Though the carburetor linkage was relocated for the AMC application, the carburetor rebuild kit is the same for both.

6. Several years ago I had the opportunity to attend a meeting where a hobby trade group was formed. Approximately 30 of the top restorers and parts suppliers in that particular hobby niche gathered to talk about the quality of reproduction parts. The restoration shop owners were quite outspoken about parts quality issues they had. They were concerned about having to redo engine rebuilds following failures of poor-quality camshafts they had purchased from vendors. Since that time, when planning any major repairs, I use the Internet to query people in clubs and newsgroups I belong to about the best parts to use. About 90 percent will tell you something you already know or try to sell you something, but you'll also get a little great advice.

7. When buying thousands of dollars worth of parts for a restoration, deal with suppliers who know the car you're working on and treat you like more than a number. When Vince Sauberlich and I rebuilt the engine in my MG Magnette, Cecelia Bruce at Scarborough Faire (a British parts supplier) helped us get the right parts for a rare car. She gave us personal attention, quality parts and free advice. Cecelia researched what we needed, made a complete list of every component, put it together as a kit and gave us a dealer price discount, too!

8. You would think that hobbyists drive their cars in spring and summer and work on them in winter, but most do not. This forces suppliers to borrow money in the winter to keep the business humming. Some parts vendors use lower seasonal pricing or midwinter sales to boost sales during the off season.

9. Most collectors consider properly rebuilt original parts to be better than reproduction parts. Rebuilt antique car parts aren't necessarily cheaper than reproductions, but they have the advantages of being all-American-made and usually have matching numbers that count when a car is judged at a show.

10. Shipping parts has gotten very expensive, so buying parts at a swap meet can save you a lot of money. Some vendors also give show discounts. In addition, a number of companies like Al Knoch Corvette Interiors and the Bumper Boyz (chrome plating) have car show delivery programs. Vendors, like Coker Tire, will bring goods to shows if you make arrangements in advance.

Shop Rates and Time Investment

Modern, fully computerized restoration shops are very sophisticated about keeping track of the hours expended on a restoration project. Each restorer has a shop rate, which is the amount you pay for each man-hour that shop employees work on your car. The shop rate may be $50, but if three employees are working on the vehicle, the charge is $150 for that hour. When the restoration bill is totaled up, it's simple arithmetic:

Shop rate x man-hours + materials + tax = Final Cost.

In the December 2008 issue of *Sports Car Market*, Colin Comer—a reputable muscle car expert from Milwaukee, Wisconsin—wrote an outstanding article called "Restoration 101." He estimated the time needed to do a top-notch restoration at 600 hours minimum for body and paint, 300 hours for chassis, 80 hours for an interior kit install, 40 hours for an engine compartment and 100 hours for final assembly and detailing. His materials cost estimate was $30,000. According to Colin, with a $75 shop rate, that puts the cost at about $130,000!

The $75 an hour shop rate is by no means uniform. In 2001, I attended a meeting where about two dozen shop owners from across the country were asked to raise their hands when their

A computer kept in a home restoration shop can help keep track of the work that you do on your car.

shop rate was called out. That was seven years ago and the number of hands up at $90 an hour took the cake. However, there were still quite a few charging $50 an hour, which is the rate I hear mentioned most when I visit shops where I live in central Wisconsin.

If you're general contractor on your own restoration, you'll want to find as many subcontractors as you can in the $50 an hour range. If the restoration is going to require an investment of 1,120 hours, you could theoretically save $28,000 by carefully selecting subcontractors with the friendliest shop rates.

In the real world, there are going to be a few rebuilders who are the only known source of a particular service and you may have to pay them more. For example, I once located a man in Dayton, Ohio, who was supposedly the only person

who knew how to rebuild MG T-Series vacuum turn signal switches. The cost was $75 an hour and there was no getting around it. However, his rebuilt switches were better than reproduction switches that sold for $150 back then.

Another factor you have to consider is that even a general contractor restoration will require you to do a little of the work yourself or farm it out locally. For example, chassis cleanup, parts washing, technical research, shipping and receiving, record keeping, parts chasing and computer entry are steps that you'll deal with at home. However, a restoration shop might charge you for this time.

I have a friend who maintains a personal 140-car collection and he has a lot of these chores done by local high school students who work on his cars on weekends. He enjoys teaching them about how to work on old cars and he pays them, but he does not pay them as much as a commercial shop would charge. With all things considered, if you do a good job as general contractor, you can probably get that $130,000 restoration whittled down to $90,000 just by managing the shop rate x man-hours part of the pricing structure. Then, if you do a good job shopping for parts and materials, you can easily slice another $10,000 off your cost. That gives you a $130,000 restoration for $80,000.

Of course, that is still way too high for the average hobbyist like you and I, but the thing you have to remember is that we are not shooting for a $130,000 restoration in the first place. I have judged Colin Comer's muscle cars against some very nice owner-restored muscle cars at The Masterpiece of Style & Speed show in Milwaukee

Cleaning chassis parts, like brake drums and steering boxes (right photo) is a task most home restorers can do to save money. Other tasks in this category are washing, research, shipping and receiving, record keeping, parts chasing and computer entry.

and it's obvious that they are restored to concours-winning standards that easily add a certain percentage to the restoration bill. You and I are more likely to stop at the almost-as-nice stage, save some money, and wind up with a total cost of $25,000–$50,000 for a very nice car.

One tool I have recently added to my shop is an old computer. Due to a recent upgrade to DSL Internet service, I had to get a newer computer with high-speed Internet capabilities. I put the one I bought in 2000 in the garage. It works well, except for no longer having an Internet connection. I use it to keep track of the work that I do on my vehicles, print out service sheets, scan pages from shop manuals (better to get greasy fingerprints on a copy) and record my expenses. I also plan to inventory my parts, tools and manuals for insurance purposes.

Using the Internet to Save Money

A few years ago, a member of the Fox Cities British Car Club in Oshkosh, Wisconsin, wanted to give his dad a special Father's Day gift. His father had purchased an MG TD roadster years ago and for years he dreamed about restoring it. Raising kids and paying bills prevented him from achieving that goal, but eventually his kids got the idea to sneak the car out of the garage and surprise him by restoring it. They ordered the parts they needed from one of the catalogers who sell British parts, got the complete job done and surprised him on Father's Day with the restored MG.

This was a great project and a terrific story, but my friend has since admitted that the project would have been a lot cheaper to do if eBay had existed when they started it. People are selling exactly the same parts that we bought at full retail for about 20 percent less through the online auctions.

To a large degree, online auctions aren't true auctions where the part goes to the highest bidder. Sellers on eBay can place a minimum or reserve price on their item, they can add in a set buy-it-now price that a bidder can pay to end the auction immediately, they can sell for a set price through an eBay store offering or now they can even sell on a make-me-an-offer basis. There are also websites like Craigslist (www.craigslist.org), that are short, free classified ads.

With so many ways to make transactions online, prices on old-car parts sold via the Internet tend to go all over the ballpark. People who clean out their garages and find an old part they never installed may try to sell it for a few bucks on Craigslist with a free listing. They may also choose to offer it in an eBay auction. In this case, they will have to pay fees

Some parts that are rare and desirable—like this 1957 Chevrolet Rochester fuel-injection unit—may be offered in an eBay auction.

and commissions, so the part will typically cost you more. If a commercial vendor has an identical part, he may list it for sale in his eBay store. Items in such listings typically have higher starting prices than auction items. Some parts that are rare and desirable may be sold in an eBay auction, draw lots of bids, and wind up bringing thousands of dollars.

I have personally done lots of parts shopping on eBay. In some cases, I got tremendously low prices on very nice parts. In other instances, I paid the same price a part would have sold for at a swap meet, but it was easier to find the part online and I did not have to burn up $50 in gas getting to the swap meet. I have also wasted money on parts that were totally—and I'm sure inadvertently—wrongly described by sellers who took a guess at what they had found.

Like most auctions, the online variety requires the buyer to be aware of problems like overenthusiasm and outright fraud. Don't get too excited when bidding and watch out for swindles. If the auction site has a feedback system, pay attention to the ratings that other buyers have given the seller. Make sure the parts you are bidding for are correct for your car and fit your car.

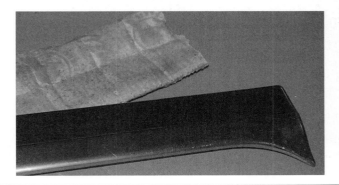

NOS (new old stock) means the same thing as OEM, but NORS means the part is an aftermarket replacement from the old days. This is a valuable NOS fender skirt molding for a '53 Pontiac. It is in the original factory wrapper.

Be aware of the differences in appearance and quality between OEM (original equipment manufacturer) parts and NORS (new old replacement stock) parts. Do not confuse NOS (new old stock) with NORS. NOS means the same thing as OEM, but NORS means the part is an aftermarket replacement from the old days. Also keep in mind that NORS is not the same as reproduction. An NORS part is an American-made replacement and a reproduction is a modern replica that might come from the United States or from another nation. NORS and reproduction parts come in varying qualities—not all good and not all bad.

You can find good buys on parts online without going the auction route. Just go to a search engine like Yahoo! or Google and type in some search words like 1953 Chevrolet starter or starter for 1953 Chevrolet. This will take you to a list of Websites that may lead you to the part you need. Some will take you to eBay and some will take you to general auto parts sellers who really don't carry obsolete parts. However, if you check out the source listings (or hits) you'll eventually get to companies like Fondy Auto Electric or www.rockauto.com that can really help you. In fact, when you search for a part at www.rockauto.com you'll see a chart comparing their prices to those of other suppliers. Their prices will usually be lowest, but don't forget to factor in the shipping cost of that item. Rock auto doesn't maintain a parts inventory. It brokers parts for manufacturers and the shipping charges will be calculated from the manufacturer's location.

Record Keeping Counts

You are not going to know if you're a good general contractor unless you keep track of what you do and how much you spend for your restoration project. The easiest way to keep track of

what you do on a car is to take digital pictures as the work moves along. You can set the camera to mark the date and time on each photo so that you know the exact sequence of the work. You will also want a notebook nearby to jot down little details that the camera doesn't quite capture, such as which direction a nut spins in (in rare cases, you'll find a reverse nut).

At the end of your session in the shop or garage, you can review the photos and jot down a description of what you did that day. If you do set up a computer or laptop in the shop, you can immediately enter your daily progress. In addition to the work you did, these entries should include a list of parts and supplies you will need for your next session of working on the vehicle. It may be a good idea to also jot down any expenses that you incurred that day, particularly any small expenses that you did not get receipts or invoices for.

Once a week or so, you can total up all your expenses and enter them in a ledger or a similar computer program to keep a permanent record of what you spend on the restoration of your vehicle. One well-organized collector I visited lately maintains a complete file on every car in his collection. Here are some of the interesting things he has in each file:

• Documents related to his purchase of the vehicle, including any paperwork that he received from the previous owner.
• A copy of the original dealer invoice available for many postwar collector cars from Triple A Enterprtises.
• A photo CD of the restoration and all invoices associated with restoring the car.
• Copies of articles about his car or similar cars and copies of pages from books about his car.
• Title, registration and insurance documents.
• Copies of pages from *Old Cars Price Guide* that give ballpark values for his car.
• A spare set of keys for the car (just in case the regular keys get lost).
• An original owner's manual for the car.
• When available, the original Protect-O-Plate (GM) and other dealership paraphernalia that new owners received when buying a car.
• A CD with images that photographically document the car's condition, in case he has to show his insurer what it looks like or file a damage claim.

Keeping good records is just one of the steps to a successful restoration. But don't ever lose sight of your main goal, and that is to have fun!

SOURCES

Body & Exterior Trim

A & A Plating (chrome)
9400 E. Wilson Rd.
Independence, MO 64053
800-747-9914
www.aaplating.com

Advanced Plating & Powder Coating
(bumper restoration)
1425 Cowan Ct.
Nashville, TN 37207
800-588-6686
www.advancedplating.com

Allan Heywood Enamels
(cloisonné emblem restoration)
5 Montgomery St.
Skipton, 3361 Australia
+61 (0) 353402265
www.heywoodenamels.com

All-Brite Metal (chrome plating)
2148 E. Tucker St.
Philadelphia, PA 19125
215-423-2234 or 267-872-0935

Allied Technical Services
(pot metal trim repair)
6239 Airport Way
Seattle, WA 98108
206-763-3346

Auto Hardware Specialties
(GM body hardware)
3123 McKinley Ave.
Sheldon, IA 51201

Bennett Coachworks LLC
(metal fabrication)
1500 North 4th St.
Milwaukee, WI 53212
414-298-2068
www.hotrodbuilders.com

Bill Oldenberg
4426 N. Sullivan La.
Galena, IL 61036
815-777-9204

Bolt Locker
(powder coating)
Eau Claire, WI

Bud Ward's Antique Cars
13001 Interstate 30
Little Rock, AR 72209
888-6860-9664
www.budwardsantiquecars.com

California Polishing
(stainless steel restoration)
714-931-6131
www.californiapolishing.com

Carey Classic Metals
(stainless steel restoration)
3 Fallen Arrow Dr.
Hilton Head Island, SC 29926
908-209-6340
tlcarey@roadrunner.com

Charger Metal Works (chrome)
215-289-9227

Chrome Company, Inc.
630-543-5252

Classics Plus Ltd.
(stainless steel restoration)
601 Lakeshore Dr.
N. Fond du Lac, WI 54937
888-923-1007
www.classicsplusltd.com

Cliff's Classic Chevrolet Parts
(mirror resilvering)
619 SE 202nd Ave.
Portland, OR 97233
503-667-4329

Custom Plating (bumper restoration)
3030 Alta Ridge Way
Snellville, GA 30078
770-736-1118

Custom Plating Specialists
(chrome plating)
W 797 County Road K
Brillion, WI 54110
920-756-3284
www.customplatingspecialist.com

Dan's Classics, Inc.
(stainless steel restoration)
13676 Serena Dr.
Largo, FL 33774
727-595-7997
dneumann@tampabay.rr.com

Detail Plating (chrome)
2496 N. Zediker
Sanger, CA 93657
559-875-0290
www.detailplating.com

Emblemagic
PO Box 420
Grand River, OH 44045-0420
440-209-0792
www.emblemagic.com

The Finishing Touch, Inc.
(chrome plating)
5580 Northwest Highway
Chicago, IL 60630
800-403-4545
www.thefinishingtouchinc.com

Fixit Rubber Parts (rubber restoration)
W6903 Kenyon Rd.
Oakfield, WI 53065
866-654-4480
www.fixitrubber.com

Fond Du Lac Bumper Exchange
1285 Morris St.
Fond du Lac, WI 54935
800-236-2570
www.fdlbumper.com

Frank Laiacano Jr.
(custom fabricated body panels)
29120 Badet St.
Westland, MI 48185
734-522-0797 or 734-425-9302
classicparts4U@aol.com

Glassworks, The Hardtop Shop
113 McGovern Blvd.
Crescent, PA 15046
724-457-0680
www.thehardtopshop.com

Graves Plating (chrome)
4230 Chisholm Rd.
Florence, AL 35630
256-764-9487
www.gravesplating.com

Hamilton Classics (metal fabrication)
W04271 Ledge Rd.
Fond du Lac, WI 54937
920-924-9000

Hanlon Plating Co. (chrome)
925 East 4th St.
Richmond, VA 23224
804-233-2021
www.hanlonplating.com

House of Powder (powder coating)
100 S. 1st St. & Route 71
Standard, IL 61363
815-339-2648

Iverson Automotive
(stainless steel restoration)
14704 Karyl Dr.
Minnetonka, MN 55345
800-325-0480
www.iversonautomotive.com

J & P Custom Plating, Inc. (chrome)
807 N. Meridian St.
PO Box 16
Portland, IN 47371
260-726-9696
www.jpcustomplating.com

Jewel's Body Shop, Inc.
(1950s T-bird/Ford reproduction parts)
W 797 County Road K
Brillion, WI 54110
920-756-2549
jam55tbird@aol.com

L & L Antique Auto Trim
(custom running board moldings)
403 Spruce St.
PO Box 177
Pierce City, MO 65723
417-476-2871
blandoll@hotmail.com

Lakeside Custom Plating, Inc.
(chrome)
373 Commerce St.
Conneaut, OH 44030
440-599-2035
www.customchromerestoration.com

M+M Custom Finishing
(wood grain & carbon weave finishes)
9318 Corneils Rd.
Bristol, IL 60512
630-553-3143
www.mmcustomfinishing.com

MCB Performance Center
(stainless steel restoration)
14500 Foley Rd.
Capac, MI 48014
810-543-0088
www.tuffwheelrestoration.com

N.E.L. Metal Restorations
2127-35 Margaret St.
Philadelphia, PA 19124
215-289-4944
www.precisionchrome.com

North Star Bumper Exchange
5085 Wren Drive
Appleton, WI 54913-7606
920-731-3030

Nu-Chrome
161 Graham Road
Fall River, MA 02720
800-422-8012
www.nu-chrome.com

Paul's Chrome Plating, Inc.
90 Pattison St.
Evans City, PA 16033
800-245-8679
www.paulschrome.com

Pot Metal Restorations
4794-C Woodland Circle
Tallahassee, FL 32303
850-562-3847
www.customcoatings.net

Professional Plating, Inc.
705 Northway Dr.
Brillion, WI 54110
920-756-2153
www.proplating.com

Quality Pot Metal Works
2810 Parkway St. #5
Lakeland, FL 33811
863-640-0079
www.chromeplus.com

Realistic Auto Restorations
(stainless steel trim restoration)
2519 6th Ave. S.
St. Petersburg, FL 33712
727-327-5162
www.realisticrestorations.com

The Reflected Image
(mirror resilvering)
21 Westwind Dr.
Northford, CT 06472
203-484-0760

Resto-Trim (stainless steel restoration)
250 Akron St.
Lindenhurst, NY 11757
631-226-7982
www.eastcoastrestorations.com

Restoration Specialties & Supply, Inc.
(body hardware)
PO Box 328
Windber, PA 15963
814-467-9842
www.restorationspecialties.com

Restoration Supply Co.
(body hardware)
15182-B Highland Valley Road
Escondido, CA 92025
800-306-7008
www.restorationstuff.com

Ron's Corner (mirror resilvering)
27169 State Hwy 6
Winston, MO 64689
660-749-5473

Rowland Hall (hood hinge restoration)
1901 Jackson St.
Burbank, CA 91504
818-845-3574

SMS Auto Restoration Services
(hood hinge rebuilding)
42 Manchester Rd.
Derry, NH 03038
800-989-6660
www.sms-auto.com

Speed & Sport Chrome Plating
404 Broadway St.
Houston, TX 77012
713-921-0235

Spence Industries, Inc. (powder
coating)
1505 Cornell Rd.
Green Bay, WI 54313
920-662-0720
www.spencepowdercoating.com

T & M Plating Service (chrome)
N3503 Highway 55
Chilton, WI 53014
920-439-2099

Thompson Hill Metalcraft (panel beating and metal parts fabrication)
21 Thompson Hill Rd.
Berwick, ME 03901
207-698-1800
www.thompsonhill.com

Tri-City Plating Co. (chrome)
218 E. Mill St.
Elizabethton, TN 37643
800-251-7536
www.tricityplating.com

Turners
(stainless straightened and buffed)
4388 S. Willow
Fresno, CA 93725
559-237-0892

Vickerman's Chrome (chrome)
211 South McKinley Street
South Beloit, IL
815-389-4700
www.vickermanschrome.com

Vintage Vehicles Co.
(stainless steel restoration)
N-1940 20th Dr.
Wautoma, WI 54982
920-787-2656
www.vintagevehicles.net

Vintage Woodworks
(exterior automotive wood; trimming)
315 Depot Street
Iola, WI 54945
(715) 445-3791

Woodgrain Specialists
1480 White Hall Rd.
Littlestown, PA 17340
717-359-4597
woodgrainingpros@earthlink.net

Brakes

Antigo Auto Parts (reline service)
1025 Fifth Ave.
PO Box 140
Antigo, WI 54409
800-472-0089

Automotive Friction (relining service)
20251 SE Highway 212
Damascus, OR 97089
800-545-9088
www.autofriction.com

Brake & Equipment Warehouse
(sleeving and rebuilding)
455 Harrison St N.E.
Minneapolis, MN 55413
800-233-4053

Brake Boosters
2496 N. Zediker
Sanger, CA 93657
559-875-0290
www.brakeboosters.com

Brake Tech Solutions
10806 Reames Road
Charlotte, NC 28269
704-509-9210
www.braketechsolutions.com

Classic Tube
80 Rotech Drive
Lancaster, NY 14086
800-882-3711
www.classictube.com

Inline Tube (brake and fuel lines)
15066 Technology Drive
Shelby Township, MI 48315
800-385-9452
www.inlinetube.com

Power Brake Exchange
(power brake booster rebuilding)
260 Phelan Ave.
San Jose, CA 95112
800-322-1775

Power Brake X-Change, Inc.
(power brake booster rebuilding)
336 Lamont Pl.
Pittsburgh, PA 15232-2006
800-580-5729
www.powerbrakex-change.com

Sierra Specialty Automotive
(brake/clutch relining services)
3494 Chandler Road
Quincy, CA 95971
800-4-BRASS-1
www.brakecylinder.com

Stainless Steel Brakes Corp.
(stainless steel rotors)
11470 Main St.
Clarence, NY 14031
800-448-7722
www.ssbrakes.com

White Post Restorations
(sleeving and rebuilding)
One Old Car Dr.
White Post, VA 22663
540-837-1140
www.whitepost.com

Convertible Tops

Auto Tops, Inc. (convertible top kits)
320 Howell St.
Bristol, PA 19007
800-937-2947
www.autotopsinc.com

Convertible Service
(convertible top parts)
5126-D Walnut Grove Ave.
San Gabriel, CA 91776
800-333-1140
www.convertibleparts.com

Convertible Top Specialists
(convertible tops & accessories)
1760 N. U.S. Highway 41
Inverness, FL 34450
800-272-2394
www.topsdown.com

Electron Top Manufacturing Co.
(convertible top kits)
126-15 89th Ave.
Richmond Hill, NY 11418
7148-846-7400
600-221-4476
www.electrontop.com

Haartz Corp. (maker of Hartz cloth)
87 Hayward Rd.
Acton, MA 01720
978-264-2654
www.haartz.com

Hydro-E-Lectric
5530 Independence Ct.
Punta Gorda, FL 33982
800-343-4261
www.hydroe.com

Kee Auto Top (convertible top kits)
800-438-5934
www.keeautotop.com

Prestige Autotrim Products
(British car convertible tops)
Oak Tree Place
Rock Ferry, Birkenhead CH42 1NS
United Kingdom
800-659-2649
www.prestigeautotops.com

Robbins Auto Top Company
(convertible top kits)
321 Todd St.
Oxnard, CA 93030
805-604-3200
www.robbinsautotop.com

Scarborough Faire (MGA trim)
1151 Main St.
Pawtucket, RI 02860
401-724-4200
MGAParts@aol.com

SMS Auto Fabrics (upholstery fabrics)
350 South Redwood St.
Canby, OR 97013
503-263-3535
www.smsautofabrics.com

Spinneybeck Leather
(Rolls-Royce trim)
800-482-7777
www.spinneybeck.com

Victoria British Ltd.
(British car interior kits)
PO Box 14991
Lenexa, KS 66285-4991
800-255-0088
www.victoriabritish.com

XKs UNLIMITED (Jaguar soft trim)
850 Fiero Lane
San Luis Obispo, CA 93401
800-444-5247
www.xks.com

Cooling

Al's Radiator & Auto Repair Inc.
502 W Wolf River Ave.
New London, WI 54961
800-954-2188

Arthur Gould Rebuilders
(water pump rebuilding)
5R Main St.
Kings Park, NY 11754
631-269-0093

Bill's Antique Radiator Restorations
(radiator restoration)
1134 Walnut St.
Chillicothe, IL 61523
309-645-0606
www.billsantiqueradiators.webserveplus.com

Classic Heaters (heater cores recored)
566 Fulton St.
Farmingdale, NY 11735
516-293-2175
www.classicheaters.com

Classic Radiator (radiator rebuilding)
Long Island, NY
516-293-2175
www.classicradiator.com

Elizabeth Radiator
(radiator and fuel tank repair)
1550 Hayden Blvd.
Elizabeth, PA 15037
412-384-5340

Four Seasons Radiator Service, Inc.
(radiator restoration)
Madison Heights, MI
248-585-6484
www.fourseasonsradiator.net

Howard Stewart Restorations
(water pump rebuilding)
North Carolina
336-476-9834
www.howardstewartrestorations.com

Joe Hudacek
715-392-6169
hudacekjj@chartermi.net

Mike Gadaleto (heater control valves)
New Jersey
856-753-6788

O & G Water Pump Co.
4402 Ave A
Lubbock, TX 79404
800-365-1981
ogwaterpump@nts-online.net

Powell Radiator Service
1277 W. Main St.
Box 427
Wilmington, OH 45177
800-448-7722

R & R Radiator (heater cores recored)
1418 Tower St.
Superior, WI 54880
715-392-2099

Revcore Radiator
(radiator, gas tank, heater restoration)
Woodstock, IL
815-337-6858
revcore@mc.net

Water Pump Specialist
(water pump rebuilding)
10005 North Country Road 2750
Lubbock, TX 79401
806-746-5310
www.powersteeringparts.com

Dashes, Consoles and Trunks

American Classic Restorations
(dash and console restoration)
680 Douglas St.
Uxbridge, MA 01569
508-278-0020
www.american-classic.com

Dashboard Restorations
Brush Prairie, WA
360-892-4075
sales@dashboardrestorations.com

Dash Specialists
(dashes rebuilt & recovered)
1910 Redbud Lane
Medford, OR 97504
541-776-004

JC Auto Restoration
(Chrysler dash restoration)
20815 52nd Ave. W
Lynnwood, WA 98036
425-672-8324
www.jcauto.com

Just Dashes (dash covers)
5941 Lemona Ave.
Van Nuys, CA 91411
800-247-3274
www.justdashes.com

Performance Restorations
(dash bezels restored)
Texas
817-433-0001 or 817-431-1888
www.newdash.com

Phoenix Restoration
(gauge face restoration)
2418 Wilkes Ave.
Davenport, IA
563-326-5744

Tomco Tops (convertible tops)
202 Kefauver Dr.
Madisonville, TN 37354
423-420-9071
www.tomcotops.4t.com

Ultimate Rides (dash pads)
11540 Gateway East
El Paso, TX 79927
877-DASH-PAD

Electrical

Ace Alternator (starter and alternator
rebuilding)
Wichita, KS
239-821-6548 or 316-529-8854
www.acewichita.com
gcheancy@aol.com

Advanced Distributors (British cars)
1149 Quincy Street
Shakopee, MN 55379
612-804 5543
www.advanceddistributors.com

American Autowire (vintage wiring)
150 Heller Pl. #17
Bellmawr, NJ 08031
800-482-WIRE
www.americanautowire.com

Bob Soucy Performance Automotive
Ignition (distributor rebuilding)
Tennessee
800-556-1365

British Car Part Restoration
(SU electric fuel pump rebuilding)
E. Lawrie Rhoads
7 Knollwood Rd.
Medfield, MA 02052
508-359-2077
info@british-car-part-restoration.com

Burton L. Norton
(distributor rebuilding)
0-1845 West Leonard
Grand Rapids, MI 49534
616-677-1208
burtonlnorton@yahoo.com

Fondy Auto Electric (electrical part
rebuilding)
765 Sullivan Drive
Fond du Lac, WI 54935
800-236-2701
www.fondyautoelectric.com

Harnesses Unlimited (wiring harnesses)
Box 435
Wayne, PA 19087
www.harnessesunlimited.com

Jack Marcheski (rebuilt gas tank
senders)
100 Dry Creek
Hollister, CA 95023
831-637-3453

Philbin Rebuilt Products (distributor
rebuilding; electric motor rebuilding)
28 N. Russell St.
Portland, OR 97227
503-287-1718
www.philbingroup.com

Precision Power, Inc. (starter and
generator rebuilding)
630 Park Pl.
Lansing, MI 48912
800-794-5962
www.precision-pwr.com

Rhode Island Wiring Service, Inc.
(wiring harnesses)
Box 434H
West Kingston, RI 02892
401-789-1955
www.riwire.com

Wilton Auto Electric LLC
(British car electrical restoration)
10 Stoney Brook Dr.
Wilton, NH 03086-5151
603-654-9852
wiltonae@comcast.net

YnZ's Yesterdays Parts
(wiring harnesses)
333 E. Stuart Ave. Unit A
Redlands, CA 92374
909-798-1498
www.ynzyesterdaysparts.com

Engine, Transmission and Differential

A & C Casting Rebuilders
(casting repairs)
3560 Big Valley Rd.
Kelseyville, CA 95451
866-935-3227
www.accastingrebuilders.com

Advanced Engine Rebuilding
(engine rebuilding)
176 Main St.
Wareham, MA 02571
508-295-2288
www.enginesbyadvanced.com

Alan Taylor Company
(French Cotal transmission rebuilding)
1220 Industrial Ave.
Escondido, CA
760-489-0657
www.alantaylorcompany.com

The Babbitt Pot (babbitting)
1693 State Rt. 14
Fort Edward, NY 12828
518-747-4277

Benchwick Carburetor, Inc.
(carburetor rebuilding)
2747 Glenwood Ave.
Youngstown, OH 44511
330-782-3767
www.ohiocarb.com

Casting Salvage Technologies
(casting repairs)
Virginia
800-833-8814

CCS (carburetor rebuilding)
1020-A Princess St.
Wilmington, NC 28401
800-792-2077

Classic Carburetors
(carburetor rebuilding)
3116 East Shea Blvd.
Phoenix, AZ 85028
602-971-3300

Dale Manufacturing
(harmonic balancer rebuilding)
3425 Fairhaven Ave. NE
Salem, OR 97301
503-364-8685
www.dalemfg.com

Damper Doctor
(harmonic balancer rebuilding)
1055 Parkview Ave.
Redding, CA 96001
530-246-2984
www.damperdoctor.com

Daytona Cams
(cam grinding)
Florida
800-505-2267
www.camshafts.com

Daytona Parts Co.
(carburetor rebuilding)
1191 Turnbull Bay Rd.
New Symrna Beach, FL 32168
386-427-7108
www.daytonaparts.com

Delta Camshaft (cam grinding)
19838 Tacoma Ave.
Tacoma, WA 98402
800-562-5500
www.deltacam.com

Diesel Machine Service, Inc.
9795 Lincoln St.
Amherst, WI 54406
800-236-3674

Effingham Regrinding, Inc.
(rebabbitting)
Effingham, IL
217-342-4186

Egge Machine Company
(engine rebuilding)
11707 Slauson Avenue
Santa Fe Springs, CA 90670
866-534-EGGE
www.egge.com

Engines by Schmitts
554 E. Butler Ave.
Doylestown, PA 18901
215-348-4747

Fort Wayne Clutch (clutch rebuilding)
Ft. Wayne, IN
800-CLUTCHES
www.fortwayneclutch.com

Harkin Machine Shop
(rebabbitting/rebuilding)
903 43rd Street N.E.
Watertown, SD 57201
605-886-7880

Hedworth Carburetors
(custom rebuilding)
707 S. Missouri St.
Macon, MO 63552
660-385-2536

J & A Engines/Machine
(engines and water pump rebuilding)
Washington
888-334-5811
j_aengines@yahoo.com
918-333-3444

J & M Machine (engine rebuilding)
40 Mt. Vickery Rd.
Southborough, MA 01772
508-460-0733
www.jandm-machine.com

Jim Taylor
(SU carburetor/fuel pump rebuilding)
1222 Harned Dr.
Bartlesville, OK 74006

Joe Curto, Inc.
(SU carburetor specialist)
22-09 126th St.
College Point, NY 11356
718-762-SUSU
www.joecurto.com

Jon W. Gateman & Son
(casting repairs)
PO Box 413
Beatty, NV 89003
775-764-0976

Kar-Go Carburetors, Inc.
(carburetor rebuilding)
30952 Ford Road
Garden City, MI 48135
734-425-4590

Larry Isgro (carburetor rebuilding)
1604 Argyle Rd
Wantaugh, NY 11795
516-783-1041

Lawson Carburetor
(carburetor rebuilding)
1109 N. Dort Hwy
Flint, MI 48506
810-232-5881

Marx Parts (head gaskets, ignition)
7323 County Trunk N
Arpin, WI 54410
715-652-2405
www.marxparts.com

Ohio Pattern Co. (casting repairs)
614-875-9599

Precision Carburetor
(carburetor rebuilding)
287A Skidmores Rd.
Deer Park, NY 11729
631-667-3854
prpcarb@optonline.net

Promar Precision Engine Rebuilders, Inc.
(engine rebuilding)
10 Peach St.
Paterson, NJ 07503
800-422-6022
www.promarengine.com

Rick's Carburetor Repair
135 Blissville Rd.
PO Box 46
Hydeville, VT 06750
802-265-3006
robinric@sover.net

Southland Clutch
San Diego, CA
800-310-2588
www.southlandclutch.com

Surge Clutch and Driveline
(clutches and drive shafts rebuilt)
South Holland, IL
708-331-1352
surgecdi@aol.com

Terrill Machine, Inc. (fuel pump
rebuilding)
1000 CR 454
DeLeon, TX 76444
254-893-2610

Van Hook Vintage, LLC
(SU and Weber carburetor rebuilding)
Upper Black Eddy, PA
215-262-8547
www.vanhookvintage.com

Vintage Engine Machine Works
(engine rebuilding)
5959 N. Government Way
Coeur d'Alene, ID 83815
208-651-1161

West Amity Machine Shop
(engine rebuilding)
61 Toledo St.
Farmingdale, NY 11735
631-845-4604
www.westamitymachine.com

Wyoming Carburetor Technology
(carburetor rebuilding)
307-672-7512
www.wyocarb.com

Glass

American Restorations Unlimited TA
PO Box 34
Rochelle Park, NJ 07662
201-843-3567
www.american-restorations.com

Auto City Classic (cut-to-pattern glass)
800-828-2212
Heritage Auto Glass, Inc.
623-533-6918
www.heritageautoglass.com

Auto Glass Specialists
302 South Park Pl.
Madison, WI 53715
(608) 829-1900

Old Car Lenses
(headlight, taillight and cowl light
lenses)
802-362-1808
www.oldcarlenses.com

PPG AutoGlass Vintage Group
(vintage glass)
877-855-8100
vintageglass@ppg.com

Pilkington Classics
(reproduction curved glass)
4458 Alum Creek Drive (Ste C)
Columbus, OH 43207
800-848-1351
www.pilkington.com

Ragtops & Roadsters
(British sports car windshields)
203 South Fourth St.
Perkasie, PA 18944
215-257-1202
www.ragtops.com

Sanders Reproduction Glass
(Ford glass)
Vancouver, WA
360-883-4884
www.sandersreproglass.com

Vintage Glass USA (cut-to-pattern
glass)
Connecticut
860-872-0018
800-889-3826

Lights

Chicago Corvette
7322 S. Archer Road
Justice, IL 60458
708-458-2500

Classic Autopart Reproduction Service
(brass headlights)
789 Furlong Road
Sebastopol, CA 95472
707-824-0657
www.brassauto.com

Corvette Clocks by Roger
(headlight motor restoration)
24 Leisure Lane
Jackson, TN 39305
800-752-3421
www.corvetteclocks.com

Corvette Specialties of Maryland
(headlight motor restoration)
1912 Liberty Road
Eldersburg, MD 21784
410-795-3180
www.corvettespecialtiesofMD.com

D & M Restoration
(headlight motor restoration)
46 Grand Ave.
Greenville, SC 29607
800-722-0854
www.dandmrestoration.com

Donald Axlerod (headlight lenses)
35 Timson St.
Lynn, MA 01902
781-598-0523
hdlthqtrs@aol.com

Steve's Auto Restorations, Inc.
(headlight resilvering and parts)
4440 S.E. 174th Ave.
Portland, OR 97236
503-665-2222
www.stevesautorestorations.com

Vintage Headlamp Restoration
International Ltd.
Limestone Cottage Lane
Wadsley Bridge
Sheffield S6 1NJ
England
www.vintage-headlamp-restoration.co.uk

Little Things

American Classic Restorations
(clock repairs and quartz conversions)
680 Douglas St.
Uxbridge, MA 01569
508-278-0020
www.american-classic.com

Bob's Speedometer
(cables and casings and clocks)
10123 Bergin Road
Howell, MI 48843
800-592-9673
www.bobsspeedometer.com

Clockworks
(clock repairs and quartz conversions)
1745 Meta Lake Rd.
Eagle River, WI 54521
800-393-3040
www.clockwks.com

Convertible Service
(relays and switches)
800-333-1140
www.convertibleparts.com

Convertible Top Specialists
(reconditioned top pumps)
1760 N. U.S. Hwy 41
Inverness, FL 34450
800-272-2394
www.topsdown.com

David Lindquist
(clock repairs and quartz conversions)
12427 E. Penn St.
Whittier, CA 90602
562-698-4445
www.autoclock.com

Hydro-E-Lectric
(reconditioned convertible top cylinders)
5530 Independence Ct.
Punta Gorda, FL 33982
800-343-4261
www.hydroe.com

Instrument Services, Inc. (clock and
gauge rebuilding)
11765 Main St.
Roscoe, IL 61073
800-558-2674
www.clocksandgauges.com

Instrument Specialists
14 Church St.
Oxford, MA 01540
508-932-3349
www.instrument-specialties.com

Key Men
Monroe, NY 10950
www.key-men.com

Nisonger Instruments
(Smiths and Jaeger instruments)
225 Hoyt Ave.
Mamaroneck, NY 10543
914-381-3600
www.nisongerinstruments.com

Palo Alto Speedometer
(clock repairs and quartz conversions)
718 Emerson St.
Palo Alto, CA 94301-2410
650-323-0127
www.paspeedo.com

R S Gauge Works (rebuilding gauges)
Phoenix, AZ
602-978-1746
www.rsgaugeworks.com

Vintage Lock
(lock service and key making)
144 S. Main St.
Cambridge, MN 55008
763-689-0877
Vintagelock@msn.com

Williamson's Instruments
(clock repair and quartz conversion)
2018 E. Front Ave.
Chester, AR 72934
479-369-2551
www.williamsons.com

Optional Equipment

Andover Restraints (rebuilt seat belts)
Andover, MD
410-381-6700
www.andoverrestraints.com

Cadillac King
(rebuilt seat belts and computers)
9840 San Fernando Rd.
Pacoima, CA 91311
818-890-0624
www.cadillacking.com

Classic Auto Radios & Clocks
(radio restoration)
7908 Gillette
Lexena, KS 66215
913-599-2303
www.fredsclassicradios.com

Classic Auto Radio Service
(8-track tape player restorations)
23502 Shelby Ave.
Port Charlotte, FL 33954
800-880-1409
www.classicautoradioservice.com

D & D Automobilia
(steering wheel re-casting)
813 Ragers Hill Rd.
South Fork, PA 15956
814-248-9696
www.danddautomobilia.com

Gary's Steering Wheel Restoration
(steering wheel restoration)
866-879-6525
www.garyssteeringwheel.com

J.B. Donaldson Co.
(steering wheel restoration)
2533 W. Cypress St.
Phoenix, AZ 85009
602-278-4505
www.steeringwheelsusa.com

Jim's Sales & Service
(1920s–1970s radio restoration)
455 Gerdes St.
Breese, IL 62230
618-526-8492
mp3amradio@yahoo.com

Precision Stereo Repair
(radio restoration)
8441 Seneca Turnpike
New Hartford, NY 12413
315-797-5219
oldstereo@hotmail.com

Quality Restorations, Inc.
(steering wheel restoration)
858-271-7374
www.qualityrestorations.com

Tayman Electrical
(radio restoration)
244 Shopping Ave. #288
Sarasota, FL 34237
941-371-8924
www.taymanelectrical.com

West Coast Auto Radio
(radio restoration)
9260 Gainford St.
Downey, CA 90240
562-869-6491

Williamson's Instruments
(tachometers)
2018 Front Ave.
Chester, AR 72934
479-369-2551
www.williamsons.com

Vintage Car Radio Restorations
(radio restoration)
30422 Mountain Lane
Waterford, WI 53185
888-514-3811
www.vintageautoradio.com

Services
Bumper Restoration
Advanced Plating & Powder Coating
1425 Cowan Ct.
Nashville, TN 37207
800-588-6686
www.advancedplating.com

The Bumper Boyz
2435 E. 54th St.
Los Angeles, CA 90058
800-995-1703
www.bumperboyz.com

Custom Plating
3030 Alta Ridge Way
Snellville, GA 30078
770-736-1118

Fond Du Lac Bumper Exchange
1285 Morris St.
Fond du Lac, WI 54935
800-236-2570
www.fdlbumper.com

North Star Bumper Exchange
5085 Wren Drive
Appleton, WI 54913-7606
920-731-3030

Restoration Chrome
509-534 N. Lake Road
Spokane, WA 99212
509-534-0456
www.restorationchrome.com

Casting Repairs
A & C Casting Rebuilders
3560 Big Valley Rd. Unit A
Kelseyville, CA 95451
866-935-3227
www.accastingrebuilders.com

Casting Salvage Technologies
Virginia
800-833-8814

Jeff Goodhart
Lessport, PA
484-269-9450
www.polish-this.com

Jon W. Gateman & Son
PO Box 413
Beatty, NV 89003
775-764-0976

Lite Metals Company, Inc.
100 North Walnut St.
Ravena, OH 44266
330-296-6110
www.litemetals.com

Ohio Pattern
614-875-9599

Metal Fabrication
Bennett Coachworks LLC
1500 North 4th St.
Milwaukee, WI 53212
414-298-2068
www.hotrodbuilders.com

Frank Laiacano Jr.
29120 Badett
Westland, MI 48185
734-425-9302
classicparts4U@aol.com

Precision Welding & Repair
E2235 King Rd.
Waupaca, WI 54981
715-258-5405

Plastic Chrome (Metallizing)
Auto Instruments.com
2125 Virginia Ave.
Collinsville, VA 24078
877-450-0110
www.autoinstruments.com

Chrome-Tech USA
2314 Ravenswood Rd.
Madison, WI 53711
608-274-9811
www.chrometechusa.com

CV Vacuum Platers
(Business Address)
Unit #3
7160 Beatty Dr.
Mission, B.C. V2V6B4
877-763-2323
www.cvvacuumplaters.com

CV Vacuum Platers
(Shipping Address)
446 Harris St.
Sumas, WA 98295
604-820-9371

M & M Metalizing Sales
16478 Beach Blvd. #393
Westminster, CA 92683
714-822-6086
www.mmmetalizing.com

Mueller Corp.
530 Spring St.
East Bridgewater, MA 02333
508-583-2800
www.muellercorp.com

Plastic Resin Parts
Indian Bonnet
Chris Daniel
Mooresville, NC
cdaniel677@aol.com

Pot Metal Repair
Allied Technical Services
6239 Airport Way
Seattle, WA 98108
206-763-3346

Pot Metal Restorations
4794-C Woodlane Circle
Tallahassee, FL 32303
850-562-3847
www.customcoatings.net

Quality Pot Metal Works
2810 ParkwaySt. #5
Lakeland, FL 33811
863-640-0079
www.chromeplus.com

Resilvering
The Reflected Image
21 Westwind Dr.
Northford, CT 06472
203-484-0760

Ron's Corner
27169 State Hwy 6
Winston, MO 64689
660-749-5473

Woodwork/Woodgraining
Bill Gratkowski
515 N. Petroleum St.
Titusville, PA 16354
814-827-1782

C.D. Hall
1351 Locust Ave.
Long Beach, CA 90813
562-714-9118

Classic Wood
Nampa, ID
208-467-2988

Classic Woodgraining
(wood restoration)
Springfield, OH
866-472-4648
www.classicwoodgraining.com

Custom Graining (wood restoration)
New York
315-729-5060
www.customgraining.com

Grad Davis (wood restoration)
Washington
206-463-6110

KAT Performance Coatings
(wood restoration)
21838 Moens Rd
Atkinson, IL 61235
309-936-1323
www.katcoatings.com

Lauren Matley
Washington
253-350-3604

Lokays Woodgraining
Florida
727-375-1797

Madera Concepts
800-800-1579

Main Street Custom Finishing
www.mainstreetcustomfinishing.com

MAT Fabrication LLC
8124 Secura Way
Santa Fe Springs, CA 90670
562-693-6700
www.matfabrication.com

Nichols Automotive Woodworking
Michigan
231-342-2090 or 231-922-9648

R. L. Bailey
27902 45th Ave. S.
Auburn, WA 98001
253-854-5247
www.rlbaileyrestoration.com

Ron Lawless (wood restoration)
California
626-797-0266

Royal Coach Works (wood restoration)
Georgia
404-414-4952

Vintage Woodgraining, Inc.
(wood restoration)
Asheville, NC
828-254-0755

William Rau Automtive Woodwork
(wood restoration)
310-445-1128
www.rau-autowood.com

Wood Doctor (wood restoration)
5511 Silver Lake Dr.
West Bend, WI 53095
262-338-1033

Woodgrain 4 Wagons
(wood restoration)
Lakewood, CA
562-425-6009
www.woodgrain4wagons.com

Woodgrain by Estes
(wood restoration)
2001 Charles St.
Lafayette, IN 47904
765-490-5634

Woodgrainings (wood restoration)
Elk Grove, CA
916-683-2172
www.woodgrainings.com

Steering
Chicago Power Steering
5836 W. 66th St.
Bedford Park, IL 60638
800-634-5829
www.pwrsteering.com

Lares Corporation
855 South Cleveland
Cambridge, MN 55008
800-555-0767
sales@larescorp.com

Rare Parts, Inc.
621 Wiltshire Avenue
Stockton, CA 95203
209-948-6005,
www.rareparts.com

Supplies
Coatings
Bill Hirsch (restoration supplies)
396 Littleton Ave.
Newark, NJ 07103
800-828-2061
www.hirschauto.com

Central Mass Powder Coating
(powder coating)
978-365-1700
www.centralmasspowdercoating.com

Miller's (coating)
4251D Wayside Ct.
Lilburn, GA 30047
770-931-1505
www.millerpowdercoating.com

Next Generation (coatings)
Massachusetts
413-562-4700

Peacock Laboratories (coatings)
PCchrome
1901 S. 54th St.
Philadelphia, PA 19143
215-729-4400
www.Pchrome.com

PM Industries (coatings)
800-833-8933
www.nomorerust.com

Restomotive Laboratories
(POR-15 rust preventative coating)
PO Box 1235
Morristown, NJ 07962-1235
973-887-1999
www.por-15.com

Hardware
Auto Hardware Specialties (hardware)
3123 McKinley Ave.
Sheldon, IA 51201
712-324-2091

Mr G's Enterprises (hardware)
5613 Elliott Reeder Rd.
Fort Worth, TX 76117
817-831-3501
www.mrgusa.com

Restoration Specialties & Supply, Inc.
(restoration supplies)
PO Box 328
Windber, PA 15963
814-467-9842
www.restorationspecialties.com

Restoration Supply Co.
(restoration supplies)
15182-B Highland Valley Road
Escondido, CA 92025
800-306-7008
www.restorationstuff.com

Totally Stainless
(stainless steel restoration)
PO Box 3249
Gettysburg, PA 17325
717-677-8811
800-767-4781
www.totallystainless.com

Polishes
Kreem Products (metal polish)
4510 Donlon Road
PO Box 399
Somis, CA 93066
805-386-4470
www.kreemproducts.net

Luster Lace Polishes (polish)
104 Trade Center Dr.
St. Peters, MO 63376
636-272-1885
www.lusterlace.com

Pot Metal Repair Supplies
Caswell Electroplating
(pot metal repair)
7696 Route 31
Lyons, NY 14489
315-946-1213
www.caswellplating.com

Muggy Weld (pot metal repair)
360-357-4770
866-684-4993
www.muggyweld.com

Tools
Eastwood Company
(specialty restoration tools)
263 Shoemaker Road
Pottstown, PA 19464
610-323-2200
www.eastwood.com

Harbor Freight (automotive tools)
3491 Mission Oaks Blvd.
Camarillo, CA 93011-6010
www.harborfreightusa.com

Lefthander Chassis
(metal fabrication tools)
13750 Metric Dr.
Roscoe, IL 61073
815-389-9999
www.lefthanderchassis.com

Lincoln Electric (welders)
115 E. Crossroads Parkway
Bollingbrook, IL 60440-3538
630-783-3600 or 773-412-5153
www.lincolnelectric.com

Martin Autobody Tools
(auto restoration tools)
New Hampshire
603-669-1475
www.performancemetalshaping.com

Mittler Brothers Machine and Tool
(sheet metal fabrication tools)
10 Cooperative Way
Wright City, MO 63390
636-745-7757
www.mittlerbros.com

Northern Tool + Equipment
(automotive tools & equipment)
PO Box 1499
Burnsville, MN 55337-0489
800-556-7885
www.northerntool.com

Park Tool USA (motorcycle hand tools)
6 Long Lake Road
St. Paul, MN 55115
651-777-6868
www.parktool.com

Restomotive Laboratories
(POR-15 rust preventative coating)
PO Box 1235
Morristown, NJ 07962-1235
973-887-1999
www.por-15.com

Woodward Fabrication (tools)
800-391-5419
www.woodwardfab.com

Woodgraining Supplies
GIT Technologies, Inc (woodgraining)
334 Commerce Court
Winter Haven, FL 33880
863-299-4494
www.woodgraining.com

Performance Metal Shaping (sheet
metal fabrication tools)
New Hampshire
603-669-1475
www.performancemetalshaping.com

Suspension

Accurate Alignment
(cold setting springs)
3020 W. Franklin St.
Appleton, WI 54914
(920) 731-5442

Apple Hydraulics
(shock and carburetor rebuilding)
1610 Middle Road
Calverton, NY 11933
800-882-7753
www.applehydraulics.com

Eaton Detroit Spring, Inc.
(spring reshaping)
1555 Michigan
Detroit, MI 48216
313-963-3839
www.eatonsprings.com

King Pin Rebuilding
(king pin rebuilding)
New York
607-273-5049

Rudy Rosales (leaf spring covers built)
4086 E 71st.
Cleveland, OH 44105
800-248-7839
rudysrrparts@aol.com

World Wide Auto Parts of Madison,
Inc. (shock rebuilding)
2517 Seiferth Rd.
Madison, WI 53716
608-223-9400
www.nosimport.com

Tires & Wheels

British Wire Wheel
(wire wheels restored and mounted)
800-732-9866
www.britishwirewheel.com

Calimer's Wheel Shop
(wood spoke wheel restoration)
30 East North St.
Waynesboro, PA 17268
717-762-5056
www.calimerswheelshop.com

Chuckwagon Restoration/First Shot
Carriage (wagon wheel restorations)
PO Box 282
Gonzales, TX 78629
830-857-6521
www.texaswagonworks.com

Coker Tire (antique & classic tires)
1317 Chestnut St.
Chattanooga, TN 37402
800-251-6336
www.cokertire.com

Custom Tire FX
(tire customizing services)
Cleveland, Ohio
216-670-0867

Dayton Wire Wheel Restoration Dept.
(wire wheel restoration)
115 Compark Rd.
Dayton, OH 45459
888-559-2330
www.daytonwirewheel.com

Denman Tire Corporation
(Denman Classic IV tires)
400 Diehl South Road
Leavittsburg, OH 44430
800-334-5543
www.denmantire.com

Diamond Back Classics (classic car
radial tires)
Conway, SC
888-922-1642
www.dbtires.com

Hansen Wheel & Wagon Shop
(wagon wheel restorations)
40979 245th St.
Letcher, SD 57359
605-996-8754
www.hansenwheel.com

Kelsey Tire Company (classic car tires)
PO Box 564
1190 East Highway 54
Camdenton, MO 65020
800-325-0091
www.KelseyTire.com

Lucas Tires (East)
2141 West Main St.
Springfield, OH 45504
800-735-0166
www.lucasclassictires.com

Lucas Tires (West)
2850 Temple Ave.
Long Beach, CA 90806
800-952-4333
www.lucasclassictires.com

Mobil Tire Customizing (tire
customizing services)
6808 N. 77 Lane S. and W. Lamar Dr.
Glendale, AZ 85303
623-930-6553

Motorspot, Inc.
(discount vintage whitewall tires)
Orange, CA
760-731-8303
www.widewhitetires.com

Pfahl's Mack & Antique Truck
Restorations (hard rubber truck tires)
73 East St.
Bethlehem, CT 06751
203-266-6455
www.macktruckrestorations.com

Universal Tires (vintage car tires)
2994 Elizabethtown Rd.
Hershey, PA 12033
800-233-3827
www.universaltire.com

Viking Wheel Service
3901 N. Market St.
Wilmington, DE 19802
866-392-5569
Vikingwheel@verizon.net

Wallace W. Wade (antique car tires)
PO 560906
530 Regal Ave.
Dallas, TX 75247
800-666-TYRE
www.wallacewade.com

Wheel Repair Service of New England
317 Southbridge St.
Auburn, MA 01501
508-832-3222
www.wheelrepairservice.com

Upholstery & Interior Trim

ABC Auto Upholstery
(1955–'62 Ford interiors)
PO Box 6
6 Chestnut St.
Amesbury, MA 01912
800-221-5408
www.LeBaronBonney.com

Abingdon Spares
(British car trim parts)
South St. PO Box 37
Walpole, NH 03608
603-756-4768
www.abingdonsparesllc.com

Al Knoch Interiors
(Corvette, Camaro, Firebird)
9010 N. Desert Blvd.
PO Box 484
Canutillo, TX 79835
800-880-8080
www.alknochinteriors.com

Auto Custom carpets, Inc. (carpets)
PO Box 1350
Anniston, AL 36201
800-633-2358
www.accmats.com

Auto Trim Manufacturing (soft trim)
730 Orange Ave. Ste. 1
Altamonta Springs, FL 32714
407-869-7777
www.automobiletrim.com

BAS, Ltd. (Jaguar trim parts)
250 H St.
PMB 3000
Blaine, WA 98230
360-332-9302
www.basjaguartrim.com

Bill Hirsch (upholstery supplies)
396 Littleton Ave.
Newark, NJ
800-828-2061
www.hirschauto.com

British Parts Northwest
4105 SE Lafayette Highway
Dayton, OR 97114
503-864-2001
www.bpnorthwest.com

CARS, Inc. (Chevy interior kits)
2600 Bond St.
Rochester Hills, MI 48309
248-853-8909
800-CARSINC

Corvette America
(Corvette interior kits)
100 Classic Car Dr.
Reedsville, PA 17084
800-458-3475
www.corvetteamerica.com

Cut-and-Sew Headliners
405-495-1212

D and M Classic Auto Restoration
46 Grand Ave.
Greenville, SC 29607
800-722-0854
www.dandmrestoration.com

Dante's Parts (Mopar interior kits)
PO Box 963
Sicklerville, NJ 08081
609-332-4194
www.dantesparts.com

Dearborn Classics (Ford upholstery)
PO Box 7649
Bend, OR 97708-7649
800-252-7427
www.dearbornclassics.com

DeLuxe Automotive Interior Stylists
(trimmer)
960 S. Lay Avenue
St. Clair, MO 63077
636-629-6996
www.deluxeautointeriors.com

Fasnap (snap fasteners)
800-624-2050
www.fasnap.com

Flocking Restored
New York
516-796-2984

Gary Goers (Chrysler interiors)
37 Amdahl Lane
Kalispell, MT 59901
406-752-6249
www.garygoers.com

George's Antique Auto Upholstery
(trimmer)
42 Terry Road
Smithtown, NY 11787
631-265-3561

Hampton Coach (upholstery supplies)
8 Chestnut St.
Amesbury, MA 01913
888-388-8726
www.hamptoncoach.com

Heritage Upholstery & Trim
(British car interiors)
Blaine, WA 98230
360-332-3022
www.heritagetrim.com

Hilborn Motor Car Interiors
(Rolls-Royce interiors)
7025 Reseda Blvd.
Reseda, CA 91335
818-345-2113

Hoover Pres-N-Snap (snap install tool)
427 Grand Ave. Unit A
San Jacinto, CA 92582-3829
951-654-4627
www.HooverProducts.com

Jenkins Restoration and Interiors
PO Box 1509
North Wilkesboro, NC 28659-1509
(336) 667-4282

Justice Brothers (Mustang interiors)
2734 E. Huntington Dr.
Duracate, CA 91010
626-359-9174
www.justicebrothers.com

Katzkin (automotive leather)
800-842-0590
www.katzkin.com

Kip Motor Co. (British car trim)
2127 Crown Road
Dallas, TX 76229
888-243-0440
www.kipmotor.com

KoolMat Insulation
(noise & heat floor insulation)
704-662-9099
www.koolmat.com

Kopecky's Klassics (restorer)
PO Box 473
N6871 Highway 49
Iola, WI 54945
715-445-4791
www.kopeckysklassics.com

L'Cars Corporation (trimmer)
110 Poplar St.
PO Box 324
Cameron, WI 54822
715-458-2277

LeBaron Bonney Company
(upholstery supplies)
8 Chestnut St.
Amesbury, MA 01913
800-221-5408
www.lebaronbonney.com

LDC (upholstery supplies)
6121 Midway Road
Fort Worth, TX 76117
817-222-9700
www.larrydennis.com

Legendary Auto Interiors, Ltd.
(interior kits)
121 W. Shore Blvd.
Newark, NY 14513
800-363-8804
www.legendaryautointeriors.com

Mac's Antique Auto Parts (118-1952
Ford truck interiors)
6150 Donner Rd.
Lockport, NY 14094
877-470-1554
www.cartoucheupholstery.com

Madison Landau Ltd. (trimmer)
15 W. Beltline at Nob Hill
Madison, WI
608-251-7161

Mark's Custom Auto Interiors
(trimmer)
14409 W. Edison Dr.
New Lenox, IL
815-458-2277

McCluskey Auto Trim (trimmer)
203 South Fourth St
Perkasie, PA 18944
(610) 360-9589

Metro Moulded Parts (molded rubber)
11610 Jay St NW
Minneapolis, MN 55448
800-878-2237
www.metrommp.com

Mid America Motorworks
(Corvette upholstery & accessories)
One Mid America Pl
PO Box 1368
Effingham, IL 62401
800-500-1500
www.mamotorworks.com

Moss Motors (British car trim kits)
440 Rutherford St.
PO Box 847
Goleta, CA
800-667-7872
www.mossmotors.com

Muncie Imports & Classics (British car
trim kits)
4301 N. Old State Road 3
Muncie, IN 47303
756-286-4663
www.muncie-imports.com

National Chevy Association
(1949–'54 Chevy Interiors)
947 Arcade St.
St. Paul, MN 55106
651-778-9522
www.nationalchevyassoc.com

New Coast Fabrics (automotive vinyls)
1955 Davis St.
San Leandro, CA 94577-1262
800-772-3449
www.newcoastfabrics.com

Northwest Import Parts
(British car trim kits)
10042 SW Palmer
Portland, OR 97219
503-245-3806
www.northwestimportparts.com

NTG Motor Services Limited (British
car trim parts)
282-284 Bramford Road
Ipswich, Suffolk, England IP1 4AY
www.ntgservices.co.uk

Original Falcon Interiors
(Falcon and Comet interiors)
6343 Seaview Ave. NW
Seattle, WA 98107-2664
206-781-5230
falconcomet1963@earthlink.net

RagTopp
(convertible top care for Hartz cloth)
800-377-4700
www.Wolfsteins.com

Steele Rubber Company
(molded rubber and weather stripping)
6180 E. NC 150 Highway
Denver, NC 28037-9605
800-230-7126
www.steelerubber.com

Tony Handler, Inc. (Bentley trim parts)
2028 Cotner Ave.
Los Angeles, CA 90025
310-473-7773
www.tonyhandler.com

Trim Parts (soft trim parts)
2175 Deerfield Rd.
Lebanon, OH 45036
513-934-0815
www.trimparts.com

World Upholstery & Trim
800-222-9577
www.worlduph.com

Woodies
AMS Woodie Restoration
('49–'51 Ford wood)
38 Fargo Road
Waterford, CT 06385
860-447-3972

Cincinnati Woodworks ('40-'48 Ford,
'46-'48 Chrysler)
1974 Central Avenue
Cincinnati, OH 45214
513-721-8221

Ford Wood Art ('32-'48 Ford interior
framing, seats, floor boards)
1125 Mallard Court
Manteca, CA 95337
209-239-1530

Hercules Motor Car Co.
('33–'34 Ford wagons)
2502 N. 70th Street
Tampa, FL 33619
813-621-2220

J.B. Donaldson Co.
('46–'53 Buick wagons)
2533 W. Cypress
Phoenix, AZ 85009
602-278-4505

Pleasantville Manufacturing Co.
(Ford Model T & Model A wagons)
5534 Centralia-Hartfield Road
Dewettville, NY 14728
716-753-2238

Rick Mack Enterprises
('49–'51 Ford &Mercury woodie kits)
PO Box 39631
Tacoma, WA 98439
253-539-0432

The Wood 'n Carr
('49–'51 Ford wood)
3231 E. 19th Street
Signal Hill, CA 90804
562-498-8730

Woodgrain 4 Wagons
Lakewood, CA 90712
562-425-6009
www.woodgrain4wagons.com

ABOUT THE AUTHOR

John Gunnell—"Gunner"—is best known for his books *Standard Catalog of American Cars 1946–1975* and *75 Years of Pontiac Oakland*. His first professional writing job was with National Corvette Owner's Association in the mid-'70s. He has written thousands of articles about classic cars, motorcycles and airplanes. His 85-plus automotive books include the Standard Catalog series. He also updated *75 Years of Chevrolet* for George Dammann's Crestline Publications. John originally hoped to be an industrial designer. He studied fine art in his hometown of Staten Island, New York, before moving to Iola, Wisconsin, in 1978, to work as an editor for *Old Cars Weekly*. He has contributed to over 50 periodicals.

John currently has ten automobiles and fifteen motorcycles in his collection, including several vehicles that are in various phases of restoration. He owns cars and trucks from 1936–2009 and motorcycles from 1940–2001. Twenty of his vehicles qualify for blue and red Wisconsin collector license plates.

GENERAL MOTORS

Big-Block Chevy Engine Buildups: 978-1-55788-484-8/HP1484
Big-Block Chevy Performance: 978-1-55788-216-5/HP1216
Camaro Performance Handbook: 978-1-55788-057-4/HP1057
Camaro Restoration Handbook ('61–'81): 978-0-89586-375-1/HP758
Chevelle/El Camino Handbook: 978-1-55788-428-2/HP1428
Chevy LS1/LS6 Performance: 978-1-55788-407-7/HP1407
The Classic Chevy Truck Handbook: 978-1-55788-534-0/HP1534
How to Customize Your Chevy Silverado/GMC Sierra Truck, 1996–2006: 978-1-55788-526-5/HP1526
How to Rebuild Big-Block Chevy Engines: 978-0-89586-175-7/HP755
How to Rebuild Big-Block Chevy Engines, 1991–2000: 978-1-55788-550-0/HP1550
How to Rebuild Small-Block Chevy LT-1/LT-4 Engines: 978-1-55788-393-3/HP1393
How to Rebuild Your Small-Block Chevy: 978-1-55788-029-1/HP1029
Powerglide Transmission Handbook: 978-1-55788-355-1/HP1355
Small-Block Chevy Engine Buildups: 978-1-55788-400-8/HP1400
Turbo Hydra-Matic 350 Handbook: 978-0-89586-051-4/HP511

FORD

Ford Engine Buildups: 978-1-55788-531-9/HP1531
Ford Windsor Small-Block Performance: 978-1-55788-323-0/HP1323
How to Build Small-Block Ford Racing Engines: 978-1-55788-536-2/HP1536
How to Customize Your Ford F-150 Truck, 1997–2008: 978-1-55788-529-6/HP1529
How to Rebuild Big-Block Ford Engines: 978-0-89586-070-5/HP708
How to Rebuild Ford V-8 Engines: 978-0-89586-036-1/HP36
How to Rebuild Small-Block Ford Engines: 978-0-912656-89-2/HP89
Mustang Restoration Handbook: 978-0-89586-402-4/HP029

MOPAR

Big-Block Mopar Performance: 978-1-55788-302-5/HP1302
How to Hot Rod Small-Block Mopar Engine, Revised: 978-1-55788-405-3/HP1405
How to Modify Your Jeep Chassis and Suspension For Off-Road: 978-1-55788-424-4/HP1424
How to Modify Your Mopar Magnum V8: 978-1-55788-473-2/HP1473
How to Rebuild and Modify Chrysler 426 Hemi Engines: 978-1-55788-525-8/HP1525
How to Rebuild Big-Block Mopar Engines: 978-1-55788-190-8/HP1190
How to Rebuild Small-Block Mopar Engines: 978-0-89586-128-5/HP83
How to Rebuild Your Mopar Magnum V8: 978-1-55788-431-5/HP1431
The Mopar Six-Pack Engine Handbook: 978-1-55788-528-9/HP1528
Torqueflite A-727 Transmission Handbook: 978-1-55788-399-5/HP1399

IMPORTS

Baja Bugs & Buggies: 978-0-89586-186-3/HP60
Honda/Acura Engine Performance: 978-1-55788-384-1/HP1384
How to Build Performance Nissan Sport Compacts, 1991–2006: 978-1-55788-541-8/HP1541
How to Build Xtreme Pocket Rockets: 978-1-55788-548-7/HP1548
How to Hot Rod VW Engines: 978-0-91265-603-8/HP034
How to Rebuild Your VW Air-Cooled Engine: 978-0-89586-225-9/HP1225
Mitsubishi & Diamond Star Performance Tuning: 978-1-55788-496-1/HP1496
Porsche 911 Performance: 978-1-55788-489-3/HP1489
Street Rotary: 978-1-55788-549-4/HP1549
Toyota MR2 Performance: 978-155788-553-1/HP1553
Xtreme Honda B-Series Engines: 978-1-55788-552-4/HP1552

HANDBOOKS

Auto Electrical Handbook: 978-0-89586-238-9/HP387
Auto Math Handbook: 978-1-55788-020-8/HP1020
Auto Upholstery & Interiors: 978-1-55788-265-3/HP1265
Custom Auto Wiring & Electrical: 978-1-55788-545-6/HP1545
Engine Builder's Handbook: 978-1-55788-245-5/HP1245
Engine Cooling Systems: 978-1-55788-425-1/HP1425
Fiberglass & Other Composite Materials: 978-1-55788-498-5/HP1498
High Performance Fasteners & Plumbing: 978-1-55788-523-4/HP1523
Metal Fabricator's Handbook: 978-0-89586-870-1/HP709
Paint & Body Handbook: 978-1-55788-082-6/HP1082
Practical Auto & Truck Restoration: 978-155788-547-0/HP1547
Pro Paint & Body: 978-1-55788-394-0/HP1394
Sheet Metal Handbook: 978-0-89586-757-5/HP575
Welder's Handbook, Revised: 978-1-55788-513-5

INDUCTION

Holley 4150 & 4160 Carburetor Handbook: 978-0-89586-047-7/HP473
Holley Carbs, Manifolds & F.I.: 978-1-55788-052-9/HP1052
Rebuild & Powertune Carter/Edelbrock Carburetors: 978-155788-555-5/HP1555
Rochester Carburetors: 978-0-89586-301-0/HP014
Performance Fuel Injection Systems: 978-1-55788-557-9/HP1557
Turbochargers: 978-0-89586-135-1/HP49
Street Turbocharging: 978-1-55788-488-6/HP1488
Weber Carburetors: 978-0-89589-377-5/HP774

RACING & CHASSIS

Chassis Engineering: 978-1-55788-055-0/HP1055
4Wheel & Off-Road's Chassis & Suspension: 978-1-55788-406-0/HP1406
Dirt Track Chassis & Suspension: 978-1-55788-511-1/HP1511
How to Make Your Car Handle: 978-1-91265-646-5/HP46
How to Build a Winning Drag Race Chassis & Suspension:
The Race Car Chassis: 978-1-55788-540-1/HP1540
The Racing Engine Builder's Handbook: 978-1-55788-492-3/HP1492
Stock Car Racing Engine Technology: 978-1-55788-506-7/HP1506
Stock Car Setup Secrets: 978-1-55788-401-5/HP1401

STREET RODS

Street Rodder magazine's Chassis & Suspension Handbook: 978-1-55788-346-9/HP1346
Street Rodder's Handbook, Revised: 978-1-55788-409-1/HP1409